OPEN BLIND EYES

OPEN BLIND EYES

Rachel Timothy

Library of Congress Control Number:		2020923346
ISBN:	Hardcover	978-1-6641-4368-5
	Softcover	978-1-6641-4367-8
	eBook	978-1-6641-4375-3

Print information available on the last page.

Rev. date: 11/19/2020

To order additional copies of this book, contact:
Xlibris
844-714-8691
www.Xlibris.com
Orders@Xlibris.com
820768

CHAPTER 1

A story like this is not an easy one to write. Putting words to the events of my life has been something I've struggled with for years, but there is healing in the process (or so I've been told). So I write this for both you and me. I write this for you, to inform you of this other world that so many know nothing about. But also for me, to cleanse my soul of the dirt and garbage that lingers from my past.

My story isn't all bad. In fact, some memories bring me so much joy that my heart literally bursts, and I can't help but smile as I think back.

Growing up, I was a perfect balance of tough but soft. Face me with a challenge, and I would meet that challenge and more. I had to be tough if I wanted to hang with my two older brothers. However, there was also a soft side to me. I had a huge heart for people. It didn't matter how they looked or smelled, or what they wore, or what they did, I tried to be kind to everyone. I never wanted anyone to hurt, and I wanted to make sure that they knew they were loved. Loved by me, but more importantly, by God.

I had a knack for seeing the good in every person I met. My heart was kind and thoughtful of how others might be feeling. It would be a constant battle in my mind. I could be sitting on my mom's lap watching TV at night, and I would begin to wonder if my dad needs me to cuddle with him for a while, just so he knows I love him too. So most nights at home, I would go back and forth from one parent to the next, thinking I was making them both feel loved and happy. It was how my young mind worked. It also was one of the first signs that I was a people pleaser and was always thinking about how I could make others happy.

And we know that for those who love God
all things work together for good, for those
who are called according to His purpose.
—Romans 8:28

Every aspect of my life—the good, the bad, the ugly—has been tied together to form who I am. It shows the "why" of God choosing to make me. To take a piece away would completely disassemble my being. Who I am. The core that provides me the strength to follow God's purpose in my life.

Christ with me, Christ before me,
Christ behind me, Christ in me.
—St. Patrick's Breastplate

I wish I could say that I've never wavered from that thought, but that would be untrue. I haven't always felt the Lord. Many times during my life, God seemed light-years away. Along with His comfort and His peace. So often I have wished to be back in that nine-year-old body when I felt God clearly and powerfully. His strength and peace in my heart were undeniable. When you know the feeling of the Lord working in you and then you seem to lose it, you are desperate to do all you can to get it back.

Let me jump back to the beginning. Not the beginning of my physical life, not even the beginning of my spiritual life. But the beginning of when I was being transformed, broken down, to be built back up in the way God needed me.

This was going to be a new school for me. My family had just left the only home I'd ever known. My dad was a minister and was hired as the new head preacher at the local Christian church. So we had moved as a family from a large and beautiful home in the country that my parents had built to a small town in the Midwest of America. We left our friends and church family and came to a place where I knew no one. This move, this change, was all one big adventure in my young nine-year-old eyes.

I was bouncing with excitement at the thought of a new school. Our new house was owned by the church and was called the parsonage. The bedrooms were much smaller than we were used to, plus my two older brothers had to share a room and a tiny closet. I'm not sure they were as excited about the move as I was. They had more going on in their life than I did. They were leaving behind girlfriends, buddies, and teams. My oldest brother was entering his junior year of high school, and the other was going into eighth grade. Apparently, those were tougher years to have to change schools. I was entering the fourth grade and truly didn't have a care in the world.

Our house was smack-dab in the middle of this new small town and was walking distance to the school and the church. In fact, the school track was in our backyard. It was such a small town that you were basically walking distance to everything. The sign leading into our new town said it was a village and was approximately the home of two hundred people, so it wasn't even classified as a town, technically. The best part as a kid was that you could ride your bike all over town. I felt like big stuff, riding around on my own. It seemed like a dream come true to a nine-year-old. I'd make daily trips up to the small mom-and-pop grocery store to buy candy. My favorites back then were candy cigarettes or a simple lemon that I would peel and eat like an orange.

Oh, how I wish you could've known me before my fourth-grade year. I had a confidence and self-esteem that seemed untouchable. I was going to be somebody. I already felt like God had a purpose for me. I enjoyed every day and took pride in being a Christian, in my family name, and in being a preacher's kid. I almost always had a smile on my face and a bounce to my step. My long blonde hair would sway back and forth with each step I took. I knew who I was and where I was going in this life. I had spunk—plain and simple.

I had bright blue eyes, a tan from the summer sun, along with extra natural blonde highlights in my hair. I had just led our baseball team to become World Series champions back in our old town. I was the only girl on the baseball team. Actually, the only girl in the league, and I loved every minute of it. A new school, a smaller school, a smaller town, I was certain I would have no trouble. And no matter what, I was ready for the challenge.

I was goal driven, even at an early age. I was also a cocky little thing. Being a professional baseball player was my first goal, but then I was told at this new school that I was required to play with the girls on the softball team. I was disappointed because I had fallen in love with baseball, and softball seemed so different. I grew to love softball; however, my favorite sport to play after baseball and where all my dreams developed was with basketball.

Friends didn't matter to me as much as winning, success, and being the best. The first few weeks at my new school were a blur. There were a lot of new things to learn and new people to get to know. I learned quickly that I needed to tone down my confidence around my new classmates. I was the new girl, and at first, the girls were standoffish with me and the boys were shy. But it wasn't long before I was making friends and fitting in with my classmates.

A few weeks in, I was walking down the long school hallway with my class, heading to the cafeteria. The walls were made of cement blocks painted tan and covered in motivational posters and kids' artwork. We walked together as a class on the right side of the hallway, an arm's length away from the person in front of us and the person behind us. Never speaking a word. We were on our way to lunch, and I knew better than to disobey the rules, especially in the hallway. The hallway monitors were the toughest teachers in the school. I quietly stayed along the wall.

This particular day, however, I was called out of line. I hadn't been talking. I wasn't following too close to the person in front of me. Maybe I had broken a rule that I didn't know about. Just like how I was a people pleaser, I was also very much a rule follower. The hallway was full of kids walking in their class lines on their way to lunch. We were about to walk past the front doors of the school's old gym when a teacher called me out by name to come talk to him. I had seen this teacher before. I knew he was the other fourth-grade teacher, but I didn't know his name or how he knew my name. Needless to say, my heart was in my throat waiting to see what this teacher wanted. My eyes were big in fear, but right away this teacher had a huge smile for me. A smile that said I wasn't in trouble. That I hadn't broken any rules and that everything was okay.

"You're Rachel, right?"

"Yes."

"And your cousin is Erin, the famous girls' basketball player at a nearby high school. Am I right?" Now I was excited. This man knew me and my cousin, and he was talking about basketball. He had my full attention.

"Yes, she's my cousin."

"I heard that you play basketball, too. Are you going to be as good as your cousin?"

Remember that cocky blonde-haired, blue-eyed girl I was describing earlier? Yeah, she didn't skip a beat.

"My cousin is really good," I said with a big smile, "but I'm going to be even better." He smiled at me with a twinkle in his eye. He seemed to like my confidence and assurance in myself. He went on to explain that he was the school's varsity girls' basketball coach and he thought it was great that my family had moved here. I got back in line with my class, and we walked on to the cafeteria. I'm sure pride was written all over my face. The varsity coach was glad I was here. This might've meant nothing to some girls, but to me, it was very exciting. I was more motivated than ever to work at my basketball skills. I wanted to back up my statement. I wanted to be even better than my cousin. I hadn't thought of that as a goal before, but now it was. And you better believe I was ready to work my butt off to make it happen.

Looking back at my innocence from those days, my eyes well up with tears. I had no reason to assume anything bad about this teacher. He didn't say anything inappropriate or wrong. The conversation had sparked an excitement in me that immediately got me anxious for the next time I could talk basketball with him.

If my coach would've kept our relationship at that level, then it would've been a healthy coach-player relationship. I went home that day and was proud to tell my parents that the varsity basketball coach had heard about me. And he was excited about our family moving here. My parents were as excited as me. They had hoped each of us kids would easily fit in at our new schools. That it would be a painless transition. My folks knew my drive and love for sports, especially basketball, so their excitement was right up there with mine. This adventure of a new home, a new church, and a new school was turning out wonderful. I would lie in bed at night, dreaming of basketball. Life was good. Life was simple. Life made sense.

I had no idea that these first conversations with my coach were the beginning stages of grooming. *Grooming* is a term I learned in the last few years, as I've gone to counseling to help me heal from the hurt that started my fourth-grade year of school. *Grooming* is defined as preparing someone for a particular activity. To prime, tailor, and\or condition. I had no idea that this simple conversation with the teacher was all part of the grooming process.

However, this was not truly the start. This coach had done his homework. He knew everything about me. He knew my family, where I lived, where I came from, and he had watched me enough to know that I was perfect prey for what he had planned. I saw it as special attention. I had no reason not to trust a teacher. His smile, his behavior, and his likes and interests gave me every indication that he was a fun teacher and coach. And that he was only interested in me to help me achieve my basketball dreams.

When I first was told about grooming a few years ago, it was hard to believe. I spent countless hours mulling over these thoughts of his actions actually being planned out for the purpose he later showed me. I tried convincing counselors that my relationship with this teacher was real. That it couldn't have been grooming. That these counselors just didn't see how he had truly cared about and loved me. There was no way that this was all an act just to get me to do what he wanted. That would mean it was years of lies and years of me being an idiot, believing it. I just couldn't see how that could be true in my situation. Maybe it's true for others, but not me. This teacher really meant all those things he said; he just had trouble making mistakes at times. That was the excuse I typically made for him.

I was twenty-eight years old when I started going to counseling and learning about grooming. So I was twenty-eight years old and still believing his lies, as if emotionally I was no older than that nine-year-old little girl. But the lightbulb turned on when I was posed with the question, "Why would a forty-year-old man want to be around a nine-year-old girl so much?" When I thought of it that way, I saw how crazy it sounded. My emotions went from disbelief to devastation. I understand that judgment will most likely come from those reading this because it doesn't make sense why it bothered me so much. But I trusted this man. I was loyal to him and believed all that he said. I was fooled. I felt like an idiot for falling for every tactic he used. It broke my heart that it was all fake. I went months truly trying to grasp how tactful he was in fooling me. I struggled almost hourly with going back and forth from thinking he really did love me, to understanding he was fake and conniving and had a purpose for each compliment he gave me. That he truly was grooming me. The embarrassment that followed was crumbling. How could I be so dumb to not understand what he was doing?

It took me another several months to comprehend that I was a nine-year-old little girl who was brainwashed by a mastermind. A professional groomer. An adult who knew exactly how to manipulate my emotions and my mind to do exactly what he wanted me to. I wish I hadn't fallen for it, but I was up against a professional. And I've also realized that I'm not the only one who fell for his lies. The school fell for his lies, the church where he served as an elder fell for his lies. My parents fell for his lies. I wasn't the only one fooled by his grooming process.

What I've learned from being groomed is that you can't assume everyone's intentions are innocent and pure. Just because someone holds a title or a status, it doesn't mean they won't hurt you. Oftentimes, perpetrators seek a certain job or title that will give them accessibility to children or give them power that leads them to believe they don't have to follow the laws and rules. That they are above it.

One question I've started asking myself when it comes to trusting men, whether it's with me or with my kids, is "Would my dad say or do something like that?" Now that I'm married, I can also ask myself if it's something my husband would say or do to another woman or child. If the answer is "No," then I stay cautious around this person. If it pertains to my kids. then I make the effort to never let them around that person without me, and I discuss with them in an age-appropriate manner that the comments or actions of this individual were wrong.

The reason I use my dad and husband as the gold standard is because I am 100 percent certain of their heart and intentions. It's not saying that any person who acts differently than them is a bad person, it's just my standard. It gives me a chance to critically think about the behavior in question compared to people who I know always have pure intentions.

An example would be when a man waits till I'm alone in a room to then come in and hug me. I know that my dad or my husband would never seek out another woman to hug in private. Therefore, even if the man seems sincere and naïve, I would have found a reason to share the experience with my husband and proceed with caution.

Another example would be if my daughter's Sunday school teacher asks her to stay after class to be his special helper to clean up. I know that my dad or husband would never seek out a little girl and try to get her alone. Especially the same girl on multiple occasions. It's easy to get caught up in the pride that your daughter was selected as the special helper, or that your daughter was praised by the principal, saying how pretty she is. Or that a newspaper reporter has taken interest in your son and wants to do some private interviews with him and continues to call him and praise him on how skilled he is in his sport.

As parents, we can't be naïve, and we must have a standard and then a plan to enforce when the standard isn't met. There are many good people in this world, and living in fear is not the answer. God does not want us to choose fear.

> For God gave us a spirit not of fear but
> of power and love and self-control.
> —2 Timothy 1:7

I think even more than having a standard and a plan, it is important to always turn to prayer for guidance in the situation. Ask for God's wisdom. For your eyes to be opened that God may reveal to you the character of the person in question so that you can learn their intentions, whether good or bad.

Grooming is scary and can begin before you even realize it. Looking back at how the grooming process started for me, it was very similar to how other adults had interacted with me. The simple conversation that this coach had with me was not wrong in and of itself. Really, there wasn't much for me to have picked up on at that point except that he had done his homework and obviously knew a lot about me. The grooming continued daily after that, and I was quickly brainwashed. Thankfully, grooming is being more and more talked about today and it even is considered a crime.

Perpetrators are smart. Have your standards and stay in prayer. The result of grooming can be life changing and even life-threatening.

As my story continues, you will see the progression of grooming and how I continued to ignore my good judgment for the chance to make this coach happy. The story gets dark, but hang with me. Even as I write this book, I am not fully healed, but God is doing amazing things. I have miracles to share with you, as well as how I came to learn about what God's love really means. And where Satan came into play. There are times in my story where I reach rock bottom and cry out to God, only to feel like there is no answer. I get to the point where I feel like I'm so far down that my prayers must not be reaching God anymore. The hardship is real, the battle is intense and devastating at times, but stay with me because today I stand victorious.

> The victory is ours through our Lord Jesus Christ.
> —1 Corinthians 15:57

CHAPTER 2

I didn't stop and think about why this coach was interested in spending time with me. My thoughts were on basketball, and my assumption was that his were too.

I was sitting in class one day, learning about maps and directions. "Never Eat Soggy Wheaties" was being instilled in my brain to remember north, east, south, and west, when there was a knock at the door. My emotions were flying high with excitement, hoping that the knock on the door was for me. On the other side of the door stood a blonde-haired little girl with a note for my teacher.

Once before, earlier in the week, the same girl had come with a note saying that the other fourth-grade teacher wanted to see me. I sat at my desk, trying not to appear too obvious at my desire for this message to be for me once again. I watched closely as my teacher silently read the note.

My teacher was one of the sweetest, kindest teachers. She hardly ever raised her voice. However, she did know how to raise one eyebrow when you're doing something questionable. Oftentimes, she just did it to be funny. She easily showed her students that she loved teaching and loved us. She was definitely in the right profession. My guess was that she had been teaching for many years, but I'm basing that guess on the fact that she seemed really old to me. But everyone seems old to a nine-year-old. I really liked her as a teacher and as a person. Probably the best part about her was her obsession with Elvis Presley. She had so many knickknacks and memorabilia of Elvis, along with all his songs. If we listened to music in her class, it had to be Elvis. January 8 was the biggest day of the year, and as a class we celebrated Elvis's birthday. Her obsession wasn't weird; it was actually cute and enjoyable. Especially with how she liked to play like she believed Elvis was still alive. At least, I think she was playing when she said that.

"Rachel, would you come here please?" As soon as she called my name, I jumped out of my chair and walked to the door where she was standing. I was trying my hardest to play it cool. As if I was used to this kind of special treatment. I was just certain all my classmates were jealous that I was getting out of class again. Isn't that every kid's dream? To get out of work.

"It seems you are needed in the other fourth-grade room." She had a big grin on her face, with one eyebrow raised, and she jokingly said, "You tell that other teacher that he better quit stealing you away from us all the time."

"Okay," I replied, feeling even more special that my teacher loved having me in her class too. I was really feeling like I belonged and fit in at this new school. She signed the hall pass, and I walked with the other little girl to her classroom.

Right away I heard "Colors of the Wind" playing from the TV in the corner of the room when I walked into the other fourth-grade classroom. It must be movie day again for his class, and they were watching *Pocahontas*. They seemed to have movie day more than any other class I knew, but I was excited because this meant I could spend time talking basketball with my coach while the class watched the movie. All of the lights were off, and it made the classroom look more like a movie theater than a school.

I walked past several rows of kids and found my way to the back corner of the room where the teacher's desk was. He first looked at the girl who had brought the message to me. He reached out and put his hand on her back and thanked her for being his special helper. He gave her the same smile he gave me. I instantly felt a twinge of jealousy inside of me when I saw that. It didn't make sense to me. She didn't play basketball, so what would his interest in her be? Granted, she was beautiful and one of the most popular girls in our class. I was more of the tomboy, sweaty, would-do-anything-to-beat-you-in-dodgeball type. The little girl smiled back at the teacher and said, "You're welcome," then the teacher turned his focus on me. His large smile was flashed my way this time, and I was glad. It didn't make sense to be jealous of the other little girl. It was a weird feeling for me. I barely knew this teacher. Why should I care if he smiled at another student? I was embarrassed for even letting that twinge of jealousy sneak in.

Before I could think any more on it, I heard the teacher say in his typical soft, deep voice that he was glad to see me. And from there our conversation flowed. We were positioned behind his desk. He was sitting in his desk chair, and he had me kneel behind his desk so our conversation was more private.

In the next several weeks, I was often called into his classroom. It became something I looked forward to each day. He was always praising me and telling me how special I was and how great I was going to be. My classmates obviously noticed how often I was getting out of class to go see him, and they started asking questions.

"He likes to talk basketball with me," I would explain. And for the most part, that was true. Although, our conversations were beginning to progress from how good I was going to be at basketball, to how good my body could be for basketball. He became interested in my muscles and having me become stronger. One time in particular, I knew in my heart that he had gone too far, but I also knew I couldn't tell anybody. If I alluded to anything at all about how our relationship has become more than just about basketball, then I wouldn't be able to get out of class anymore. I wouldn't be special. And I would hurt this man who I respected and cared for, my future coach.

We had been talking about ways I could get stronger, and he was asking me what exercises I was doing to help me get stronger. He felt my quads and my biceps. He would always make the face like he was shocked at how strong I was. He had recently started checking my abs and would have me lift my shirt so he could see. He taught me how to flex my abdominal muscles so he could feel them better. Of course, I had to be careful to be hidden behind the desk completely so no one saw us. He would smile at how fun it was to be secretive. It all made sense to me for the coach to be concerned about my muscles. Especially since I was his future star player.

On one occasion, he asked about push-ups. He believed I should begin doing daily push-ups. That it would be good for many different muscles. He rubbed his hands up my back under my shirt while I stood still. I was hoping he would think my back was strong too. He was very gentle and quietly whispered to me that I had a beautiful back. And as I blushed at him using the word *beautiful* with me, his hand went around to my front and up my chest. I jumped and pulled away quickly out of embarrassment. My eyes were even filling up with tears. I was nine and wasn't developed at all in my chest, but something about his large man hands going up there felt wrong. He saw my immediate reaction, and I could tell I had made a mistake.

"I was trying to feel your abs. I didn't mean to . . . Rachel, I am so sorry." I felt like an idiot. Why had I reacted that way? He obviously didn't do it on purpose. My reaction probably hurt his feelings. I could've just kicked myself. He looked so sad and so embarrassed.

"Do you believe me that it was an accident? I would never do anything to hurt you." I wanted so badly to make up for what I had done. I smiled at him and told him that of course I believed him and that I trusted him. I tried to hide the tears that had welled up during my initial reaction. I was acting like a child, and it made me frustrated at myself. I didn't want to hurt him.

"I trust you, too, Rachel." He paused for a while and then looked at me with his serious face. I learned at that point that I didn't like his serious face. In fact, it was scary.

"Rachel," he went on, "even though it was an accident, I need to trust that you won't say anything to anyone. If you do, I could lose my wife and my job."

My eyes probably got as big as saucers. There was no way that I would hurt him like that. He didn't deserve that at all. I promised him I wouldn't tell. A smile returned to his face, and I was glad. I was very uncomfortable with his serious face. I never wanted to see it again. All I could think about the rest of the day was how I had hurt him and the look on his face. Days went by, and I didn't hear a single word from him. I would sit in class hoping that a knock would come from the door and a note would be given to the teacher saying that I was needed in the other classroom. But the knock never came. I would look for him in the hallway, but each time I saw him, he wouldn't even look in my direction. I was heartbroken. Of course he was mad at me after the way I had acted.

At night, I would lie in bed thinking about him and how I could get him not to be mad at me anymore. It was the people pleaser in me. One day at school, my teacher announced to our class that we were going to be doing a joint project with the other fourth-grade class. My ears perked up at this news. Maybe I could get a chance to talk to him. To apologize again. As I walked with my class across the hallway to his classroom, I was excited and hopeful. But when I entered the room, I immediately saw that the lights were off and that blonde-haired girl was kneeling behind his desk. Instantly, jealousy began raging full force inside my little body. We were walking in as a class when he told his "special helper" to find her seat.

Both teachers took turns explaining the project. I would keep looking at him, but he was still acting as if I didn't exist and wouldn't look my way. We were put in groups, and as luck would have it, I was put in the same group as the other blonde-haired little girl. At this point, I was in a foul mood and I could hardly even stomach looking at the other girl. I quickly realized that she wasn't too fond of me either.

As the project was coming to an end, we were all asked to clean up our area. Together, my group and I grabbed all of our supplies and walked down the hallway to the girls' bathroom to use the sinks to clean the paint out of some of our droppers and bowls and brushes. I have always been a rule follower and was pretty good about choosing right over wrong. But on this particular occasion, I let my emotions win, and out of anger and jealousy, I grabbed one of those dirty paint droppers and filled it with water and squirted it right into the beautiful blonde curls of that little girl.

She let out a scream of horror and looked at me with straight disgust. With an ornery half grin on my face, I said to her, "It was an accident."

Her reply was a classic fourth-grade response: "I'm telling." And she marched off, back to the classroom. Normally, I would instantly regret a bad decision like that where I let my emotions win, but this time was different. I had zero remorse for my actions.

The rest of my group and I gathered up the clean supplies and headed back to the classroom. I knew that she was going to tell on me, but a big part of me believed that the teacher would hear that it was an accident and it would be fine.

When we walked into the room, the girl was standing behind the teacher's chair with her arms crossed and large tears in her eyes, and in front of her sat a very mad coach. The anger in my coach's eyes matched the anger in the little girl's. Saying it was an accident didn't matter, and then trying to explain that it was just water in the dropper didn't help me any either. Granted, there might've been a little green paint mixed in with the water, but it was, no doubt, majority water.

He didn't yell loudly at me, but with a quiet, mean voice, I was told to apologize and to never bother that girl again. I left the classroom in tears. I didn't understand why I felt the way I did. And why I would do something mean like that. I was very confused and extremely heartbroken and embarrassed.

This was the beginning of the mind games in the grooming process. My emotions were being played with. My self-esteem and confidence were starting to dwindle, and this teacher knew exactly what he was doing.

It took weeks before the teacher would look my direction again. I had pretty much resigned myself to the fact that he wasn't a fan of me anymore and that was okay. My old spunk and confidence started to return.

Every morning at school, we would file into the old gym and sit with our class, waiting for the first bell to ring. This coach would often sit down at the corner of the gym in a folding chair next to the school's PE teacher, and they would visit each morning while they drank their coffee. For a while, every morning this teacher would find me in the crowd of students and, from a distance, smile at me. But the last several weeks, he wouldn't even look my direction. Out of nowhere, one morning, I looked across the gym floor and he motioned for me to come talk to him.

I was hesitant. I wasn't sure what to expect. I had gotten used to not having him in my life, so the walk across the gym to meet him was filled with lots of conflicting feelings.

"Rachel . . ." He dragged the syllables out in my name in a playful way. "How ya been, girl?" I was still utterly confused at his smile and nice words.

"Good."

"Have you been able to shoot around much lately?" he asked me.

"Yes, every day," I said.

"You're going to be a superstar, girl. I just know it. Hey now, you promise me that when you get famous, you won't forget about me."

I smiled and most likely blushed. Going pro was my dream. Instantly, all my old emotions of wanting to impress this teacher came rushing back. He smiled ear to ear and winked at me where the PE teacher couldn't see, and said, "I'll come get you today so we can talk." I smiled and nodded and walked back to my seat with my class. When I sat down, I looked back in his direction and he was still looking at me and smiling. Then he turned his attention back to the PE teacher. Again, I blushed. He did like me after all. Maybe it had all been in my head the last few weeks. Maybe he wasn't mad after all. All I knew was that I was looking forward to that knock coming on the classroom door saying that I was needed in the other fourth-grade classroom.

The emotional roller coaster that I went on during my school years was exhausting. My days of simply being a kid and enjoying my childhood had started to evaporate. I was having to untangle the mind games and work to stay in his good graces, even though his roller-coaster behavior had very little to do with me. But I didn't understand that back then.

He was playing my heart against my head and my head against my soul. What made sense to my heart didn't make sense to my mind. What the teacher instilled in my mind as right and truth contradicted the feelings in my soul. He would convince my mind that something was good, but my soul would be screaming, "No!"

Very little had happened physically at this point, but inside, I was changing. My world was no longer steady and predictable. Life didn't always make sense anymore. And my confidence was becoming dependent on this man.

The mind games were all part of the grooming process. When he played with my innocent nine-year-old heart, he began to take control of who I was. He became in control of my emotions and my thoughts. He could push certain buttons and get certain reactions and responses from me. It was all part of his plan. It was not a quick process, but my heart and mind were being stolen more and more each day.

The isolation that I began to feel was very painful. Because I was not allowed to talk to anybody about my relationship with this teacher, I was left to figure the mind games out on my own. I had to hide all the ups and downs he put me through. It wasn't difficult during the times when he was happy with me, but when he would shut me out for weeks, sometimes for no apparent reason, I would feel completely alone. Nothing made sense, and there was no one I could talk to. I would try to think of anything I could do to get him to like me again. I had become emotionally dependent on him. Without him, I had to deal with the secrets and confusion on my own, and it was too much for my nine-year-old mind and heart to handle.

At this point, there probably wasn't a whole lot that could've been noticed from the outside. It was obvious to all that he favored me and that other little girl and he spent extra time with us. However, it became the norm for everyone around us. It was accepted as normal and okay, which also led to my nine-year-old mind believing that all of this must truly be normal and okay. The teachers knew about the time we spent together. No teacher ever asked me about why he wanted to see me so much. Their blind eye was very much a part of the struggle and confusion.

Why did nobody ask questions? Why not err on the side of caution? Asking a child questions is not wrong. Asking an adult questions is not wrong. In fact, whether the adult is guilty of anything or not, questions show that others are watching and that they care. Had someone questioned this coach's alone time with me, perhaps he would've been forced to change his behavior. Or if early on, before I was completely brainwashed, if they had asked me questions, perhaps things wouldn't have led to where they did next.

> Speak up for those who cannot speak for themselves;
> ensure justice for those being crushed.
> —Proverbs 31:8

At this point in my story, I didn't know I needed help. I didn't understand the seriousness of what was happening. I had no way to express concern to someone since I didn't see anything to be concerned about. However, the amount of time I spent with this man should've been picked up on by another adult. I am not blaming or criticizing anyone, but it's something we all can learn from. Be a voice for those who can't speak for themselves. Don't cower down and be afraid to ask questions pertaining to the well-being of a child. They need you to keep your eyes and ears open for anything suspicious.

And pray. Pray that God will give you a gut feeling or a sixth sense when no one else would maybe notice something. These types of perpetrators are crafty and educated in evil schemes and in hiding their intentions and plans. I fully understand that the mind games that were played with me were most likely, to some extent, played with other adults to acquire trust and respect for this coach. He worked very hard to get the reputation he had. We need God's help to see what as humans we often miss. So pray for wisdom, and then trust Him when He reveals something to you. Trust the instinct He's given you. We live in a world of sin, and God is asking us to be His hands and feet, the angels these children need to get them out of the dark world that they don't deserve to be in. It takes all of us.

CHAPTER 3

I knew our relationship was wrong. I may have only been nine, but each time he would mention his wife, my heart would sink. Something in my mind knew that if we had to keep everything a secret, then we must be doing something wrong.

We were sitting in our usual positions, with him in his desk chair and me kneeling next to him behind his desk. All the lights were off, and his class was busy working quietly at their desks. He got a shy look on his face, and he said that he wanted to show me something that was special to him. He pulled out what looked like a very old yearbook. It looked similar to the yearbooks my dad had stored away in our garage. In fact, my coach and my dad went to the same high school, and they weren't that far apart in age. My coach set the yearbook on the desk and started flipping through the pages. He eventually stopped on a particular page and slid the book over to me. He placed his finger down on a picture of a kid in the yearbook.

"Do you know who that is?" he asked me.

"Is it you?"

The picture was of a kid probably close to my age. The kid had the same smile as the teacher sitting next to me. The same dimple on his right cheek. But this child's skin was as dark as the night sky. And he had a black 'fro that was high above his head. My coach sitting next to me was not near that dark. He was very light skinned, and his hair was now cut short and had specks of gray through it.

"Do you think I was cute?"

I'm not sure why I was so shocked by his picture and then even more shocked by his question. I knew he was a little bit darker skinned than me, but I just saw him as a white person. It really didn't bother me, but it caught me off guard to see how dark he had been. I tried very hard to hide the surprise on my face.

"I think you were cute," I told him. He smiled big at me, and then he gave me these big puppy-dog eyes and began explaining his purpose for showing me his old yearbook.

"If I was your age, would you be my girlfriend?"

My heart was beating faster at this point. I knew the right answer would be to say "Yes." Right? Or is the right answer to say "No?" He was my coach, so maybe that's why this feeling was more of fear than excitement. In one sense, I was excited that he thought of me so highly, but what did all this mean? I knew one thing for sure: I didn't want to make him mad, and so I had to be careful with my response.

"Yes," was the best I could say, and then he looked me in the eyes and reached out and grabbed my hand.

"I would love to be your boyfriend."

What was happening? This was good, right? I couldn't tell anymore. I didn't know what I was supposed to be feeling. But I could easily tell he was happy, and that made me very happy. It was very uncomfortable after that. He was acting like an awkward nine-year-old boy who didn't know how to act around a girl. He told me that I was beautiful. That he loved everything about me. From the small mole on my hand to the blonde highlights in my hair.

He went on to share stories about himself. He told me about how high his vertical used to be. And how he could dunk a basketball easily even though he topped out at five feet, nine inches.

Before the bell rang, he told me that I could take his yearbook home. It wasn't really something I wanted to do, but I quickly learned that he had a reason behind it. His plan was for me to take it home and then return it to him on Saturday, to his house. He had recently been talking about how close we lived and that he wanted me to come for a visit. Taking the yearbook home meant we had the perfect excuse for me to actually go to his house. From where I lived in the parsonage, he lived in a blue A-frame house about three houses down.

As I walked back to my classroom, my head was spinning. Was my coach now my boyfriend? Something about this felt wrong, but yet it also made me feel special. He was a good Christian man who was even a part of a Christian quartet and very involved in the Baptist church in town. Everything about him contradicted the feelings that said this was wrong. He was an adult. A Christian adult. I was confused by what my heart was saying and what my mind was saying. A teacher is a safe person. A Christian is a safe person. Then why was my heart telling me that something is wrong? With him being a Christian, it just made things even more confusing.

> Like a muddied spring or a polluted fountain is a
> righteous man who gives way before the wicked.
> —Proverbs 25:26

Saturday rolled around, and I had held on to the yearbook as planned and was waiting till the afternoon to take it to him at his house, just as he told me. I spent the morning riding around town with friends and then came home for lunch. When I was finished eating, I asked my mom if it would be okay to return a book to my coach that he had let me borrow. She agreed to it, and as easy as that, my coach's plan worked.

I walked down the street to his house and knocked on the side door. He poked his head out and smiled and said to come on in. Something about his smile always put me at ease.

I walked into his house, and I was immediately amazed at how dark it was inside. It was a beautiful sunny fall day outside, but you couldn't tell that in his house. All of the lights were off and the blinds and curtains were shut. He kept his house dark, just like he kept his classroom. A dark house just made me even more uncomfortable.

I had butterflies in my stomach as we walked through the kitchen and into the living room. I had never been to a teacher's house before. It seemed like a very big deal in my nine-year-old mind.

Our relationship had grown slowly up until this point. It was a rapid change of pace after this first visit to his house. He used the foundation that he had set, the mind games, to guide me right into the plans he had set for me from the beginning. It was as if once I got to this point, there was no going back.

He had told me that the music room was his favorite room in the house. He walked me outside, through his garage, and to the little room attached to the other side. This small room was packed full of more music equipment than I had ever seen. His Christian quartet would go there to record their songs, and he even had a soundproof area with a mic and headphones. It was the real deal. It was really neat looking to a nine-year-old.

He smiled and asked me to go into the soundproof area. It felt a little bit like playing pretend. Like what a typical nine-year-old should be playing. He asked if I could sing. He wanted me to sing him a song. I was a confident little girl, but there was no way I was going to sing right here, alone in a room, with my basketball coach. It maybe would've been different if I had a good singing voice, but I learned early on in life just how off-key my voice really is.

I vividly remember years earlier practicing with all the kids at church for a church musical we were going to perform. We were in a classroom toward the back of the church building and were going over all the songs for the musical. I was my usual happy-go-lucky self and very proud of myself for knowing all the words to the songs that we were practicing. The songs were a lot of fun to sing, and I really enjoyed the practice. But when I got home, my brother, who had also been at the practice, asked if he could talk to my mom in private. After a few minutes, my mom called me back into her room along with my brother and sat me down. She asked me how practice had gone. I told her it was great. She proceeded to ask if I would sing her one of the songs. So I did. I started singing my favorite song. Smiles immediately came to their faces. My mom proceeded to give me my first voice lesson. I apparently needed to learn how to change my pitch from high to low to match the melody of the song. Not just loud to soft. For high notes, I wouldn't change my pitch at all. I would just sing louder. And apparently, I completely embarrassed my brother during the entire practice. At the next practice, I was much more aware of my voice and made sure to sing quietly. Our teacher seemed very pleased that I was no longer yelling the song back at her. Hey, not everyone can sound like Mandisa.

So standing in my coach's music studio and being asked to sing, I was quick to politely shake my head no. He smiled and seemed to think my shyness was cute. He said that I didn't need a pretty singing voice, I had the physical beauty to make up for it. I still couldn't get comfortable being alone with him like that, no matter how many compliments he gave me. We shared a long hug. It felt like I was hugging my dad, but my dad didn't hold on to me that tight or for that long.

I walked home feeling almost as if I had just gone on my first date. I wanted to share with my parents all the nice things my coach had said about me. But I remembered my coach's words about how sharing anything about us would get him in trouble. I wouldn't do that to him. So I went home and said very little, but in my stomach I still had butterflies that were making their presence known. I looked forward to seeing my coach at school on Monday. The weekend couldn't go fast enough.

Sunday, I spent most of my time thinking about my coach and how happy I was that he was so pleased with me. I rode my bike around town after church and went multiple times by his house, hoping he would invite me in. But I saw his wife's car there, so I kind of figured that I wouldn't be getting an invite.

I hustled to school on Monday morning, thinking that he might want to talk to me before school. But he wasn't sitting in his spot in the gym next to the PE teacher. I went on to class once the bell rang, and I noticed as I walked by his classroom that all the lights were on and a woman teacher was standing behind his desk, smiling at the students while they walked in. He had a sub. He wasn't at school. The day ended up being a waste for me, as I spent a huge chunk of my time trying to figure out if I was in trouble and if this was his way of avoiding me or if he really was sick. I had no idea, and I was very disappointed that I had no way to know what the truth was. So my little nine-year-old heart worried.

Grooming works so well on a child's mind that they become paranoid, and nervous, and anxious even when there isn't anything purposefully hurtful being done by the perpetrator. My coach wasn't sick, I found out. He wasn't avoiding me either. He was missing work because of being out of town. My mind had gone a thousand different ways, but knowing eventually that he was just out of town, I was finally able to relax and enjoy school. I even believed that he was probably missing me as much as I was missing him while he was away. Come Wednesday, when he was finally back at school, he had a lot to catch up on with work, so he couldn't make the time for me that I had hoped for. He made sure to let me know that he did miss me, though, and he asked if I could come by after school. It was getting darker earlier, so I knew I would only get to stay at his house for a short time. My folks didn't want me riding my bike around town after dark.

I walked over to the church building after school and sat at my dad's desk and did all my homework. I worked as fast as I could, and then I told Dad I was going to play for a bit and then go home. I ran home, dropped off my backpack, grabbed my bike, and took off for my coach's house. I rode by the front of his house three or four times before he finally peeked his head out and motioned for me to come. His wife worked at a high school in another town, and he had a bit of time alone. I brought my bike in with me and set it in a room that possibly had been a screened-in porch at one time. After setting my bike down, I followed him into his house. He gave me a big hug as soon as I walked in the door. Even though this was only my second time there, I felt more comfortable. I was still nervous, but not near as much as the first time I had come to his house. He got me a snack, and he talked about where he had gone out of town, then he asked me a question.

"Do you remember me saying that your beauty will take you places?"

I immediately felt shy at the question. I'm sure my face turned red, but I'm guessing he didn't notice since it was still so dark in his house. I nodded in response.

"I want to show you something," he quickly replied, and then he walked toward the door. I followed him back to his music room, and he shut the door behind us. I watched as he slid his hand between the wall and some of his large music equipment. Hiding back there was a large envelope that he pulled out and started opening. Inside were several pictures of kids. Some were pictures of kids cut from magazines, but some were the actual hard-copy photographs. The kids were posing and smiling in all the pictures. My coach looked through some of them, passing them to me. They were happy kids, you could tell. As I looked through the pictures, I expected to see someone I knew, but I didn't recognize a single girl.

"Each girl here is beautiful, but not one of them is as beautiful as you."

I was flattered by his nice words, but I wasn't understanding what he was getting at. He asked me if I wanted to help him. Before I could answer, he went on to explain that by me allowing him to take my picture, he could submit the best ones to these companies and get paid big money, just like these kids had done. It could help him, his wife, and my parents. He made it seem amazing. It felt like I was doing a secret Christmas present for my parents. That I was going to be able to give my parents whatever they wanted because of all the money we would make. Filled with excitement, I followed him back into the house. He walked into his bedroom and I saw him pull out a camera. It wasn't anything fancy. In fact, from what I could tell, it was just a disposable camera. He was almost hopping around as he walked, seeming so excited. He asked me to stand between the doorframe of his bedroom, and he took my picture. Actually, several pictures.

It was surprisingly fun, but that was mostly because my coach was being extra goofy, trying to make me laugh for the camera. He was pretending to be like a real photographer and getting all sorts of angles and telling me to pose in goofy ways. He was cracking me up with all he was doing. And when he was done, he held me close again and told me that I was beautiful. He made me feel like the most special girl in the world.

This secret plan of success was fun for a nine-year-old. I was also excited because soon we would be able to tell my parents and his wife about what we have been doing. I couldn't wait to see how proud my parents would be of me. Plus, I wouldn't have to hold all these secrets in anymore.

After our goofy photo shoot, it seemed as if all the days were flying by. My coach was showing me a lot of attention at school, and I was, no doubt, enjoying it. Eventually he pulled me aside and gave me the great news that our plan was working. The pictures turned out great, but we needed more. I was invited back over to his house again so we could take more pictures.

I rushed through my homework after school that day, and I got to his house as quickly as I could. I couldn't wait for my coach to play "photographer" again. I waited for the go-ahead to come in, just like before, and I parked my bike in the same spot and followed him into the house. He wasn't quite as hospitable this time. There wasn't a hug when I first entered, and he didn't offer me a snack. He seemed a bit more serious this time.

With concern on his face, he had me sit on his couch that was positioned up against his big picture window, facing toward his television.

"Your pictures were incredible," he said.

"Thanks. Maybe it was because you had me laughing so hard." I chuckled, thinking back to how funny he had been the last time I was here, but it became obvious he wasn't in the mood.

"Yeah, possibly. I am going to be honest with you. I only want what is best for you and even though your pictures were incredible, they could be better."

This was starting to sound more like a job than a fun plan we had. I felt awkward and uncomfortable. I am a rule follower and a people pleaser. To hear that he wasn't pleased with me made me instantly want to fix whatever I had done wrong. He pulled out another folder that he had sitting on the couch. He placed it on his lap as he explained to me that he didn't want to settle for mediocre. He thought I could be big. Really big. But if I wanted to be the best, it meant I needed to be okay with showing everything that God had made. Holding nothing back.

I was very confused about what he was explaining to me. What was he wanting me to do differently? He took the folder that was sitting on his lap and handed it to me. I opened up the folder and immediately became aware of what he was trying to tell me. The pictures in this folder were different than the ones he showed me the time before. I noticed right away that these little girls weren't smiling like the girls from the previous folder. These girls had sad eyes and forced grins. But what made me gasp out loud in shock was that the little girls in these pictures weren't wearing any clothes.

> You have kept count of my tossings, put my tears in
> your bottle. Are they not in your book? Then my
> enemies will turn back in the day when I call. This
> I know, that God is for me. In God, whose word I
> praise, in the Lord, whose word I praise, in God I
> trust; I shall not be afraid. What can man do to me?
> —Psalm 56:8–11

CHAPTER 4

Outside, the leaves were changing colors. More leaves were piled on the ground than hung in the trees. Halloween was only a few days away, and I still hadn't decided on a costume yet. It felt like yesterday, I was walking in my cowboy outfit with my third-grade class at my old school in our annual Halloween parade. We would walk down a few blocks from the school, through a nearby nursing home, and then back to the school. It was always followed by a Halloween party in our classrooms. It was a fun day. A nice memory. How was that already a whole year ago? How has so much happened since then?

I sat on my coach's couch, feeling a pain in my chest that I had only felt one other time, back when my coach unexpectedly put his hands on my chest in his classroom. Last time, I reacted quickly in shock. And this time was no different, except I was trying hard to hide it. I didn't want him mad at me again. Like he was the last time. I needed to be strong.

I didn't understand why I was being shown these pictures of girls my age without any clothes on, and I was very confused about what exactly my coach was expecting me to do. But I knew he wouldn't hurt me. I was certain of that.

"It's really no big deal. It's just going to show exactly how beautiful you really are. I can't wait to see all the beautiful things about you."

He talked on and on, and I listened. If I said "No," then he would be mad. He would be hurt. I couldn't bear the thought of hurting him. I would lose my best friend. He was the only one who knew my deepest secrets. And I would be hated by the varsity basketball coach for the next four years. I would lose my favorite sport and my dreams. Nothing about saying no seemed to be in my best interest.

"Okay. I trust you. I'll do it." I was sort of expecting a big response from him about how happy he was that I would do what he was asking. At least one of his famous smiles. But I didn't. He let out a quick "Great!" and then quickly jumped off the couch and went to his bedroom. He came back out a minute later and said he was ready.

He didn't keep his bedroom dark. The blinds were shut, but the bedroom lights were on. Sitting on his dresser were three disposable cameras. He was walking quickly around the room, seeming to get ready for whatever was about to happen. The last time, he was goofy and acted as if he had never taken pictures like this before. This time, he seemed to have a plan and he knew exactly how to set up. Almost like he had done this many times before.

I stood and watched until he was ready. He walked toward me and finally gave me the smile I needed to ease my nerves. He put his hands on my shoulders and softly spoke words of encouragement to me.

"Don't be nervous. Don't make this a bigger deal than it is. You're beautiful and I'm so proud of you."

I nodded and swallowed hard. I probably should've been more nervous about how wrong this felt, but what I was most nervous about was if he would like how I looked. No one had seen my body without clothes on except my mom, and I had no idea if I looked right. Or normal. What if something was wrong with me?

"Why don't you keep your panties on this time, so you feel more comfortable?" I was glad to hear that. He held up a white sheet that he had gotten out of his closet, and he had me take off my clothes while he held up the sheet to hide me.

"Are you done?"

"Yes."

He took a step forward, draping the sheet around my shoulders and covering my body. He hugged me from behind, holding me tight.

"You're shaking," he said while he held me. I tried to give him a smile that showed I wasn't scared, but I'm not sure I succeeded.

"It's cute how nervous you are." I wasn't sure what that meant. He had me turn around and face him. I clung to the sheet tightly around me, and he started taking pictures. I tried to smile, but it felt weird. He said it wasn't a big deal if I smiled. I was really wishing it could be fun like it was the time before. I didn't like him acting so serious.

"I want you to kneel down on your knees and sit on your feet." I followed his instructions.

"Now let the sheet fall to the floor." For the next several minutes, he instructed me all sorts of ways to stand and sit and lie. It was a good distraction having to follow his directions instead of focusing on the fact that I was only in my underwear. He seemed so happy with me. So proud. I must've been good at this, just like he thought I would be.

"I have one more camera left for pictures," he said while he reached for the final camera sitting on the dresser.

"Do you want me to take my underwear off?" He gave me a fast nod and a big smile that showed me how excited he was.

"Thank you for trusting me. You know I would never hurt you."

"I know. I trust you."

I posed in similar ways as I did before, following his directions. He promised me he wouldn't tell anyone that I had done this. He wouldn't want me to get in trouble.

"You are more beautiful than I even imagined and strong, too. You're officially my all-star. In fact, I think that will be my nickname for you. All-Star."

When his last camera was out of film, I put my clothes back on. I was surprisingly not as shy at that point about being naked. We didn't say a whole lot afterward, and I knew I needed to get home before it got dark. He left me with a hug and a smile. I smiled back at him and was honestly very proud of myself for being strong, until I started walking home. I instantly felt dirty the closer I got to our house. I felt like God was furious at me.

Remember that little girl who was always wanting to do the right thing? The rule follower? She didn't know how to handle the guilt that hung over her as she walked into her house.

Usually, anytime my guilt got bad because of something I did, I would have to tell my mom. Confess it to her and then I would feel better. But this time, I couldn't do that. I went straight to my room and sat on my bed. Mom was in the kitchen and was making supper. It was just me and her at home. Usually I would go out and watch TV or talk to Mom, but I needed to come up with a plan. A plan to make my heart feel better. I had to get rid of this guilt. After just a few minutes, I had figured out what I needed to do. The next day at school, I had decided, I would tell my coach how I was feeling. I knew he would not want me struggling. I decided I would just tell him that I was feeling rough, and I knew he would know how to make me feel better.

The next day I tried to talk to him before school, but I got to school just as the bell was ringing. My only chance to talk to him now would be if he called me into his classroom at some point during the day. The day hadn't gone well for me at all. I was preoccupied and wasn't able to focus on anything my teacher said. My guilt was eating me alive, and I began to wonder if guilt was hurting my coach like this too. No matter how good our intentions were, what we did was not okay.

The day was almost over, and finally a knock at the door came. The same little girl had a note for me, and I was finally going to be able to see my coach and make things right.

"Rachel . . ." He liked to drag out the syllables when he would say my name. I always knew he was in a good mood when he would do that. Before he could say anything else, my heart started pouring out to him.

"I'm not doing good." Tears were already dripping down my cheeks. "I feel so guilty about yesterday."

I was nervously and anxiously talking. I had held all this in since yesterday, and I was about to burst all day long waiting to talk to him. It became like a flood of words as I explained my guilt and embarrassment. I paused for a moment to let him talk too. I just knew I was right about this. But he didn't talk. He actually laughed. Like a loud belly laugh.

"You're joking with me, right?"

I was not getting the response I thought I would get. He seemed to laugh harder and harder. Finally, he slowed down and he realized that I was being serious.

"You're my beautiful all-star. I enjoyed yesterday with you. If something happened that made you feel bad, I'm sorry. But I didn't force you to do anything. In fact, you're the one that asked me if you could . . ." He paused to double-check that no one was listening. When the coast was clear, he finished what he was saying.

"You're the one who wanted to take off all your clothes."

I had never felt so ashamed. He was right. Then he held my hand and leaned in real close.

"Don't allow yourself to feel bad about yesterday. You were simply thanking God for how beautiful He made you. That's all. God has a purpose for you. Don't stop now. Together we can do amazing things, but I have to be able to trust you."

What was he saying? That God would be proud of me? I was always trying to make God proud of me. It was a daily goal of mine. This just didn't feel right. I didn't feel like my coach was right. And I definitely didn't feel like my God was proud.

"So, can I trust you?" he asked.

I felt a little bit backed into a corner. Not by anything he did or said, just by my own actions.

"Yes, you can trust me." My mind was still racing. I had so many questions. Questions I thought my coach could answer for me. Well, I guess, technically, he did. Just not the way I had hoped.

"Okay, so I can trust you, but can you trust me?"

Our time together had drawn us closer, and I could feel a connection with him because of it. Our secrets, however, were pulling me away from everyone else. I nodded yes to his question.

"Amazing." His face lit up. "Now please tell me you feel better, and that what happened yesterday with the pictures, we can do again. Because, my beautiful all-star, I thought about you all night long."

It took me a long time to fully understand that what I did that day in his bedroom was not my fault. I carried that guilt around for a long time. The perpetrator works hard to twist your thinking and your emotions to get you to think that you're to blame. It's easier to see the innocence in other little girls, but I viewed myself differently. I should've known better. Either way, it's a guilt that my God doesn't want me to carry.

> My guilt has overwhelmed me like
> a burden too heavy to bear.
> —Psalm 38:4

Things had pretty much gone back to the way they were before. It was a little while before I was invited back to his house, which was okay with me. Basketball season had started, and he was busy with practices. In fourth grade, we were able to play basketball for our school, but it was the peewee league, and it didn't start till January.

I couldn't wait for the season to start. My coach for peewee basketball was actually the brother of the varsity coach. My understanding was that he wasn't as nice as the varsity coach. I had a few nerves because of that, but they were mostly due to excitement.

The year 1995 came to an end. I was still getting special treatment from the varsity coach. I would often get called out of class. He seemed to still like me, but it also was odd to me that he hadn't brought up having me come visit him at his house or anything about pictures.

He even stopped calling me his all-star. I still thought about it every day, but somehow he seemed to completely forget. I was glad he hadn't mentioned it, and I was beginning to believe that God had a hand in it and showed my coach that what we were doing was wrong. If that were true, then I would be the happiest little girl alive. But where my mind kept going was what if he stopped because he didn't think I was beautiful anymore. Or if he stopped liking me. If something was wrong with me and he was just too nice to tell me. I didn't want to bring it up to find out his reasoning, but it was on my mind a lot.

Christmas vacation was amazing. We had a lot of snow over the break, which was both good and bad. It was good because right at the beginning of January is my birthday and I would usually get a new sled. With all the snow we got, I was going to be able to test it out. But the snow was also bad because my cousin had come over for my birthday and we were going to go to Chuck E. Cheese, but we were snowed in.

This year, for my birthday, I was really wanting a baby doll. I had never been much of a baby doll or Barbie doll type girl. I'd rather play ball with the boys and make mud soup and climb trees. But I had been adamant to my mom about wanting a baby doll this year for my birthday. She kept telling me that I was going to be ten years old and that's too old to have a baby doll. Oddly enough, I was sad.

The night of my birthday when we were all snowed in, I opened up my two presents from my mom and dad. One was a new sled, and the other was a baby doll. I was completely shocked and really excited. I looked at my mom, and she gave me an ornery smile.

"I bought it for you weeks ago. I thought it would be a fun surprise. But this is it. That's the last baby doll I'm buying for you."

I smiled real big and ran over and gave my mom a huge hug. Maybe this was my way of saying that I didn't want to grow up so fast. I was learning a lot of adult things rather quickly, and maybe my subconscious was desperately wanting to be a kid. I don't know, but having that baby doll brought me a lot of comfort, especially in the weeks ahead.

The snow melted enough over the next few days that when Christmas vacation was over, schools were open and ready to start the second semester.

I hadn't seen Coach all break, so I had some excitement about school starting up. That, and the fact that my basketball season would be starting soon.

My coach seemed to have missed me too because almost immediately he asked if I could find a way to come to his house on Saturday afternoon. His wife was going to be gone, and he was really wanting to see me and spend time alone.

I had no idea our family schedule so I didn't have the authority to say yes, but I did anyway. Mainly because I really wanted to see him too. I was enjoying all of the basketball talks and God talks the last few months, and I felt good about our relationship.

"Amazing. I am needing my beautiful all-star. I've missed her."

My heart jumped at his words. I was excited to hear his fun nickname for me, but I was also a bit nervous about where his mind was at and what his plans were for Saturday. He never said, and I wasn't going to ask.

"I'll see you at two thirty tomorrow," he said to me Friday before school. "Don't be late."

This was new to me. I was not used to him giving me a specific time to be there. Always in the past, we just picked a day, not a day and a time. I was surprised, and a ripple of fear ran through my body, but I shrugged it off, thinking that it probably had something to do with his wife and the timing of when she was gone.

It wasn't the right weather to be riding bikes around town on Saturday, so I made a plan to go to the neighbor's house across the street that had a little girl a few years older than me. The coolest thing about this girl's house was that she had a hamster. My parents wouldn't let me have a hamster, so I had fun with hers.

I only stayed at my neighbor's house for a half hour or so and then I said I was going home. But instead, I ran as fast as I could to my coach's house. To the best of my ability, I was able to get there close to two thirty. Or so I thought. I was apparently late by about ten minutes. I knocked on the side door, and immediately my coach opened the door and almost pulled me in with him.

Everything was dark as usual. I got a soft but not-nice earful about being late. At this point, I still hadn't said a word. Something in me sensed danger, but that didn't make sense since I didn't see my coach as dangerous. After my talking-to from Coach, I was hurried along into his bedroom. As I walked up to the door, I right away realized why I sensed danger. There stood my coach's brother. He was standing by the window and was holding a video camera. Then my eyes turned and to my left, sitting quietly on the bed, was the other little girl from school. Tears streaming down her face and anger in her eyes.

> I was forcibly carried off from the land of the
> Hebrews, and even here I have done nothing
> to deserve being put in a dungeon.
> —Genesis 40:15

CHAPTER 5

She was angry. Not scared. Not worried. Not embarrassed. Just flat-out mad. I had a million emotions running through my heart and just as many questions going through my mind.

Why was she here? Why was his brother here? Why did he have a video camera? And why was the little girl so angry?

My coach started to talk, saying something about sunshine. But he was cut short when the little girl burst out, crying in anger, and yelled at both men in the room.

"No! No! No! I'm not doing this! You can't make me! Take me home, now!"

And she jumped off the bed and ran as fast as she could toward the door. My coach grabbed her and kept her from running, and immediately his brother set down the camera and helped hold her. The brother looked straight at my coach and then at me with the most hateful eyes.

"You sit and don't move. This one needs to learn a lesson. If you even think about leaving, then I will personally teach you a lesson too."

I did exactly as I was told and sat on the bed. My hands were shaking. The men carried the little girl out of the room while she continued to kick and scream and fight. The door slammed shut behind them, but nothing in the world could've drowned out the cries I heard coming from the other side of the door.

This little girl had been my least favorite person at school. Maybe my least favorite person in the world. Mostly because I was jealous of her. She was my coach's favorite, his number one girl, and I knew I could never compete with her. She was beautiful, and even though my coach would tell me I'm beautiful, I knew better. I knew what beautiful was.

Even though I hadn't cared for this other little girl, at that moment, hearing her cry my heart broke for her. I was pretty certain that the brother was hurting her. Somehow teaching her a lesson. I knew better than to think it was my coach. He wouldn't hurt a soul, but his brother was a different story.

Looking back, I tear up remembering her cries, her fight. She had so much fight in her and I had none. She wasn't going to do anything she didn't want to. She wasn't going to let them hurt her, at least not without a fight. I admire and envy her strength. If only I had a similar strength, then maybe I wouldn't have listened to the brother's directions. Maybe if I had strength like hers, then I would've jumped off that bed, ran out the door, and together we could've fought them. We could've gotten free and never returned.

Why did I have no fight? Why was I so accepting of the circumstances and following the instructions? Why didn't I see myself as someone I should fight for?

Eventually, I didn't hear any more cries. In fact, it got extremely quiet. I stayed exactly where I was told to and waited. But the longer I waited without hearing any noise, the more scared I got. I wasn't going to move from that spot. If no one ever came back in that room, I would be perfectly fine. My eyes stayed glued to the door handle, praying it wouldn't turn. When it did, I held my breath, waiting to see what had happened to the other little girl.

First came my coach, with his stern, serious face. Then came the little girl. Her arms were tightly hugging herself as she slowly walked to the bed and sat by me. Finally, the brother came through the door. And he was smiling. The biggest, most evil smile I had ever seen.

My coach was just five feet, nine inches, but his brother seemed at least three or four inches taller. And bigger around too. Coach was darker skinned with short dark hair, and his brother was white. Very, very white. With short, reddish-blond hair. He was possibly the ugliest man I had ever met. His eyes bulged out from his head. His jaw seemed crooked on his face. And his nose was massive and lumpy. Those features, plus his size and mean expressions, made me very scared of him.

I was shaking, but when I looked over at the other little girl, I noticed that she wasn't shaking at all. She sat perfectly still, staring down at the floor. She seemed to be off in a distant place. I wanted to ask her if she was okay, but I was being watched very closely. As the brother dealt with the video camera, Coach came and knelt next to us, almost like a coach on a basketball gym floor, in the team huddle telling his team which play to run next. He put one hand on my leg and the other on the blonde little girl's leg, and he smiled.

"For just a little bit we are going to play a game called 'Simon Says.' I listened very carefully to his words as he went on to explain the game.

"You both will have to do what Simon says but there is one rule to follow. You do what Simon says and you are not allowed to stop until Simon says stop."

My ten-year-old mind immediately jumped to how I could follow the rules of this game perfectly. I wanted my coach to be proud of me. But I wasn't certain why that rule was even mentioned. I always played this game that way. Where if Simon said to pat your head, then you kept patting your head until Simon said to stop. I guess my coach wasn't as familiar with this game as I was. I didn't want the brother to hear me, but I did have one question, so I leaned in and whispered it in my coach's ear.

"What happens if we mess up and do something Simon didn't say?" Coach leaned back and put both hands on my legs and smiled real big.

"That isn't going to be an issue," he said. My eyebrows scrunched in confusion. I was pretty certain that was the whole point of the game. The other little girl still wasn't saying anything, but she had stopped staring at the floor. The two men had started talking softly to each other. I wanted so badly to be brave. I felt in my gut that I needed to talk to the other little girl. I needed to see if she was okay. Ask what happened to her. But my fear took over, and I just sat there instead.

The men turned their attention back to us. We were still sitting on the bed. The brother had the large black camcorder on his shoulder, and while I was looking at him, I saw the red light turn on. He was recording. Absolutely none of this made sense to me.

"Sunshine, I want you to meet All-Star. All-Star, this is Sunshine." My coach said these words with a smile. Like what he was saying was the most exciting thing in the world. I realized quickly that I wasn't the only one he'd given a nickname to.

"Girls, you are here to make the camera happy, and how you make the camera happy is by doing exactly what Simon says."

As my coach talked, the other little girl started showing anger in her eyes again, but she never said a word and she never tried to run.

"Simon says to undress each other."

A child's mind can't process something like this. It physically is incapable to do so. So as I tried in my head to make sense of what was happening, I couldn't. I knew that my coach loved me and would never hurt me. That was one of the promises he said to me over and over. But this game that they were making us play made me feel sick to my stomach and really sad. I didn't want to touch her, and I didn't want her touching me, especially where Simon told us to.

I was like most little girls who imagined who they would someday marry, or where they would go on their first date, or what their first kiss would be like. This was definitely not how I thought my first kiss would happen. Not locked in a room with two men videotaping and not with another little girl. I still remember the taste of tears when we were told to use our tongues. And I did as I was told, but she kept her teeth clenched shut. This other little girl was still putting up what little fight she could.

I struggle so much to look back at the events of this day and know that I gave no effort to fight. When I was told to do something, the thought of not doing it never crossed my mind, even if it was something I didn't want to do or didn't understand. Why didn't I say no? Why didn't I fight? Why would I trust this man and do what he said? Something must be wrong with me that I would do such terrible awful things simply because a man told me to.

The thief only comes to steal and kill and destroy . . .
—John 10:10

Going to school on Monday morning was the last thing in the world that I had wanted to do. Honestly, I didn't want to leave my room. I didn't want to leave my bed. Sunday hadn't gone well at all. I was in my own little world, struggling with images of the day before, feeling nauseous each time I thought about it. My mom and dad picked up on me being in a bad mood. All they knew was that I was crabby, and I couldn't explain my reasoning as to why I was crabby. So in their mind, I was acting this way for no reason, and it was not going to be tolerated. As a preacher's kid, you often feel like you live in a glass bowl, and our family handled that by acting as if we never had any problems.

"Act like it doesn't hurt," was one of my dad's famous quotes. He had a huge heart for us kids and when we hurt, but he would use this phrase a lot when it came to sports. Particularly when you got hit by a pitch in baseball, you needed to run to first base and act like it didn't hurt.

I didn't want to get in trouble with mom and dad, so I quickly put on a smile and did exactly that. I acted like it didn't hurt. As the day went on, pretending that everything was fine seemed to actually help. I was able to numb my emotions and keep my focus on normal things. But when Monday morning rolled around, I was back to feeling nauseous at the thought of going to school. I had to be happy at home and I had to act normal at school, but I didn't want to see this other little girl at all.

A million thoughts ran through my head of how I could get out of going to school. I considered very seriously running away from home. I was walking the sidewalk that led to the school building, and I stopped at the end of the sidewalk. To the left was the school. To the right was the church where my dad was at. And straight ahead was a field. Do I go left to the school and face the embarrassment and shame of seeing this other little girl and my coach? Do I go right and run straight to my dad, tell him everything and squeal on my coach, and face whatever punishment I would get for what I had done and for keeping it a secret? Or do I go straight? I didn't know what was straight ahead, other than a field and, beyond that, some woods. It was still very cold outside, with some snow piled up in different places. I didn't know the first thing about surviving in the cold or finding food. The only thing I was good at was following directions, and out there, there were no directions.

I turned left and walked to the school. I felt like I could throw up at any moment, and I couldn't stop shaking. Do I talk to the other little girl? Do I say that I'm sorry? Do I act like she's not there? Do I ask her if she is okay?

I walked into the gym and sat with my class. My coach was in his usual spot, and right away he motioned for me to come talk to him. I set my backpack down and walked across the gym floor to see him. I had to work really hard to hide the tears in my eyes.

"Hey . . . how's Rachel?" He had his huge smile and happy eyes. He showed zero signs of anything being different from the week before. I knew that his question wasn't meant for a real answer, so I did the same thing I had done all weekend. I faked it.

"I'm good."

"Peewee basketball starts up this week. I can't wait to see how good you do." In all this craziness, I had completely forgotten that basketball was starting on Wednesday. I felt less sick and a bit more excited.

"I can't wait." At that moment, it hit me that my peewee coach was my coach's brother. Fear must have covered my face because my coach was quick to assure me in a quiet way to where no one could hear.

"It's okay. My brother thinks you're great and he won't ever hurt you. I won't let him. You just focus on basketball." A huge relief washed over me. I instantly believed my coach and felt better about the upcoming season. I knew my coach wouldn't let his brother hurt me. I was pretty sure that it was his brother that made him do all that stuff on Saturday, but no more.

I walked back to my spot in the bleachers and kept looking around for the other little girl. So far there was no sign of her. Later in the day, a knock came at the door in our classroom. I expected it to be the other little girl, but it wasn't. It was someone new. I wondered if she faced the same battle that I did and didn't want to come to school today. I was glad she wasn't there, but I dreaded the day she did come back.

I followed the other student to my coach's classroom. As usual, his lights were off. I went straight to his desk. He smiled at me, which was an instant comfort. We talked about basketball and the upcoming season. The peewee team was made up of boys and girls. It wasn't until the next year that I would be on my coach's girls' basketball team.

I was finally getting comfortable in our conversation, realizing it was back to our usual relationship of talking basketball, but right before I needed to head back, he said that he needed to explain something to me. I couldn't pick up on whether he was mad or sad, but he told me that the other little girl wouldn't be coming back to school.

I'm pretty sure my mouth hung open in surprise for the next few minutes. My coach explained things, and I was confused and unsure of what was going on, but I was so glad that she was gone so that I wouldn't have to face her. I wouldn't have to worry about her telling people what I did. And I wouldn't ever have to be alone with her again at my coach's house. I was also glad that I could now be my coach's favorite. It seemed like an answered prayer.

The first day of practice was Wednesday after school, and I was nervous for obvious reasons. Surprisingly, it went really well. The brother didn't act any different toward me than he did to anyone else, and he was still very ugly but didn't have that evil look. All of my practicing had paid off, for I easily held my own at practice. There were several other girls on the team and lots of boys. Because of that, there were three teams. An A, B, and C team. It became obvious that the C team was going to consist of all the girls, and the boys would play the A and B games, but by the middle of practice, I was moved up to play with the boys. This was more of what I was used to.

Our first game came, and I was amazed to see that I was on the starting five of the A team. It was exciting to me and my family; however, it was aggravating to the other families. In their mind, a girl should not be playing over a boy. My coach's brother explained that he coached to win, and he didn't care if it was a boy or a girl. If a child was skilled enough to be in the starting five, then they would be in the starting five.

Several games in, the boys were starting to hold a grudge against me. No one on the team would pass me the ball. It became obvious to everyone watching that they were boycotting having a girl on the A team, so the school set up a board meeting to discuss the complaints of the parents.

The night of the board meeting, my mom sat me down in my room and tried to convince me to quit. She said that it wasn't worth all this. That I could become a cheerleader and not worry about this.

There was no way I was going to quit. I loved basketball too much, and I was good. It was a dream that I wasn't willing to part with. My dad left for the board meeting to go support my coach's brother. He respected the brother for being bold enough to play me. We went through something similar back in our old town with the baseball team I was on. There was a meeting held to discuss who deserved to be on the all-star team, and statistically, I should've easily made the team. I had better stats than anyone on my team and better than several other teams, but it was decided at that meeting that a boy should not be passed up for the all-star team because of a girl. My dad was afraid that the same thing was going to happen with this meeting, so he went to try and help defend me.

Several families came to try and get the brother fired from coaching our peewee team. Majority of the complaints had to do with me, but one family was there because they feared this man being around their daughter. Their comments were basically ignored, and the board decided that this man should not be fired for starting a girl and that the players could no longer purposefully keep from passing me the ball.

Dad came home and shared the good news with me that the brother wasn't fired. It would've been a perfect opportunity to tell my parents about the Saturday at my coach's house, but my mind was racing about basketball. I pushed the bad thoughts behind and focused on what made me happy, and that was basketball.

I believe that my coping mechanisms were many, but my number one tool to keep myself from going crazy was focusing on basketball. Still to this day, I could be struggling, but put a basketball in my hands, and instantly I'm at home. That peewee season went on, and I continued to be in the starting lineup. Not once did the brother make me feel uncomfortable or say or do anything to hurt me. My confidence seemed to be coming back. With the other little girl gone, I was able to push that memory to the back of my mind.

> Like a roaring lion or a charging bear is a
> wicked ruler over a helpless people.
> —Proverbs 28:15

CHAPTER 6

Basketball season came to an end, and spring was right around the corner. Through the ups and downs of the emotional roller coaster that my coach had me on, I was constantly wondering if I was in his good graces, or not. The last few months I had mostly been on a downtime with him. He always seemed preoccupied and busy. He definitely wasn't interested in me for whatever reason. It would take me a while to quit hurting from the fact that he abruptly would shut me out of his life. Usually about the time I finally would get used to it, then he would pop back into my life as if he never left.

The end of winter and the beginning of spring, things had been pretty quiet with him. When he began to talk to me more, it was always fun conversations and he would spend a lot of time making me feel good about how I looked and how I was going to be a famous basketball player someday. He explained that he felt blessed to be in my life. My ten-year-old mind believed every word and would emotionally become attached to him again, and maybe even more each time he would let me back into his life because I wanted to make sure that he wouldn't shut me out again. I always assumed that when he would shut me out, it was because of something I did wrong, so my goal was to never do anything wrong.

During a conversation in his classroom one day, he asked me why I hadn't been back to his house. I sat in a dumb moment, unsure of how to answer a question that didn't make any sense to me. He had hardly talked to me, let alone invite me back to his house. I had done a pretty good job of blocking out the last time I had gone there. I was able to remember the good things about him and the good moments, not the bad. I also always assumed the best, so when he invited me to come over on a certain day during spring break and at a certain time, I reassured my mind and heart that he wasn't going to do anything to hurt me. That he loved me.

I wasn't even the least bit nervous walking to his house on the day he wanted me to come. I just wanted so badly for him to be proud of me. My parents believed I was walking to the small general store in town to get a snack, but instead I stopped at my coach's house. He opened the door before I even knocked and was quick to embrace me in a long hug.

"You came!" He said this in a way that showed he was surprised that I actually came and he was very grateful.

"Of course I came."

In the past, when I would come to his house, he seemed to be more focused on things he wanted to show me or things he wanted me to do. This time he was focused on me. Really focused on me. My heart was racing each time he touched me in his gentle way. It was foreign for me to have a man show affection to me by hugging or touching in any way. I'm sure my body was as stiff as a board, but he continued to say nice things and to touch and hug me. It was a compliment to me that he seemed to love me so much, but in a way, it was very suffocating and scary. I think a part of me started to question what was going to happen next.

We stood between his dining room and living room, with his arms wrapped around me. I wasn't certain what to do with my hands, so they just hung by my side.

"You know you mean so much to me, right?" I nodded to his question and smiled at his kind words.

"You know that I have loved you so much that I have shared some amazing things with you?" I nodded again. "Well, I want to share something new with you, something special, that will show you just how much I love you."

"Okay," I softly said to him. Whatever he was going to show me couldn't be bad. If he was going to show me how much he loved me, then there was no way it could be bad. My thoughts went automatically to basketball and that he was probably going to share with me something that would be amazing for my game. I knew how much he cared about my future basketball opportunities. I couldn't wait to hear what he wanted to share.

"When two people love each other, they don't just say that they love each other. God taught us that we should actually make love with each other." He paused a long time, I think he was waiting to see my reaction. "To make love" was a new phrase for me. I hadn't heard it before, and I wasn't sure what it meant. I pictured that the talking and hugging we had done was the making love that he was talking about. Maybe sharing more of each other's hearts and dreams. Love is special and exciting. If God was the one who was teaching us to make love, then it had to be good. I was smiling and gave him every reason to believe I was ready for what came next.

He reached out with his left hand and grabbed my right hand, intertwining our fingers together. Then he began walking me to his bedroom. I was fine until we were about to enter his room, and then my heart started racing. I didn't understand why we would make love in his room. I didn't pull away but continued to walk with him. I was still trusting and still believing that making love had to be a good thing, that is, until I walked into his room, and once again, standing up against the wall was my coach's brother, holding the same video camera.

Everything stopped. My heart stopped. My breathing stopped. I couldn't move a muscle. I felt tears welling up in my eyes, but everything else just completely stopped.

"Rachel," he dragged out the syllables in my name and flashed me his big smile. "It's okay. You trust me, right?"

What a hard question for a ten-year-old to answer at that point. Yes, I definitely trusted him, but I didn't like anything at all that had to do with his brother and with a video camera. I didn't like how I felt after leaving his house. I didn't like the secrets that continued to be adding to the list. I didn't like always being confused. But I wasn't used to sharing my true feelings on something. I was used to being compliant, especially with adults. So I knew the correct answer was yes.

"Yes." I said it only loud enough for my coach to hear.

"Yes, what?" he quickly said back.

"I trust you."

He smiled and then went through an explanation about how important it was to capture our first moment of making love. And that I need to just pretend that his brother isn't there.

"Ignore him being here. Let's just enjoy each other. This is something I've wanted to do with you for a long time and I am thankful that God has set this up to where we can make love just how he taught us to do in the Bible."

I felt at ease hearing his words and the reassurance again that God was in charge of this. I didn't want to go home again feeling like God was mad at me for something I did.

The video camera turned on, and almost immediately I saw a change in my coach's eyes. His eyes weren't soft, but hard. And they no longer were looking into my eyes. They were looking down at my body.

He didn't have to explain a single thing after that. Not one word was said. There was no more sugarcoating of what was about to happen. His brother moved around the room, coming in closer and then further away at certain times, with the camera still on his shoulder. I kept my eyes on my coach's face more than anything else. I couldn't get over how different his face looked. It was almost like looking at a totally different person.

I can remember times when I was a kid and I got hurt. Maybe I fell on gravel or fell off my bike or bumped my head on something. And I would tear up from the pain and would go find my mom or my dad. They could tell immediately by the look on my face that something was wrong. That I was hurt. And they would go to the ends of the world to make the pain stop.

As I lay in my coach's bed with him on top of me and feeling the worst physical pain I had ever felt, along with the worst emotional pain, and I teared up. I didn't cry out loud. From my knowledge, I was able to keep from making a single noise. But tears filled my eyes from all the pain and all the confusion and hurt. And I looked at my coach with those tears, hoping that he would understand that he was hurting me. But either he didn't notice or he didn't care.

My heart broke into a million pieces that day. Just like my coach's face changed, I'm pretty sure something in me changed that day too. Slowly he had taken bits and pieces of me away. Stealing who I was. By this point, I was completely gone. I had turned off inside and began to function on autopilot.

After he had finished making love to me, I was told to grab my clothes and go to the bathroom. It hurt so bad to even move. My lower stomach and the place between my legs felt like I had been beaten with a bat. I got up and immediately felt like I had peed down my legs, but it wasn't pee. I didn't know what it was. I was scared and froze in that spot, waiting for help to come, but the only help I got was some mean words from the brother saying that I was getting stuff everywhere and I need to hurry to the bathroom to get it taken care of.

I found my clothes and walked to the bathroom that was just the next room over. I went in and shut the door. I wanted so badly to run home and to crawl up in my mom's lap and let her see the pain in my eyes so she could take it away. I needed to get home as quickly as I could. I started to get dressed in the bathroom when the door opened and in walked a lady. I stopped what I was doing and looked at her with eyes of question. Was she good or was she bad? She smiled at me and said that she wanted to help me clean up before I went home. That we needed to make sure there was no sign of what happened just now.

She taught me how to clean myself up and to get rid of any smell or leftover residue. I was bleeding. She assured me that that would stop eventually, but that I might have to find a place to throw my underwear away so that my mom and dad don't find it. When she was done helping me, I continued to watch her. I couldn't tell if she was good or bad. She opened the bathroom door, and we both walked out. I stood at the opening of the door waiting to see what was going to happen next, but nobody was there. The lady said that I needed to go ahead and go on home. And she reminded me to not make this a big deal and to keep my mouth shut.

The walk home wasn't long enough. I needed a thousand years to be able to wrap my head around what just happened. I felt lost and alone. The old spunky Rachel was gone, and she was replaced with a shy, timid, zero-confidence Rachel.

When I got home, I went into our backyard and sat down on the swing that we had. Usually I would run things through my head and would try to figure it out. Like, why did he say that or do that and what did I need to do? I would think about how to fix things, but not this time. This time I just shut down, went blank. Numb. The pain was physically and emotionally too much, that going numb was a gift.

As the school year was getting close to an end, I had been going to my coach's house more often. It had become normal to make love while I was there. I learned how to throw my underwear away before my mom could see the blood on it in order to keep her from realizing what was happening. The lady that had come the first time to help clean me up had been there several times too. I figured out she was the brother's wife, and she liked to do things to make me look more grown-up and pretty while my coach and I made love. She would put makeup on me or do my hair special. I still couldn't figure out if she was good or bad. When we were done making love, she would take off all the makeup and change my hair back to how it was before.

The last day of school, there was a big explosion across the street from the school building. There were two large oil tanks that caught on fire and exploded. Our school was evacuated and dismissed early. I walked home that day from the last day of school, and I looked back and saw the oil bins in flames and firefighters standing around, trying to keep the flames contained. I'm sure they felt like it was pointless to try and get the fire to stop from the oil bin, but they needed to keep the fire from spreading.

It seemed appropriate for how my school year had gone. It felt like my world was on fire, like it had exploded into flames, and there was no way to put it out and no point in even trying. I just needed to contain the flames so that it didn't spread. Spreading the fire would only hurt people and make things worse.

I struggled with why I felt so empty and broken when my coach was obviously a good thing in my life. Being loved and cared for by him made me special. It was a good thing to have that special treatment, so why did I hurt so badly?

During the summer, my parents had decided to move. The parsonage was nice but dated and small. My folks were able to get the church to allow us to build our own house and move out of the parsonage. We had built a home in our old town on the outskirts of town about five years prior, and it had been a fun adventure for our family. We were very excited to get the opportunity to build again. After considering lots of places to build, my parents decided on a piece of property that was just two streets down from the parsonage. So we could still enjoy the blessings of being in town. I could still ride my bike around town, still play with my friends in town, and still go see my coach.

During the summer, I began playing on a traveling softball team. I had mentioned earlier how much I enjoyed baseball, but softball seemed completely new to me. As I went to the first practice, I tried to find my place on the team. I had been a pitcher, catcher, and a shortstop on the boys' baseball team, so I waited to see where I would be needed. By the end of the first practice, I was assigned the role of catcher, which became my favorite position on the field. I met the pitcher of the team, and we decided it would be good to get together a few times a week to practice.

The first day I went to her house, I didn't want to go. This girl seemed stuck up, and I didn't want to go there and catch for her. She had to pitch one hundred strikes before we could be done, and we probably were near twenty-five before we started laughing and having a great time. She quickly became my best friend. That summer, we spent so much time together. We laughed more than anyone you would ever meet. Being with her, I was able to be a kid. To be goofy. To not have a care in the world and just laugh till my belly hurt.

I never told my friend about my relationship with my coach. Just like I never told anyone. But when I was with her, my mind was alive and free. The summer nights of playing ball together, the slumber parties, and the adventures we went on through her woods. She was a blessing to me in so many ways.

Just before my fifth-grade year, we moved into our new house. I had my room decorated with posters of boys like Jonathan Taylor Thomas and Andrew Keegan. The boy craziness had begun.

I made the school softball team and actually earned some varsity playing time as just a fifth grader. My classroom at school was out in a trailer just next to the main school building. The fifth grade had two classrooms and two bathrooms out in that trailer. Right next to the fifth-grade trailer, a new trailer was put in, and this became the fourth-grade classrooms. My old fourth-grade teacher and my coach both had their classrooms out there, along with a boys' bathroom, a girls' bathroom, and a large closet that connected the two classrooms.

My coach had a new class, and he quickly had his one or two favorite girls that would run all his errands for him, including coming to get me from class. He seemed to be more careful getting me out of class with my new teacher. But during recess, he would send his favorite girls to come find me on the playground, and I would then get to go to his classroom. I hadn't seen him much all summer, and we hadn't made love since before school let out. Our conversations consisted of talking about the upcoming basketball season and how softball was going. I even talked to him about boys.

"I have a new boyfriend." I shyly explained who this new boyfriend was and how cute he was. My coach smiled at me.

"But he's not as cute as me, right?" My coach was flirting with me. It always made me feel good when he would say stuff that showed he still liked me.

"We just started being boyfriend and girlfriend," I explained. "We hadn't made love yet."

I could tell I had said something wrong, but I wasn't sure what that was. My coach's face became the serious, scary face that I hated so much.

"How dare you even think about making love with someone other than me?! I taught you what making love meant and you better never share that with anyone else." He spoke softly but harshly. I apologized for the thought and promised him quickly that I wouldn't make love with anyone else. I wished that he would understand that I was still learning the rules, but that I am trying. His mean face seemed to leave, but he remained very serious.

"I need to explain to you how special making love is." I listened carefully because I could tell he was going to be explaining rules, and I wanted to be sure to get it right.

"Making love to someone means you belong to them. Making love binds two people together forever. I made love with my wife and now she is mine. Your mom has made love with your dad, so she belongs to him. You made love to me, so who does that mean you belong to?"

"You," I quickly replied. I followed each word he said and was certain I had the answer right, and I did.

"Yes. You belong to me. You can play boyfriend and girlfriend with your little classmates, but you are mine. Forever."

He didn't say this to scare me, but just to explain that I wasn't to interact with anyone the way I did with him. Our relationship was special and unique. He even compared me to his wife, so I knew it was important. I would feel so much older when I was around him. Nothing like how I felt when I was playing with my best friend. I had almost become two totally different people. I was the ten-year-old Rachel who could play dolls and pretend and laugh. And I was the old, mature Rachel, who belonged to somebody and who had business she had to do to keep him happy.

> You were bought at a price. Therefore
> honor God with your bodies.
> —1 Corinthians 6:20

The fact that God was used so much in the relationship with my coach led me to struggle a lot with certain scriptures and beliefs of God. I was taught a different God than what really exists. It was close to the real deal but slightly twisted to fit my coach's needs. I was told that the events that took place in his bedroom were honoring God. That I was pleasing God by pleasing him. I was left with a contradiction inside of me that I couldn't understand. And I became a robot who did as she was told without trying to understand anymore. The plan that my coach had from the beginning was working exactly how he had hoped. But this was just the beginning . . .

CHAPTER 7

We were just a few months into the school year. Softball was almost over, and we were quickly approaching basketball season. I had been in the gym shooting around when my coach walked in the door. He made his way toward me, smiling bigger than I had ever seen him. I hadn't seen him much; in fact, he had missed a lot of school lately. I was happy to see him, and I could tell by his smile that he was happy to see me too.

"Long time no see." He almost seemed to have a skip in his step.

"Where have you been?"

"Nobody told you? We had a baby last week."

"What? A baby?"

"Yes. A baby boy. He is perfect. He looks just like my beautiful wife."

My heart felt weird. Why in the world was I jealous of him and his wife? This was good news. I should be happy for him. But for some reason, jealousy was raging through me.

"I am so happy for you guys. I can't wait to meet the little guy"

My coach was on cloud nine as I watched him go from person to person, talking about his newborn son. I'd never seen him so happy.

As weeks rolled on, I saw my coach occasionally, but usually because of basketball. His mind was on things at home, and all his spare time was spent with his wife and son. Around the beginning of October, my best friend and I decided that we were going to go TP-ing. This was our first time, so we had the anxious giggles as we got ready to go. We both were dressed in black from head to toe. We then stuffed toilet paper rolls in our sweatshirts and sweatpants. We looked like sumo wrestlers by the time we were done loading ourselves with toilet paper. My mom and dad were going to be our drivers, and we decided that the best person to TP would be my coach.

We waited till it was plenty dark. Then my best friend and I wiggled our way into the van. We had to stand up the whole time in the van because we had so much toilet paper in our pants that we couldn't sit down. Truthfully, we could hardly move, but we thought it was the funniest thing.

My mom and dad dropped us off a street away, and we slyly ran over to his house and started to throw the toilet paper up the tree in his front yard. There was only one tree there. I'm not sure why we decided he would be a good one to TP. We had been wobbling our way around, trying to throw the toilet paper as high as we could and giggling at how goofy we both looked, when all of sudden we heard a baby cry from inside of my coach's house. We must've been giggling louder than we realized. A few seconds after we heard the cry, we then saw the lights my coach's house turn on. We were going to get busted if we didn't get out of there fast. Around the corner came our minivan, and we hopped in the sliding side door as fast we could, just as my coach was walking out his front door.

My dad drove away fast, and everyone was laughing and joking, except for me. I saw the look on my coach's face as we drove away. He was mad.

The next day was a Saturday, and I was out in my driveway shooting baskets. My best friend had spent the night but had already left to go home. I don't know how long my coach had been watching me, but he finally drove up slowly to the front of my house and rolled down his window. I was so proud that my coach saw me out practicing. I was certain that he would be impressed that I was working so hard.

"I saw you last night." His face was serious. Mad. My whole body started to tremble at seeing him so angry with me. I realized that he must've figured out that it was me who TP'd his house the night before and that I was the one who woke up his baby late at night. I was terrified of him when he would get angry, so I tried to play dumb.

"I don't know what you mean."

"Yes, you do. And you woke up my son."

"I still don't know what you mean."

"You woke up my son and you made my wife upset, which makes me upset. You owe me an apology." I hung my head. I don't do well with getting in trouble. I tried to hide my tears.

"I'm sorry. I didn't mean to cause a problem."

"Don't do it again." And with that, he drove off.

My heart sank, and I felt instantly sick to my stomach. I tried to keep shooting, but I didn't feel like it much anymore, so I went on inside. Why was I always making such stupid mistakes that made my coach mad?

Toward the end of October, we started getting ready for basketball. We had tryouts, and once the team was picked, we then were handed out our jerseys. My cousin, who was the famous basketball player at a high school nearby, wore the jersey number 14, so I wanted so badly to have that same number. However, the jerseys were picked out first by the eighth graders, then the seventh, then the sixth, and finally the fifth. I had talked to my coach a few times before about how badly I wanted number 14. He knew it meant a lot to me, but he couldn't promise that I would get it. If it was still there by the time the fifth graders got to pick, then it would be mine.

I was very anxious about it. I wanted that number so badly. Finally the fifth graders were called to my coach's classroom to pick out our uniforms and try them on. I was ecstatic to see that the number 14 was still there. I quickly grabbed it and ran to the bathroom to try it on. It fit perfectly. I ran back out to my coach's classroom so he could see it on me. I was smiling from ear to ear. He called me over to his desk and started to then explain that I couldn't have that jersey.

"We have a sixth grader who is home sick with mono. The number 14 jersey is her size and I have to let her have it." I was shocked. Why would he give her this jersey? Couldn't he give her any other jersey? I stood there, desperately hoping he would tell me that he was just joking. But he didn't. He then gave me the jersey with the number 41, saying that if I looked in the mirror, then it will look close to the number 14.

I went to the bathroom with the new jersey and tried it on. It was way too big, but I didn't have any other choice. I put my practice clothes back on and threw my new jersey into my duffel bag and then returned the number 14 jersey to my coach. He didn't seem to care one bit that I was heartbroken. Maybe I was just being childish anyway.

I returned to the gym to continue shooting around until everyone was ready for practice to actually begin. My coach came into the gym with his serious look again and he asked me if I had stolen the number 14 jersey. I was in shock. There was no way I would steal it. We were given a blue jersey and a white jersey, one for away games and one for home games, and I had the number 41 jersey. I went ahead and checked in my duffel bag to make sure, but only because my coach insisted upon it. I pulled out the jerseys. I had a number 41 white jersey, and a number 14 blue jersey. I must've accidentally thrown the wrong one in my bag when I was changing. But it was most definitely an accident. I went to try and explain it to my coach, but he just grabbed the jersey and said, "I can't believe you tried to steal it."

I wanted to curl up in a ball and hide in the corner. I felt two inches tall when he said that. I didn't say anything back because I had no words. I was still in shock over what just happened.

After practice, my mom picked me up and we went home. I was still very upset about what had happened with the jerseys, and as soon as I got home I started crying. My mom started to ask me questions, and I explained about how I accidentally put the wrong jersey in my bag but that my coach said that I had tried to steal it. I promised my mom that I didn't try to steal it. It was really an accident. But that my coach was really mad at me.

After dinner, I was sitting down in front of the TV watching a show, when there was a knock at our garage door. My mom went and answered the door, and to my surprise, it was my coach and his wife. I got up and walked over to greet them, but my head was hung because I was still very hurt by what my coach had accused me of. My coach, however, was very happy. He was smiling and talking a bunch, and he went on to explain that he was just joking with me when he said he thought I had stolen it. He knew that I would never do that. I was completely confused about what he was saying because I saw how angry he was at me. He definitely wasn't joking earlier at practice.

The adults talked for a little bit longer while I went back in to watch TV. My coach came in and squatted down by me and asked me if we were okay.

"I promise I really didn't mean to take the jersey." He seemed to finally believe me, and I said that we were definitely okay. A few minutes later, they were gone. I asked my mom why my coach and his wife had come over, and she said she called to explain to my coach that I didn't try to steal the jersey and that I was feeling really bad that he thought I did. She said that she didn't know that they were going to come on over, but that it was very nice of them to do so. I just smiled and went back to watching TV. I was emotionally exhausted from the day.

My coach was very nice at school and seemed to make sure that I felt his love. His niceness quickly made me forget about how mad he had gotten and about his accusation. During practice one day, he said that he needed some alone time with me. That he hadn't been able to make love with me since his son was born and he was really missing me. I didn't really have any feelings toward this. I didn't dread it, and I didn't look forward to it.

I guess my feelings were one of the things taken from me through all the events and mind games with my coach. If I had feelings toward something, then it made things worse. It was better to take it for what it was and move on. It was better to be numb. To just not feel.

It was time to meet up at his house like he had planned. I worked to come up with a reason as to why I would be gone from home for a bit. It really wasn't hard. I was able to say that I would be riding my bike around town, and that was all it took. My mom would ask that I come back and check in every once in a while, but the time in between was enough time to be with Coach.

I rode my bike over to his house and parked it in his side room. My coach was ready for me as soon as I got there. We went back to his room, and I was prepared for what was going to happen. His brother was there with the camera, and his brother's wife was there to make me look pretty. I went along with all they needed me to do.

Everything was going the way I had gotten used to, and I found comfort in the fact that there weren't any surprises. I went to his bed and sat on the edge, waiting for my coach to come. When he finally walked through the door, he wasn't alone. He had following right behind him another teacher from our school. Tears started to fill my eyes. I didn't know why there was someone new there, and I didn't want to know.

"Do you remember seeing the junior-high science teacher at school?" my coach asked. I nodded. I knew he was the science teacher, but I wasn't yet in junior high, so I hadn't had him for a teacher yet. He was very tall and had a slender build. He had black hair and glasses, and he appeared like he wore eyeliner and foundation on his face. He had a face full of pits that must've come from having terrible acne when he was younger. He looked at me with a smile that made my skin crawl.

"He has heard amazing things about my all-star and he wants to get some love from you too. So you will be a good girl and make love to him just like you have with me." My mind immediately went in a million different directions. I remembered how carefully my coach had explained to me exactly what making love was and what it meant. Why would I make love to this man? Does that mean I belong to him now too? Why would my coach want me to do that?

An anger and a fear grew inside of me. I didn't want this man anywhere near me. I couldn't stand the thought of him. I instantly wanted out of that house as fast as I could, and I jumped off that bed and ran. I ran with a force that felt like I could run through a wall. I wasn't going to let this man touch me. I ran out of the bedroom before anyone could catch me, and I made it to the front door, but it was locked. I started trying to turn the lock, but I wasn't fast enough. My coach grabbed me and carried me into the kitchen. He pushed me against the lower cabinets and grabbed my face to make sure I was looking him in the eyes.

How did this man have the ability to change his eyes so quickly? His eyes were the meanest I had ever seen them. His eyes looking at me like that made me freeze and listen carefully to his words.

"You will have sex with this man. Do you understand me?" Sex? I'd heard the word *sex* before, and I knew it was how babies were made. But I didn't know that when my coach and I were making love, it was sex. I had never told my coach "No" before. I always did exactly what he asked me to do. But not this time.

"No. I want to go home." I could see his jaw muscles tighten as I said these words.

"You get a choice," he said softly to me, and then he reached over and grabbed one of the biggest kitchen knives I had ever seen. "You either have sex with that man, or you have sex with this knife. You decide."

He still had a tight grip on my arm and was pushing me with his body up against the cabinets. I knew I couldn't win. It hurt so bad to make love, I mean have sex, with my coach that I couldn't imagine how much it would hurt to have sex with a knife. I nodded to my coach that I understood, and with his hand still tightly squeezed around my arm, we walked back into the bedroom.

I lay in the bed, feeling my body hurt in new ways, watching as the disgusting man hung all over me. His body was even more disgusting than his face, and it took everything I had not to throw up.

When he was done, I just lay there in the bed, unable to move. I had the smell and slime of this man all over my body and I lay there praying that I would die. I didn't want to be alive anymore. I didn't want to be here, I didn't want to go home. I didn't want to exist at all anymore.

The lady came in the room while the men talked and while the brother put away the video camera. She walked me into the bathroom, and I stood there while she cleaned me up with washrags and soap and water. When she was done, I was told to go on home, and I walked out of the house and grabbed my bike and started to ride home. It hurt too bad to even sit on my bike seat, so I had to ride standing up all the way home.

No tears came. The temperatures were getting chilly, but I didn't even notice. As I got closer to home, I knew that I needed to act normal, or else my mom would ask questions. She was most likely going to ask me where I had been. I decided to grab some rocks from the train tracks and take them home; that way I could say that I had been collecting pretty rocks from the train tracks.

I showed my mom the rocks, and I tried to act excited as I explained how fun it was to pick out which rocks I wanted. Mom was busy with laundry and cleaning, but she took some time to hear my excitement, and she said she was fine if I went back out for a little bit longer. I was very glad to hear this because I needed some time alone. I didn't want to have to act happy for a while.

I went back to the train tracks and just sat. As I sat there, I saw the science teacher drive by. He looked over at me and winked and then drove on. Who had I become?

What do they call people like me? The Sunday school teacher at church would talk about women like me in the Bible. At least, I thought so. They would try and use nice words and sugarcoat what these women were really doing, but I knew what she meant. These women would be with all sorts of men. They called them prostitutes, I thought.

Now let them use her as a prostitute, for that is all she is.
—Ezekiel 23:43

Most nights as a kid, when I would lie in bed trying to sleep, the only thing that would bring me peace was thinking about basketball. I wish I could say that it was God who brought me peace. But even though I was certain God existed, I was still very confused about His feelings toward me. Something there wasn't right, and I was sure it was my fault.

Basketball was always there, it was something that I could put my heart and soul into and be happy with the results. Basketball season was going well. I was starting JV and even dressing for varsity. Coach was extremely happy with me because I was becoming a star on the court, and I was his all-star behind the scenes.

At the beginning of school one morning, my coach motioned for me to come talk to him. I had a feeling it had something to do with how good I played the night before in our basketball game. The PE teacher actually talked first.

"Great game last night."

"Thank you."

My coach smiled big and seemed very proud of me. He rested his hand on my lower back and rubbed it around slowly while I stood next to his folding chair. I could tell he had something he wanted to tell me, but the PE teacher kept talking about the game the night before. I enjoyed hearing all of the PE teacher's positive comments, but I was anxious to see what it was that my coach was wanting to tell me. Finally the PE teacher got distracted by another student, and my coach turned to me and said he had a surprise.

"The high school coach was wondering if you would want to come and practice with his team today after school." I couldn't believe my ears. My face lit up with excitement.

"Yes, of course."

He went on to explain that he was going to find someone to drive me over to the high school so I could practice. But that I needed to keep this a secret so that my teammates didn't get jealous. I was completely fine with that. I could not believe that the high school coach wanted me to practice with them, especially since I was only a fifth grader.

The day dragged on and on until finally it was time for practice. I made sure to tell no one about getting to practice with the high school team. I had gotten very good at keeping secrets. I put my practice clothes on and then headed to the gym. My coach was sitting on the bleachers. He was just as excited about this opportunity as I was. He said that his car was parked in the back of the gym. He was having someone drive me over there and drive me back so that he could still lead his practice at the grade school. The timing of it should be the same as our two-hour practice at the grade school. I was nervous and excited. This was going to be the best day ever.

I grabbed my basketball shoes and headed out the back door of the gym toward my coach's car. I was about to open the back door to get in when I realized that it was my coach's brother driving the car. Instantly I felt like this was some sort of setup. I didn't know what to do. The brother saw me, and he told me to get in the car and to lie down on the floor in the backseat. He was not a person that I would tell no to. He was big and mean and meant business. I did exactly what he said. There was still a small part of me that was hopeful that maybe, just maybe he would really take me to the high school practice, but when we started driving down country roads, I knew we weren't going to the high school.

CHAPTER 8

"Stay on the ground until I tell you to get up!" He had a very deep, raspy voice. I lay on my stomach at first, but I began to get scared, so I rolled to my back, hoping that as long as I didn't sit up, then I wouldn't get in trouble for moving. I didn't want to be surprised by anything, so I didn't want my eyes hidden. The brother noticed me rolling over and shot me a look.

"Don't try anything smart."

My mind wasn't thinking about possibilities of how to get away. My mind was focused on where he was taking me and what I was going to have to do when we got there. My mind didn't even comprehend a way to escape. My coach had always been with me, even when I was forced to be with the other teacher, at least I had my coach there. I could feel some comfort in knowing he wouldn't let anyone hurt me. At least not really bad. But I knew my coach was nowhere near me this time to protect me. He was still back at the school for practice.

I wished so badly that I was at practice too. I didn't want to be on the floor of this car. I wanted to be in the gym practicing with my team like I was supposed to be. I could picture the team going through our normal beginning-of-practice routine. Maybe some of the girls were beginning to wonder where I was. Honestly, I was beginning to wonder where I was.

At first I was able to keep track of where we were based on how smooth the roads were and what turns he made. But after a while, I was completely turned around. We were probably in the car for only five minutes or so, but it felt like we drove all over the place. I was scared but anxious to see where he had taken me. I expected to hear commands on what to do, but he didn't say a word. He stopped the car, got out, and then opened the back door, where I was still lying on my back on the floor. He grabbed my leg and started to pull me out like I was nothing more than a duffel bag or something he needed from the back. He still didn't say a word, but his eyes said enough. I felt the need to hustle and get out of the car fast. I had my practice basketball clothes on, and it was dark and cold outside.

As soon as I got out of the car, my eyes caught the attention of an old white house about thirty yards in front of me. Next to it was a large shed that I assumed was used for tractors and such.

Everywhere else, there were trees and fields. The only light I saw came from a light pole near where we were parked. I couldn't see a single light shining inside of this white house. Maybe nobody was home. Maybe the brother got the wrong time or the wrong place. The brother's hand had turned the back of my shirt into a ball that he squeezed tightly and then used to pull me toward the house. I was scared, but I stayed close to him. Whatever or whoever was in this house was scarier in my mind than the man holding on to me. I stayed close to his side as we walked up the porch steps. I went to pause in my walking, thinking that he would stop and knock on the door, but immediately he opened the screen door and then the front door, and together we walked in.

Hell is described in the Bible as a place of "weeping and gnashing of teeth" (Matthew 25:30), a place of "outer darkness" (Matthew 22:13), a place of "torments" (Luke 16:23), a place of "sorrows" (2 Samuel 22:6), and a place of "everlasting destruction" (2 Thessalonians 1:9).

From a ten-year-old's standpoint, the inside of this house equaled everything that the Bible says about hell. Except I don't remember it being hot. That is probably the only exception. Otherwise, it hit all the criteria of hell on earth. It was a place of torment. I could hear sounds of crying and screaming. It was very dark, even spiritually dark, inside that house. I can't imagine a place on earth that could be any further from God. It was a place of sorrow and destruction. When I think of hell, I think of this place, and I'm reminded of what a life without God looks like and what a terrible eternity awaits those who don't choose Jesus as their Savior.

As I walked in, I continued to cling closely to the brother. The brother was probably my least favorite person in the whole world, but he was the only one I knew in that house, and I wasn't about to take my chances with anyone else.

The first thing I noticed was a horrific smell. I had never smelled anything like this before. My eyes instantly welled up with tears. This was not a place I wanted to be. Just the feeling inside the house was cold and dirty.

The inside of the house hardly resembled a house at all. It definitely wasn't a home. Along the right side of the house was what looked like makeshift rooms. Rooms that didn't seem to belong there. The walls and doors didn't seem to fit exactly right, and there were way more doors and rooms than you would expect. To the left was a small open area that had a couch and a few other chairs, but nobody was sitting there. There were a few lights on, but I realized that the reason I couldn't see any light from outside was because the windows were completely covered in what looked like cardboard. In front of me stood a man.

The man looked like a normal person that you would see at the grocery store. Nothing out of the ordinary about him. He wasn't dressed junky. With how bad it smelled in this house, it seemed like you should be seeing trash all over and people who were unclean and poor. But this person didn't seem poor at all. And there wasn't an ounce of trash seen from where I was. Maybe they hid all the yucky-smelling trash in the back. One smell that I did recognize, though, was the smell of slime. The same slime that my coach and the other teacher put all over me. I hated the smell of it, the taste of it, and the way it made my body feel. But recognizing that smell gave me a pretty good idea of why the brother had brought me here. I was physically trembling with fear.

Somewhere in the back, I could hear crying. The saddest cry I had ever heard. And there was moaning and groaning that was echoing throughout the house. My mind started to think about running. I didn't know where I was or where I would go, but even the woods seemed better than a place like this. But the brother had a tight grip still on the back of my jersey. I wasn't going anywhere. And if I tried, it could end up being even worse.

The man at the house and the brother talked for a bit. The brother seemed aggravated at something and I thought he was going to punch the man, but he calmed himself down and agreed to whatever the man wanted. In an instant, when the man turned his eyes on me, he no longer looked normal anymore. His eyes weren't right. They were evil. It was as if I could see all the plans in his head about what he wanted to do to me. His creepy smile told me even more.

We followed the man to a room toward the back that looked to be the kitchen in the house. It was small with a fridge, a sink, and a microwave sitting on the small counter against the wall. Again, the room was nice and clean. In the center of the room was a small dining room table, and three men sat there. They only had cups in front of them, and they were laughing and talking. The man walked over toward the other guys and started talking.

"You boys need to decide on this one here. Do we want to keep her?" He was still looking me over with a smile. The man went on.

"This one is ten years old. She's been in the porn industry so she isn't a newbie. But she sure is pretty." The man went on to say that he voted yes.

The other men had the same eyes and the same smile as the first man.

"I haven't seen enough. I need to see more," one man said. None of the men seemed to be out of the ordinary except for their eyes. I couldn't get over the way their eyes looked at me.

I wasn't certain what the comment meant, that he hadn't seen enough. I was about to turn my head around to see if there were other girls they were going to see, but then the man directed the brother to let the men see more. The brother still didn't say a word to me. He let the back of my jersey go, only to grab both sides of my jersey and the shirt under it and pull it up over my head and completely off.

Comments were being made by the men, but I wasn't comprehending what they were saying. I had on a sports bra even though I didn't have much reason to wear one yet. As the men talked, the brother would then reach over and take more of my clothes off, and eventually I stood there with absolutely nothing on. Even my sandals and socks were forced off. I tried to hide my body with my arms, but the brother would slap my arms back down to my side. He then grabbed ahold of my ponytail the way he had done my jersey.

"Come on, you big bully, let the girl go. She's not gonna run anywhere," a man from one of the chairs said. "Bring her to me. I know how to treat a youngin' like her."

The other men continued talking as the brother pushed me in the direction of this man. His hands instantly went on my body, and I immediately flinched.

"Don't be scared. We treat little girls like princesses. You won't find better treatment than you do here. Ain't that right, boys?" All the men laughed and then continued talking.

"I know you look pretty, but do you taste pretty, too? Give me a sweet kiss." He grabbed the back of my head and pulled me toward him. His kiss was nothing more than him shoving his tongue all around my mouth. I tried to resist him, but his firm hand on the back of my head wouldn't let me. He then dragged his tongue all over me, taking breaks to talk about how good little girls taste.

Each man got their turn with me. None of them had sex with me but just looked over my body in every way you can imagine. When they were done, I was able to get dressed while the men talked to the brother. The brother finally seemed happy as the man that had been up front walked us back and then gave the brother some money. They talked some more, and then the brother grabbed hold of my jersey again, and we walked back out to the car. He still didn't say a single word to me. He just opened the back door and pointed to the floor. I went back to lying down on my back as he shut the door, and we left.

He turned the radio on to a local country station and started singing as if I wasn't even there. I lay there, struggling to understand what just happened. I could still smell that horrific smell, and I was certain that I smelled just like that now too. I wanted to get back to the school. I wasn't even thinking about basketball anymore, but I wanted to talk to my coach. I just knew he would be upset when he found out where his brother had taken me. I had a feeling that his brother was going to be in big trouble.

When the car finally stopped, I was already starting to get up before the back door even opened, but the brother stopped me from moving any further.

"Sit up in the seat and listen to every word I'm about to tell you." I scrambled up on the seat, wanting desperately to peek around to see if anyone was watching.

"You went to the high school practice today. If anyone asks you any questions, you make up about how great it was. If you screw this up, you will wish you never had been born. Your coach can't protect you from me. If I hear you disobeyed, you're mine."

I went inside, and basketball practice was still going on. I still had my shoes, so I quickly put them on and tried to join my team, acting like I was happy. But my body was still trembling. I couldn't get the words out of my head, the smell out of my nose, or the taste out of my mouth. My usual drive to improve and get better during practice was not there. I was simply a body on the court, with no heart and soul. That was beginning to be how I felt in life too. Nothing but a body, with no heart and soul.

My coach didn't talk to me after practice. He told the team he needed to head home to see his son and he left. The assistant coach stayed to make sure we were all picked up by our parents. I could tell that my teammates hadn't been told where I was. They must've assumed I had a doctor's appointment or something like that. As we waited for our ride, we talked about things like the math test we needed to study for and how our teacher was about to have a baby and we were going to be getting a sub for several weeks.

I joined in the conversation and was able to go back to the ten-year-old life, where the biggest stress was the math test in the morning. I had the boyfriend that all the girls wanted, and it was fun talking about how cute he was at lunch today or the sweet note he wrote me after recess. It was amazing how good I had gotten at turning one life off and the other on and vice versa. Oftentimes, I would get so good at going back and forth from one life to the other that I could completely block out the events that were traumatic. My mind seemed to flush that stuff out and just keep the good, happy, safe stuff.

The only problem was, the emotions remained. I still had nightmares and would feel at times like my life wasn't worth living. I struggled to understand why I could feel that way, when I had such an amazing life. Something must be wrong with me if I can't be happy with the life I have. I knew that sometimes bad things would happen, but then I would flush them away and move on. There wasn't any reason why, if I could stop the memories, the emotions that came from them didn't stop too.

The next week, I was told again that I would need to miss practice. This time my coach didn't even sugarcoat it by saying that I was going to get to practice with the high school. I had wanted so badly to bring up to him what had happened, but he never asked anything about it, and I still could hear his brother's threats in my head.

My coach seemed sad that I was going to miss practice. I couldn't say a word because my desire was to obviously be in practice. I'm sure he knew that. I definitely didn't want to go on another joyride with his brother. Even though the memories of the time before had been flushed away, they came back at the word that I needed to miss practice again.

Where was he going to take me this time? My thoughts came through with the idea that I needed to do this and get it over with so I can get back to practice. I wanted to be able to get a little bit of practice in if I could. Nothing in my mind said that I should fight or say no to going. It was more like, "Let's get this over with so I can get on with my other life."

I was anxious to see where we were going. I assumed we would go to a new place with new men who would pay money to look at me. I hoped that wherever we went, that it would smell better than the last place. Just like the time before, I was told to lie down on the floor in the back of the car. This time, though, I was keeping my mind on basketball and getting back to the gym.

Each game I was getting better and better. I had been trying really hard to learn how to take a charge on defense. It was something I had practiced and practiced, and finally, the game before, I took my first charge ever. I lay on the floor of that car, thinking back to when I was guarding the opponent's point guard full court, trying to force her left. I had been flustering her all over the court until finally she put her head down and tried to dribble by me. I put my foot on the sideline and stood my ground as she barreled her way through me. I remained perfectly still until the hit, and I flew back doing a backward summersault on the gym floor in the process. I sat on the floor and looked up at the referee, who signaled with one hand behind his head and his other hand pointed forward in a fist. It was a charge. I hopped up and pumped my fist in the air twice and ran down the floor to play offense. It was the highlight of my fifth-grade season up until that point.

I had almost completely forgotten that I was in the back of the car until the brother nailed a pothole in the road and I flew up in the air. I tried not to act like it was a big deal, but I was pretty sure I was going to be left with a bruise. The car stopped, and I was ready to hop out and get this thing done so I could get back to practice, when I looked out the front windshield and saw the same white house that we were at last time.

I was confused. Why would we be back here? They already looked at me and paid money. Wasn't I done at this place? Maybe they were wanting to do it again. I was dreading the guy with the tongue and all of the comments and definitely the smell, but I would try and make things quick so we could leave. I could handle this.

Just as before, the brother didn't say a word. He grabbed me by my jersey, and we walked inside. The smell had seemed a little bit better this time, or maybe my nose had just gotten used to it from the last time. The same man stood at the front right as we walked in. I felt sick to my stomach like I was going to throw up just by the look of him. I'm sure the smell didn't help it any.

The man started talking to the brother, saying something about the first customer wasn't there yet. I stood there trying to process their conversation, but the words I was hearing didn't make sense. I wouldn't have cared, except that I knew that their words were describing what my next hour was going to look like, and I wanted to understand.

"Go ahead and get her ready in room 4." This direction made the brother mad.

"What do you mean get her ready? I don't get them ready. Don't you have a girl that can do that?"

After they heatedly discussed who would get me ready, I was then led to the right side of the house. To me, it seemed like the hallway went on forever with door after door after door. In black marker, there was a number written on each door. I was led to room 4, and the man told us to wait just a second.

I grabbed ahold of the brother as tightly as I could while the man was gone. I begged him not to leave. To please save me. I was starting to understand what was about to happen, and I hoped that maybe the brother would hear my cries and take me home. That he wouldn't let me get hurt. The man came back in, and he had with him a tall, skinny Asian girl, who was staring down at the ground. The man instructed the brother to leave, but I wouldn't let go of him.

"Please, please, don't leave me here. Please. Take me with you. I'll be good, I promise. Please don't leave me."

He took both hands and shoved me to the floor as he walked out of the room along with the other man. I sat there on the floor with tears streaming down my face and sobs causing my body to shake. Was I going to be here forever? The girl continued to keep her eyes down as she made her way around the room. I never heard her speak a word. I couldn't figure out where she had come from. There weren't any other cars out front.

She walked toward me and started to take off my basketball practice clothes. My focus stayed on her as she took each piece of my clothing off. Her eyes were sad and empty. She didn't seem to have any life in her at all. I watched her every move, as she left me naked on the cot that was in the room. She walked over to a cabinet and pulled out a silk blanket that she wrapped me in like a towel. She sprayed me with some perfume and then she started pointing for me to lie on the bed. I lay flat on my back, still wrapped in the blanket, and she tried to turn me on my side with my body twisted and turned in a way that was painful. Before she was done getting me to lie the way she wanted, the door opened. In walked a man. He told the lady to leave, and he shut the door behind her, never once taking his eyes off me.

I write this today, still unable to describe what happened in the room with that man. For a long time, I can't even remember beyond the door of the room. My brain had blocked out this memory, and I'm thankful it has. I'm not sure if the memory will come back or not. I was honestly nervous about writing this chapter, not knowing if, as I started writing, the memories would start flooding my mind. But for right now, my memory of that room is blank after seeing the man shut the door. That can only be explained as a God thing. I'm certain that God allows me memories as He sees me capable to handle them, process them, and heal from them. This memory I must not be ready for, and maybe I never will be. Only God knows the answer to that, and I leave my life and my memories in His hands to do with what He wants. Anything else will make this pain and hurt pointless. If anything good can come from my life story, then I want that to happen, and that can only happen if God is the Author and Leader of my life.

CHAPTER 9

Taking a step back from the events of when I was a child, it obviously is hard to comprehend how so much went on and no one noticed. Or if they noticed, they assumed the best, given my coach's appearance of being a faithful Christian with high morals and a Godly character. Still today I hear many people talk of him and believe he is nothing but wonderful. It's hard for them to imagine my coach involved in such terrible acts when they see only the side he wants them to see.

I think it's hardest on those who love me the most, especially the ones who knew me growing up. They search back, trying to find the signs. Trying to remember something that should've made it obvious what was going on. But they come up empty. They remember me as the one who was passionate about basketball, who was always smiling. They remember my heart for others and my determination. But they can't pinpoint anything that would've showed them the darkness I was involved in for so many years.

How hard it must be for them to know that they walked beside me during that time in my life and they were blinded to my pain. Excuses were often made for my actions. The most common excuse was that I was a preacher's kid who was looking for attention or was rebelling. I know that my actions were from a pain I couldn't understand or describe, but no one could've possibly assumed what was really happening. If I had been point-blank asked if my coach was hurting me, my answer would've been a quick "No." I would've protected him no matter what. I would've kept our secret for as long as he needed me to. And that's something that most people don't understand. And I can't explain it. Why would I choose a life with him and the torture that went with it, instead of a life without him that involved no pain? I don't have the answers. Just the questions.

One of the things that always held true for me through it all was my love for God. I never questioned that. I always loved Him. But unfortunately, the men hurting me often used Him when they would justify what they were doing. Through all of their talks on God and the illusions they placed in my head, my love for God always remained. He was real and He was powerful and I needed Him. When the events would be on a downtime and my coach was ignoring me, my relationship with God would grow. It would be rock solid. But while the events were happening, it seemed like God was far from me. That He wasn't as easy to talk to or listen to. Our relationship was rocky during those times. As a ten-year-old who was dealing with demonic events and people and also trying to love the Lord and honor Him, it became impossible. The two didn't mix. Usually during the downtimes with my coach, my relationship with the Lord would start to rekindle, but then the events would start up again.

The two worlds just didn't seem to fit, even though the men would use God's name and scriptures often, I still knew that who they were portraying God as wasn't true. When they would tell me that God couldn't love me because I was trash, or that He was only proud of me if I did what the men wanted, or how I was made by God for the purpose of pleasing men. I knew deep down in my soul that they were wrong. At least on most days. I knew deep down that I was God's child and He saw me as beautiful, and worthy, and priceless. That I am not trash to Him.

I knew each time when I would be told to get in the car with the brother and lie down on the floor of the car, that I would be going back to that little white house in the country. Each time I wasn't only hurt physically, but also emotionally and mentally.

"You're nothing but trash."

"A dirty little girl."

"This is what you were made to do."

"God couldn't even love you."

"You're my favorite sex toy."

It was another night and another practice I would miss. Another time I was being told to get in the car and lie on the floor. I was lying on my back, looking up and out the window. I could see the sky and nothing else from where I lay. Within a few minutes, the car stopped. I started to sit up and get out of the car, but the brother told me quickly to stay where I was. Not to move. Not to say a word. I lay there frozen. This was new to me. Always before, I needed to be quick to get out of the car and into the house so that I could work as long as possible before I needed to go back to the school.

I couldn't hear noise from outside the car. I wasn't even certain if the brother was still close by. So I stayed perfectly still and kept my eyes on the sky. It was already dusk, and the stars were starting to show. Something about the stars made my mind shift to thinking about God. God couldn't be happy with me. He couldn't be happy with all the wrong things I had done with these men. But something about the stars and how beautiful they looked in the sky made me think that maybe God wasn't angry. Maybe he was smiling down on me and was wanting nothing more than for me to ask for forgiveness. Maybe He was hurting because I was hurting and was wanting to rescue me.

I closed my eyes as tight as they would go, and as tears spilled down my cheeks, I prayed. I prayed with the most sincere, honest, childlike faith.

"Dear God, I know You are there. I am so sorry for the bad things I've done. I am so scared. I need You. Please take me home. Can You send someone to come and take me home? I just want to go home. Please, God. In Jesus name, Amen."

I dried my tears and opened my eyes. The sky was getting darker and darker. I began to get butterflies in my stomach as I lay there. I was no longer scared. I was no longer waiting and dreading for the brother to come back. I was waiting and excited for the door to open and someone different to be standing there. Someone that God sent to take me home.

The door finally opened, and even though it was pretty dark outside, I knew right away from the profile and the voice that it was the brother who opened the door.

"It's your turn. Let's go!"

When I got out of the car, I didn't see anyone except the brother. He grabbed ahold of the back of my jersey, and he started pushing me to walk. But this time, it wasn't the house he wanted me to walk to. It was the large shed to the left and back of the house. As we got closer, I noticed several cars parked behind the shed. We reached the door, and the brother opened it and pushed me in.

I believe it's only natural for me to look back on this event and wonder why. Why, on that beautiful starry night, was an innocent little girl, who was crying out to God to be rescued, was instead fed to the wolves? Why did that little girl have to choose between fighting back and going numb? Why did she have to feel that abandonment?

Trust in the Lord with all your heart and
lean not on your own understanding.
—Proverbs 3:5

I can't say that I understand, because I don't. But I can say that I trust God. I trust Him better on some days than others, but I trust Him. That moment where God heard my cry but allowed the bad to still happen does not define my relationship with Him. God didn't make a mistake. Satan didn't win. But because of the sin of others, I was forced to endure hell on earth that night.

As a ten-year-old girl, my reaction was not anger toward God. In fact, that was maybe the hardest part. I understood. I understood why He said "No" to my prayer, and I knew that it was because everything that the men had been telling me all along was true. I was different. My worth must truly be in pleasing men; otherwise God wouldn't have allowed that to happen. That's what my young mind thought at that time. That there wasn't anything wrong with God. There was something wrong with me.

I was only in the shed for maybe a half hour. The events that took place inside of the shed were confusing and shameful. It appeared to be some sort of an auction, but I didn't understand the purpose. After my turn in front was over, I was then loaded back up and brought back to school. I still had been gone for most of practice but stayed a little longer afterward to shoot around. My coach stuck around to rebound for me.

"Sometimes I get confused about why you send me away to other men." My coach seemed genuine in his response back.

"Because I love you. I'm always watching out for you. We are a team, you and me. We are going to win both on and off the court. I love you so much, Rachel."

Without thinking another thought, I instantly replied that I loved him too, and then we played a quick game of one-on-one. My coach had torn his Achilles tendon a few years prior, so he couldn't move on the court like he once could. Which gave me an advantage. The game became more playful than competitive. I didn't doubt his love for me at all at that point.

"Rachel . . . Rachel, are you paying attention? Rachel, it's your turn to read." I must've zoned out again in class. It was happening more and more. I saw the frustrated look on my history teacher's face, and I knew I needed to find the right spot quickly and start reading. I looked over at a friend, who pointed to the spot on her page, and I was able get on track and begin reading where the teacher wanted me to.

These moments of zoning out were really starting to interfere with my life, but they weren't something I could ward off. They came on quick, and before I knew it, my mind was taken to another place.

I was in a period where I was being ignored by my coach. I didn't know how to handle his separation, even though these droughts would happen often. Basketball season was over, and I had another great season. As a sixth grader, I started varsity and was the second-leading scorer throughout the year. I was beginning to see my dreams play out as I continued to improve my game.

Now that the season was over, the only time I saw my coach was by invite only, and for the last month, there had been no invite. A whole month of zero contact. It would make sense to others that I would be happy to be free from the bad events that came with being close to my coach, but I was anything but free. He held on to my heart and my mind even though physically he was absent. One particular day at school, I brought a note in an envelope for my coach. Along with the note, I also had put in the envelope all the money I owned. I begged him in the letter to like me again and that he could have all my money.

I had seen money exchanged often for time spent with me, so in my young mind, it made sense to give him money so I could spend time with him. In the morning before school, in the old gym, I gave that note to a girl in his fourth-grade class. I knew exactly which girl to give it to. I found the one that was his "special helper" for the year, and I asked her to give my coach the envelope.

Later that afternoon, there was a knock at my classroom door, and there stood that same girl asking if I could leave class to go talk to my coach. I was so glad that my plan had worked. However, when I walked into his classroom and saw the look on his face, I quickly realized that my plan had been a very bad idea. I hung my head and walked toward his desk. Right away he pointed for me to go into the walk-in closet that connected the two fourth-grade classrooms together. He followed and shut the door behind him.

"What were you thinking with that note? Were you trying to embarrass me? To get me in trouble?"

Tears filled my eyes. I couldn't seem to do anything right. He continued to quietly talk in his anger.

"You're the one who should be embarrassed. You're going to look back at this someday and see how dumb and childish this is."

Just then, the door opened from the other classroom. There stood the other fourth-grade teacher. At that point, my coach was inches from my face and he had a hold on one of my wrists. When she saw my coach and me in the closet, she turned and walked out and shut the door behind her. My coach continued to give me a tongue-lashing before he told me to go back to class. He was right, I was embarrassed. As I walked back to class, I thought about how dumb I had been and how the other fourth-grade teacher had even caught us. I was certain that she was going to be suspicious of us now, but she never said a word about it to me or, from what I can tell, to anyone else.

Sixth grade had looked pretty similar to fifth grade. Lots of house visits, lots of time at my coach's house and my coach's classroom, and lots of moments when I was completely invisible to him. My heart hurt, but my mind often didn't understand why. To ease this pain in my heart, I started to cut. When I would take a knife to cut, I wouldn't be brave enough to do it fast. I would slowly and repeatedly drive the knife into my body in the same spot over and over, deeper and deeper. The physical pain would help ease the pain in my heart.

I worked to hide my cuts from others because I was afraid they would think I was crazy. One night, though, the night of our sixth-grade dance, I slipped up, and a carving on my body became visible while my mom was helping me get ready for the dance. Anger instantly flooded my mom's eyes as she looked at me with what felt like disgust.

"What in the world is that?"

"I don't know." Wasn't that the typical response of a sixth grader who had been caught doing something stupid?

"Why in the world would you carve something into your skin? What's wrong with you? Do you realize that if people saw this, they would think you are a nutjob?"

I just hung my head. I knew I had screwed up. I had no idea why I was feeling the way I was. But mom confirmed the fact that I was going to look crazy if anyone saw it.

"Your dad would be so hurt if he saw this."

That broke my heart even more. I desired for my earthly father to be proud of me just as much as my heavenly Father. I was a daddy's girl, and Mom was right. If Dad saw this, he would be so disappointed in me.

My mom got me a large Band-Aid to put over the carving, and we both said we would keep this between us. I knew that I was going to need to do a better job of hiding when I cut.

That night, mom dropped me off at school at six o'clock for my sixth-grade dance. I was really excited to get out of the house and be around my friends. And I was very boy crazy, so I was excited to see who I would get to dance with. The old gym was dark except for the colorful lights that were flashing near the back of the gym. About half of my class was probably already there by that time, as I continued to look around the gym. And then I was shocked when I looked behind the speakers and the lights and I saw my coach. He was the DJ for the dance. I hadn't talked to him in so long that I had no idea he was going to be our DJ. I wasn't sure if I was allowed to talk to him, so I walked near where he was, and when he saw me, he motioned for me to come talk to him. Instantly, I felt butterflies in my stomach just with being near him. I began hoping that he wasn't mad at me anymore.

"Dannnngggg, girl. You're looking fine tonight."

"Thanks." I was glad it was dark in the gym because along with my big smile, I could also feel my cheeks blushing.

"Who is your date for tonight?" I kind of shrugged to imply I didn't know. He leaned in close and said in my ear, "Everyone is going to want to dance with you, but make sure you save at least once dance for me."

I smiled and nodded, knowing that he was just playing with me. Obviously, no one could see us together like that, but it was nice of him to say.

I went back to being with my classmates. I had no idea how to dance, but I could slow dance. Most of the slow songs I ended up dancing with one boy in particular from my class. The same one I had liked in the fifth grade. We were at that awkward point in life where a lot of the girls were taller than the boys. And so, while we danced, I was able to easily look over his head. And most of the time I ended up moving my eyes toward my coach, and I would see him staring at me. The dance was finishing up, and the plan was for me to walk over to the church when it was over. My mom was going to pick me up there. The lights were turning on in the gym and kids were gathering their things to leave, when I noticed my coach. He wanted me to come talk to him. So while everyone was starting to leave, my coach and I snuck out the back door. Once we got outside, he grabbed my arm.

"I told you I wanted to dance." My eyes were huge in fear. Yes, I'd heard him say that, but I was certain that he was just joking. His eyes were mad.

"I'm so sorry."

"Why didn't you dance with me? Why did you dance with those other little boys? Do you not love me?"

I had no idea what to say. Obviously, I had messed up, but I was still so confused. How could I have danced with him? I didn't understand at all. He was still mad when we parted ways. He went back inside to clean up the gym with the other teachers, and I walked on over to the church. My mom's van was already sitting there, and I opened up the front door and sat in the passenger seat. My mom was obviously still mad at me. She could hardly look at me.

I felt completely defeated. I was messing up right and left. Nothing made sense anymore. The pain in my heart was back, and this time it was stronger than ever. Maybe it would be better for everyone if I just wasn't alive anymore.

When neither sun nor stars appeared for many
days and the storm continued raging, we
finally gave up all hope of being saved.
—Acts 27:20

CHAPTER 10

Where did I come from? How did I get here? My dreams from my childhood are lost. Who am I? Why am I here? What's the purpose, what's the point? Was I born to be used, abused? Was I born to stay quiet? To simply obey with no question? I can no longer tell the safe from the unsafe. The enemy from the Savior.

Who am I? This is a question I'm trying to figure out. I need to know the answer. My first thought is that I am a child of a King. The one true King. I am His child. I am broken and ashamed, but that is not what my King sees. He sees me as His precious child. I believe that my story can't go on without me bringing God into the picture a little more. Picturing where He was and what His thoughts possibly were will hopefully allow an additional perspective and will be important for my own healing. Keeping my eyes focused on Jesus is always a good thing.

Being a twelve-year-old girl is a challenge in itself. I went through the roller-coaster ride of drama between girlfriends and boyfriends. I pushed myself with basketball and did fair in my schoolwork. I had a mostly normal life, from the outside looking in. And honestly, on the inside, I was beginning to forget a lot of the darkness that my eyes had seen and that my body had endured from the previous three years. God had hidden the terrible memories in my mind for a time until I was ready to handle them. The enemy had attacked me, but as the child of God, the enemy cannot have the final say.

> The enemy meant it for harm, but
> I (God) mean it for good.
> —Genesis 50:20

I woke up early one morning for school, and I was right away distracted by the ache in my heart. I couldn't understand where this feeling was coming from. I was hurting, and I didn't know why. Basketball season had just finished up, and without it, I felt lost. My soul hurt. As a child, I only saw the surface of my life, and therefore I saw no reason for this terrible, deep pain inside of me. I was still in a close relationship with my coach, but our relationship was changing. I had begun to forget a lot of the old stuff we did back at his house and at the white country house. In my mind, my coach was not a reason for the pain I was dealing with. Not understanding the ache was not enough to make it go away. I was smart enough to know that something wasn't right, but as a child, my mind couldn't figure out what it was that was hurting me. I did know that with basketball gone, the days didn't seem to have a purpose. I wanted to play, and I wanted to see my coach. I wanted to hear his kind words and feel the excitement of getting called from my class to go see him, but the knocks on the classroom door never came.

My friends were becoming more and more a part of my life, and I often longed for their naïve thoughts and feelings. My best friend was still the pitcher from my summer softball team, and I loved my time spent with her. God knew how important this time was for me, when I would get to go to her house and play. It was a chance to be a child and be goofy and silly, the way a twelve-year-old-girl should be. There were often times when I would have to fake the childishness, but after a while spending time with my best friend, I was being just as goofy and silly as she was.

One evening when I was spending the night with my best friend, she told me that she had some big news to share with me. She had been told at school by some classmates what it meant to have sex. Her friends had put it in a silly story form, and my best friend couldn't wait to share the news with me.

"Ugh! Isn't that the most disgusting thing you've ever heard?" she said. I quickly nodded yes and acted completely grossed out and disturbed by the thought, but my heart hurt. I knew what sex was. In fact, the silly story she told me was not near the full details of what sex was. There needed to be a camera and sometimes ropes, and they didn't only do the few things that she said. Sex was so much more than what she realized. Images began flashing through my mind. I was familiar with them, and yet somehow I wasn't able to make sense of where I was in the images and who was having sex with me. I needed to act grossed out and completely shocked, so I did my best to hide what I was feeling inside. That I not only know what sex is, but that I know exactly what it feels like.

I had a million emotions running through my little body. It felt like an elephant marched in the room and had a seat right on my chest. I saw how excited my friend was to share this secret with me, and so I did my best to play along. But nothing took the pain in my chest away.

In that moment, God wanted to scoop me up in His big and mighty hands, and simply hold me. Love on me. He began to whisper to my soul just how valuable I am to Him. Just how amazing I am. But I could only feel the pain. The emptiness. The betrayal.

School was hard for me. My emotions and feelings didn't match up with my life. Why did everything seem under control and steady and good all around me, but my heart was screaming for help? History class had been going on for about twenty minutes, and the students were broken into groups to do projects together. I sat frozen in my chair. My thoughts raced. My heart hurt so bad that I couldn't swallow. And what made it worse was that I had no reason in my mind for the hurting. I had nothing at all to be sad about. That made my mind flood with more thoughts of being worthless and that I was weak and a sorry existence of a life. Before I knew it, I grabbed the teacher's scissors that had been sitting on a desk close to me and I hid myself behind my desk. I held those scissors tightly in my right hand and put them up against my left wrist. I didn't want to be alive anymore. I didn't know how to make the pain stop or why it was there, and I couldn't handle it anymore. I wanted to be done. I didn't have anything on my mind at the time except that I needed to get away from this pain. This endless, confusing pain.

As the events were playing out, I'm certain God's eyes were pooling with tears. He knew exactly why I was hurting and why I felt like calling a quits with life. He knew all the terrible things that Satan laid on me at such a young age. He knew my pain because He was feeling it too. He was nestled in my heart, bunked close to that massive amount of pain that kept aggressively making itself known. He felt every bit of pain that I felt. He had been walking in my shoes this whole time and taking the abuse right along with me. Yes, He hurt, but even more so, He hurt for His broken child. My tears were met with His tears. Looking back, I know that I was not alone during that time. But yet, I felt very much alone. Satan poured cruel lies into my mind, trying to push me over the edge.

"There is no other way."

"Spare everyone else the trouble of dealing with you."

"You just want attention. What about those children who actually have a reason to hurt?"

"What is wrong with you?"

I couldn't control the hatred being thrown at me by the enemy. I looked around and saw everyone focused on schoolwork. I was done pretending. I held the scissors tightly and began to cut the skin on my left wrist. The scissors were dull, and the first swipe barely made any mark at all. I pushed harder and harder, getting braver and braver and more determined each time. I was unsure of exactly how I was supposed to do it. I didn't think about what would happen next. I just wanted the pain deep down in my soul and the confusion to stop. No one understood my pain. No one ever tried. I held the scissors tight and continued to swipe it harder and harder against my skin. Blood was starting to show more with each swipe, but I couldn't feel anything. I couldn't feel any pain or even the tears streaming down my face.

One tear, two tears, three. Each one that rolled down my cheek seemed insignificant to me. My tears weren't seen by anyone except God. And God didn't only see my tears, He counted each one.

Four tears, five, and carefully He caught them in the palm of His hands. God didn't question the plan. He didn't second-guess how strong He knew I was, but He hurt for me all the same.

Six tears, seven tears, eight. Drip, drop, into His hands. God knew that I couldn't see past the ache in my soul. I didn't know that each hard step was going to lead me to a confident, strong woman with a purpose someday. God knew my future. He knew how it would all play out.

Nine tears, ten. But in this moment, as I felt alone and scared and unable to take another step, God stepped in and caught each individual tear that rolled down my face.

> You keep track of all my sorrows. You have collected all
> my tears . . . You have recorded each one in Your book.
> —Psalm 56:8

I continued to use the scissors against my skin, crying quietly behind my school desk, believing I was invisible to the world, but I was wrong.

"What are you doing?" a classmate next to me asked. She then yelled across the room at the teacher that Rachel was cutting her wrist with the scissors. I didn't even look up. I didn't feel anything except cheated from being able to finish what I had started. My young mind obviously didn't put together how this scene would play out. I didn't comprehend that there was very little chance of me succeeding in this attempt to end it all by using a pair of scissors and by doing it in a crowded junior-high classroom. After the declaration had been made about what I was doing, I simply threw the scissors down on the ground and sat in my desk chair, hunched over and covered in tears. I heard my teacher quickly get up from her desk and walk toward me. I couldn't manage to even look up at her.

"Let's go chat, Rachel," the teacher said. And together we walked down the long hallway to the girls' bathroom. Once we got inside, my teacher asked me what was going on. Instantly, the tears fell with force. My teacher quickly wrapped me in her arms while I sobbed. She gave me a feeling of love and care that not only came from my teacher, but was also a gift from God. Other teachers came into the bathroom after they were informed of what I had done. But in that precious moment, I was held by an angel sent from the Lord. I wanted to tell the teacher why I was hurting, but I didn't know what to say. I had no idea how to explain that I missed basketball and I missed my coach. I knew that I couldn't mention my relationship with my coach with anyone, or it could get him in trouble.

I was taken down to the principal's office, and I sat in a chair while my teacher explained to the principal what had happened. My tears had dried, and I sat scared and worried about what the principal would say. When the principal came in, she shut the door behind her and took the seat behind her desk.

"Rachel, your teacher told me what happened in class. She said you took scissors to cut your wrist. Is that true?" I nodded that yes, it was true.

"Why did you want to cut your wrist?" I shrugged to show that either I didn't know why or that I didn't want to talk about it.

"Do you think you were just wanting attention?"

The question took my breath away. Was that what was going on? My mind searched for something to say. God was wanting to scream from the heavens that His daughter had been hurt and was hurting. That she needed to be helped. But instead the principal seemed to go with the idea that it was done for attention.

"I'm going to have to call your parents in because of what you did."

Within the next thirty minutes, my mom showed up to the school and discussed with the principal what I had done. I sat there, embarrassed, as they discussed how preachers' kids have a tendency to rebel and seek attention. I began to believe that maybe that's all I was doing. My mom turned to me and asked to see my wrist. I could tell from my mom's eyes and from her voice that she was angry and hurt. So I stretched out my arm to show her my wrist, but being quick to protect myself, I tried to fool her by showing her the wrong wrist. My mom didn't buy it.

"Show me the other one." So I hung my head and stretched out my other arm.

"You drew blood," was all she said.

I didn't know what to say. I was embarrassed and confused and scared. Embarrassed because I didn't feel like I had a reason for my actions and confused with myself and how everyone else was handling it. I hadn't thought about how my actions would affect others, but by the look in my mother's eyes, I clearly could see that my choice was devastating to my mom.

The meeting ended, my arm was bandaged, and I was sent back to class. I realized that showing that I was hurting only made things worse. I dreaded seeing my classmates. I dreaded going home and facing my mom and dad. And still I didn't understand what was wrong with me.

I still desired to be seen by my coach. I desired to have him yearn for me, like he used to. I wanted him to want to be with me and to love me. Being with him gave me some kind of comfort of being needed.

God desperately wished that I could see Him and desire Him the way I did my coach. To intimately desire Him in every area of my life. To need Him. It was pure jealousy, but not judgment. God knew that my heart had been played with. That I had been purposefully confused and hurt and it left me with a sinful desire that came from Satan. God was hurting, but He knew me and that this was not the end of my story. This would not be the last time I would reach out for help. In fact, the very next year, around the same time, at the end of basketball season, I reached out again.

I had moved again, and this time it was in the country and too far for me to ride my bike to my coach's house. My coach and I had continued a relationship, but just through our time at school, in his classroom, and on the court. During school, I started realizing that my coach had more interest in some other girls. Girls younger than me. I saw how he looked at one girl in particular. She was his special fourth-grade helper. It became obvious that he wanted her, not me. At least, that was how I felt. Jealousy definitely set in. I couldn't describe the emptiness that his absence left inside of me. Who was I if he didn't want me anymore? He had told me that I belonged to him, and yet he no longer wanted me.

God knew that my coach was staying somewhat close to me to keep me from talking, but that he had no interest in me other than that. He was continuing the mind games and mind control. I was looking more like a woman and less like a kid but he needed to keep me tight under his control. It was just procedure. He had lost all desire for me, but he couldn't let me know that.

I could feel the difference but wasn't understanding. I dealt with flashbacks of other men in a dark place in my mind, but my memories didn't make sense. The place where these men were hurting me didn't make sense. Honestly, nothing made sense to me. The only thing that stayed consistent was the pain.

"Pain doesn't just show up in our lives for no reason. It's a sign that something in our lives needs to change." This quote is from one of my counselors during recent years, who has helped me heal from my past. It's a very true statement and one that I didn't understand for so long.

I learned from my suicidal attempt that, from that point on, I needed to suppress the unexplainable pain. I began reminding myself often that I had no reason to be in pain and I must just be looking for attention. That's at least what I heard others say, and it stuck in my head. My coach only saw me occasionally, and as the time away from him grew, I was able to switch my focus to basketball. My summer was filled with three-on-three tournaments, basketball camps, softball games, and sleepovers with my best friend. I was feeling settled and in control of my life. My name was beginning to circulate as the upcoming local basketball star. It was becoming my identity, and that made me very happy.

Seventh-grade year for me was a roller-coaster ride. Getting back in the routine of school and seeing my coach daily became a challenge. I wanted to impress my coach. My young heart and mind never steered away from my feelings with my coach, and as a result, seeing him every day made me think of him often. Every morning before school, I hoped that he would look my way, smile at me, and possibly even motion for me to come talk to him. I would get his flirty looks and sweet comments often, but he was spending majority of his time with someone else. Someone younger. And I knew that the younger girl was my replacement. It was confusing for my young mind and heart.

I decided that on one Monday morning I was going to take the ball into my own hands. During the gym time before school, I asked if I could go talk to my coach. I walked up to him, and right away he smiled and put his hand on the small of my back. I instantly melted.

"Heyyyyy. This is a good surprise."

I smiled at his sweet words and became very shy, but I was determined to be strong. We made small talk, and then when the PE teacher wasn't paying attention, I quietly asked if I could see him during class time today. He acted thrilled at my request, which heightened my excitement in what I wanted to talk to him about. I felt better about it and was certain he would be thrilled about my request.

I spent all morning at school going over and over in my head what I was going to say. Just like a junior high girl working up the guts to ask out a boy that she liked. But this was different. It felt wrong and it felt rebellious, but it seemed to me that it was the key to my happiness. When my coach was pleased with me, then I seemed to find more joy in my life.

The very first class after lunch, a knock came at the door, and I knew what that meant. I was already standing up from my seat even before the young fourth-grade girl on the other side of the door made the request to come with her to see my coach. I was nervous but anxious to see him and how happy he was going to be with what I wanted to ask him.

God flashed many red flags in my heart as I walked to his classroom. God's voice inside of me was yelling, *"Don't do it! Run!"*

But my excitement and anxious thoughts grew louder, and I never hesitated in my decision. I sat next to him like I always did as soon as I entered his classroom. I had a shy smile on my face, but I was determined to show him that I was the one he wanted. That I was better for him than any other girl. He spoke before I could and began flirting with me right away. He said he loved my smell and had missed touching my skin. He told me I was his girl and I was going to be a basketball star.

"Make sure you don't forget me when you make it to the pros. Remember your old grade-school basketball coach."

I was being lifted higher and higher with each kind word he said to me. I really believed at that moment that he was more in love with me than ever. So I shyly but confidently started.

"I wanted you to know that I'm okay if you want to make love to me. Actually I would do whatever you want to do to make you feel good." I smiled and looked up at him, embarrassed but certain I was going to see a huge smile stretch across his face by offering myself to him. But that was not the response I got.

"Do you know how serious this is, Rachel?"

I was instantly confused. I didn't know how to answer that.

"Do you have any idea what you are saying? Are you trying to get me in trouble? Or are you even thinking about anyone other than yourself? How in the world do you even know what making love is?"

My heart instantly fell to the floor. What in the world was going on? Did I miss something? He looked angry and very disturbed that I would say something like that. I thought I had learned about making love from him. I thought it was a good thing, that it was what God wanted from me. And I thought it was my coach that desired me in that way. I don't remember much about the process of making love but bits and pieces. And I remember how it made him happy with me. At least, that's what I thought. Maybe I was wrong. I ended up being asked to leave his classroom immediately, and I was completely puzzled by his anger and his words.

Weeks went by without even so much as a glance from my coach. Each day I would start off hopeful that he would notice me, and each day I was let down. Becoming more and more depressed and frustrated. My nightmares were getting worse, and I was more confused than ever on what was the truth. I felt like a crazy kid. I would lie in bed at night and pray that God would take the pain away and give me strength to not make any mistakes. The biggest mistake I was afraid of was seeking help from someone. I desperately wanted someone to help me, to understand the battle I was facing each day, but I was scared of the consequences of seeking help. I had to remind myself often to not seek help because of the consequences.

God saw my tears and heard my cries at night. He knew my fears, and He knew the battle that lay ahead of me. That for years no one would listen or believe. God knew that I would not be heard or understood by anyone until much later in my life. Together, He and I wanted to shout from the mountains that I was hurting, but there was a long process that had to happen before anyone would hear my cries. However, all my young mind could understand was that my pain was either from weakness or for unimportance. People choosing to not care or not believe left me feeling like what I was going through didn't matter. Or that I didn't matter. People turning a blind eye to the situation was very confusing to my young mind and aided in the brainwashing that was done to me.

Day after day, I struggled and felt a pull from God to reach out to people. To ask for help. But I didn't know what was wrong with me, so how could I ask for help? And how could I do it in such a way that there would have zero consequences? I didn't understand my pain, and I didn't want to sound crazy or like I was just seeking attention. My sweet child mind was trying to process an adult situation with only a small portion of the tools that an adult has. Which led to major problems.

CHAPTER 11

My strength was wavering. I tried to stuff my feelings and not allow the pain to overtake my soul. I tried to keep on top of the symptoms by keeping myself consumed with other things in my life, but my efforts failed me. God knew that I needed to get the pain out, not stuff it deeper within me. He knew what holding the pain inside would do to me. He also knew my future and even my cries for help would not be heard this time around, just like last time, but He knew that they would eventually be heard. And each step I would take to find help would be one more step closer to healing.

My young mind was working hard to find the correct ways to express my pain. I needed someone, anyone to understand and to lead me to a place of healing. I wasn't seeking for answers as much as I was looking for love. Someone to share the pain with. I was too embarrassed to go to my parents or my teachers, especially after the way my suicide attempt went. I was getting sadder and sadder, and my friends at school began to notice. There were four girls that I had gotten very close to in junior high. We were in sports together, and we would hang out outside of school quite often. I wasn't as close to them as I was with my best friend, but we did have fun together, and they were good girls. They noticed how sad I seemed, and they began to ask me questions.

"Rachel, you're sad all the time now. What's going on?" It seems like an insignificant question, but with all the many people in my life, these girls were the only ones who noticed my sadness and asked me about it. Tears immediately began to fall. I told them in between a lot of sobs that I was hurt by an older man and I didn't know what to do. Images began to quickly flash through my mind. I could see the flash of various men's faces, each lying on top of me. I could feel the strength of their arms holding me down. I could see my coach's smile and feel his comforting touch. I could see other flashes of things that didn't make sense. I had no verbal way to express these images in my head, so I just cried.

My friends wanted to rush to my rescue. They wanted to know who hurt me and what the man did to me, and then they wanted to tell an adult. I begged and pleaded with them not to share this with anyone because I was afraid of getting in trouble. I hurt, and I needed someone to help me not hurt me anymore. I didn't want to face the consequences of trying to get help.

Once again, I hadn't thought through my actions. Of course they would want to know this stuff. And, of course, they not only wanted to know the facts, but they also wanted to report the man that hurt me.

My brain immediately went into hyperdrive. Why was it happening this way? Why couldn't they just listen to me? I couldn't put together the pieces of who each man was, and I knew I couldn't say anything about my coach. What was I supposed to do? My heart was beating a million miles an hour. I wished I hadn't said anything at this point. I searched for reasons to not talk about it anymore. I was so afraid of being punished once adults found out. I begged my friends to please keep it a secret. But they didn't, and next thing I knew, the same teacher that had helped me during the suicide attempt was now asking me who hurt me?

My emotions were beginning to be in conflict. I felt like running and hiding, I felt like fighting and I felt like crying all at once. I was beginning to see the world from a different view. Like I was the one being blamed for pain. Like I was the one who was hurting others.

For the next year, I probably told a dozen different people that I was being hurt. That I needed help. But each time I would give up those difficult words to another human being, I was given responses that kicked me in the gut.

I wasn't certain of exactly what I needed. As a child, I couldn't explain in a reasonable way what had even happened, but no one sat down with me to work through it. I was told I was lying. I was told that I was looking for attention. I was told to tell my parents, but my parents said I was lying. That my story didn't make sense. That I don't understand what pain is compared to what they had experienced in life. That I am a sick person to seek out attention in that way. I was grounded from all my friends. My friends' parents found out that I was lying about men hurting me, and they told their daughters to stay away from me. I was told if I didn't straighten up, then my parents would take me to a hospital and have me examined. I was faced with so many people being angry with me and embarrassed of me. It was considered the black years of my life because I was seen as rebelling.

I began writing in my journal as if my journal was the only one who really would listen. I asked for forgiveness in my journal for being such a bad kid. For hurting so many people. I knew that I was both physically and spiritually dirty. One of my punishments from my parents was that I had to go and apologize to anyone who was affected by my "stories." I apologized to my friends, to my friends' parents, to my principal, my teachers, my superintendent, and to two men who had hurt me, one being my coach. My parents threatened to send me away to a correctional facility that worked with delinquent children.

I cannot explain the emptiness inside of me because of all that I went through for trying to express my pain. I wasn't angry at anybody except myself. I was unsure of what it was, but I knew that something was very much wrong with me.

One evening, during my eighth-grade year, I had begun to make new friends and was invited to one of their slumber parties. I was more hurt emotionally at this point than ever before. I wasn't understanding the path that my life had taken. I no longer showed pain. I no longer shared what memories would flash in front of my face. I began to follow every rule set by adults to gain back the good graces of those I had hurt so deeply by these "stories" I would tell. But when I was at this slumber party, I hit a point where I no longer could handle life. I went away to another room after grabbing a knife from the kitchen. And I began to cut my hand. Deeper and deeper. The knife slowly dug the skin away until a pool of blood covered my hand. The emotional pain was still there. The answers still were nowhere to be found. I cleaned up my hand and snuck out a back door.

My thoughts were racing. There wasn't anyone who understood. God was nowhere around. I couldn't figure out the pain and the hurt, let alone handle it anymore. I began to walk. I was walking with a purpose, but not aware of what that purpose was. And yet, something deep inside of me knew that I was tapping out. I was calling quits.

Looking back, I know that God wasn't in the sky at this point looking down at me. He wasn't following behind me. He wasn't beside me or in front of me. God was within me. And He was angry. He had seen my pain and my shame. He saw it, but He also felt it. He knew why I was struggling, and He knew that even though others weren't listening to me now, they would someday.

Someday I would get the help I needed. But on this day, as I felt abandoned and alone, he stayed with me. I felt too much pain to feel Him radiating inside of me, but that didn't make Him leave. He stayed every step of the way, even though each step I took was taking me closer to the highway up ahead.

The sun had just set beyond the horizon, and the streetlights were turning on automatically. My friend's house was on the outskirts of a small country town, and it was not far from one of the busiest highways in the state. Each step felt quicker and more definite than the last. I wasn't strong enough to handle this fight anymore. Something was wrong with me. Something was terribly, terribly wrong with me.

Fear was rising in my throat. But my legs were quick and determined as I got closer and closer to the highway. When my feet hit the blacktop, I froze. There was something eerily quiet about the night. I stood with one foot on that road for about a minute when a car zoomed by. I wasn't even remotely fazed and felt with every ounce of my being that I knew exactly what I needed to do.

I slowly walked to the middle of the road where the yellow lines were dashed on one side and solid on the other. I looked one way and saw no cars, and then when I looked the other way, I realized I was at the bottom of a small hill, so I couldn't see for certain if there was a car off in the distance coming toward me or not. Without hesitation I began to lower myself to the ground until I laid completely on my back along those yellow lines. I spread my arms and legs out. And I lay perfectly still and stared up at the nostalgic stars sparkling in the sky. The world was quiet, and I lay there believing I was finally doing something right.

Time didn't seem to exist at this point. I was waiting, and yet I wasn't. I had given in. I had read the writing on the wall. And my time had come. Not a single tear. Not a single fear. Nothing but trust that soon I would be okay because soon I would be gone.

Even though time didn't exist, something tugged at me to where I was able to become aware that I had spent a long time lying on that road and somehow, someway, no car ever came. Not from either direction. For such a busy highway that ran parallel to one of the busiest interstates in the country, it didn't make sense that no car had come.

I slowly got up and decided to go back to my friend's house. I was confused. I was shaking and afraid. Maybe dying wasn't what God had in store for me at that moment. And in that moment, I felt an odd sensation within me. It was a feeling of hope. I'm not sure where it came from except the understanding that my time had not yet come and that God wasn't finished with me yet. As I took my first steps back to the house, I crossed over the white line of the paved road and into the grass. I turned back and looked at the road behind me and somehow was not surprised that vehicles were once again flying up and down the road.

God rested within my heart. It wasn't a moment where I had asked Him to save me, but He did anyway. God was filled with more love for me than ever. He was sad that I hurt and sad that I felt like there was no other way, but He was also filled with even more love for His child. He knew my pain was authentic. It wasn't for attention. It wasn't to rebel or to get someone in trouble. It was real, and He felt it too. He still hadn't forgotten my future or my purpose. I was still His child, and I was still precious to Him and loved by Him. Lying in the middle of a highway giving up couldn't even change that.

My best friend was one of the girls at the slumber party, and she had noticed I was missing. She could tell something was wrong with me when I made it back to the house, so she asked me if I was okay. I assured her I was and we joined everyone else at the party.

My eighth-grade year was a big transitional year for me, it seemed. I had stopped trying to reach out for help and became good at suppressing memories and thoughts that hurt or didn't make sense. I became very close to my coach, but in a different way. The year before when I had tried to seek help, he became very angry at me for talking to people about my feelings. We decided that the best one for me to talk to would always be him. I began to feel more connected to him than ever. And I desired him in a more-than-a-coach sort of way.

He didn't touch me much anymore. We would hug and we would talk, and that was about it. We talked a lot about my transition to high school. And a lot about my new boyfriend. I had started dating a guy who was seventeen and a junior in high school. He was a part of our church and a very strong Christian. We didn't go out on dates much, but I went to his house most weekends. On our very first date, we went down into his basement where his room was. He started kissing me, and things went very quickly from there. I followed his lead, as I was used to doing. And somehow I knew exactly what to do. It felt so familiar, and yet I didn't understand how I knew this stuff so well. It had never been talked about with my parents. He seemed excited by my willingness and knowledge. This became the only thing we ever really did on our dates. I struggled with knowing the rules my parents had for me when it came to boys and doing what seemed to come so natural and easy for me. I knew how to make men happy.

Basketball season ended up being a very exciting time. I was averaging over thirty points a game and couldn't be stopped on the basketball court. I had so much confidence on the floor. I started receiving Division-1 letters from universities around me. My dreams of basketball were starting to play out. My coach and I lived the dream together. He knew I was going to be a star, and he was right. We loved talking about our games and my future. And occasionally we would take a detour and talk about my love life with this boy I was dating.

My coach didn't seem to care for my boyfriend very much. I had had many boyfriends but nothing serious, and they were just grade-school relationships. My coach seemed either jealous or just uncomfortable with me having an older boy as my boyfriend.

"He isn't good for you. He doesn't know how to take care of you like I do. He better never touch you or expect you to touch him. And you better never have sex with that boy. You will get pregnant and then lose your basketball dreams."

My coach was very passionate about me not doing anything sexual with anyone. I felt like he was jealous, and that made me feel really good. I had always been jealous of him, and now he was actually jealous of me. It seemed like a good thing.

The end of the season came quickly. We made it to state, and after blowing out a team in the first round, we then played my best friend's team for the semifinal game. I had played them two other times in the year, and we had just barely beat them each time. It was a tough game because my best friend's team had five good players and our team had four players who were very important but weren't averaging more than a few points a game. And then there was me. We had three losses all year, and those teams were ones who played a triangle-and-two defense on us, where they put two players on me and left the other three players to guard our other four. My best friend believed that they should play a triangle-and-two or at least a box and one. But her coach would not play anything other than a man-to-man defense, which was a definite advantage to me. I had a quick first step that no one could stop one-on-one. We ended up winning the semifinal game by just single digits, and we went on to the state championship game.

We were playing a team that had one good player and a few other pretty good players, and they seemed pretty confident that they were going to win. I remember the crowd. I remember watching the other team's star player and feeling pretty confident that I could beat her. If I knew that I could beat the other team's best player, then I felt confident that we could win the game.

The first half ended up being a nightmare. We were down at half, 20–12. I had only scored six points. My teammates were taking a lot of shots, and I wasn't getting my hands on the ball very much at all. At halftime, my coach didn't even take us down to the locker room. He had started this new thing of having no halftime talk a few months into the season. Which honestly, he didn't have much to say anyway, so it worked out fine.

I remember sitting on the bench feeling like I was in a fog. I couldn't comprehend what was happening. I had people try to snap me out of the fog I was in, and I still wasn't able to. I had one guy come up and tell me that we need to dance to the music that got us here. I smiled and nodded, having absolutely no idea what he meant. I was told later that he meant that we needed to do the things that we had done all season long that got us to the championship, which meant I needed the ball in my hands and I needed to score.

The second half started, and I was determined to fight our way back into this game. Every time I had the ball in my hands my coach would quietly say to me, "Shoot it." His confidence in me gave me what I needed to take over the game. And that's exactly what I did.

The final buzzer rang, and we led 38–32. I scored twenty-four of our team's twenty-six points in the second half, including four three-pointers. We got in line after the game and gave handshakes to the other team as they seemed completely overwhelmed with tears and emotions. I walked back to our bench, not sure of what I felt. I walked up to my coach, and he grabbed me and hugged me tight like he had always done before, but when we were alone. And he whispered in my ear, "You did it."

I regretted for many years following that night that I didn't respond to him with something like, "No, *we* did it." Instead I just said nothing.

I was so overwhelmed by the moment and the fact that he hugged me in public that I was left speechless.

Basketball season was always a high for me, and when it ended, I usually struggled with the pain that basketball seemed to hide so well. My eighth-grade year was a little bit different. This time I had a boyfriend and I had track, which I had a good chance of making it to state in as well. I still had enough going on in my life to distract me from the pain that still lay nestled in my soul. God knew the future and that someday, no matter all the distractions in the world, that pain would come out with a vengeance, but at this time, it was still dormant.

Track season had just begun as our basketball season ended. The high school basketball seasons were still in full swing with about a month left after our grade-school season was over. My coach called me into his room several times, and we talked about possible ways for us to get together alone one last time before I went to high school. I was excited to work on this plan with him. He seemed madly in love with me and couldn't wait for us to be alone so he could show me that love again.

We found a way that we could work, but I needed to ask my parents first for permission to go with him. After coming up with the perfect game plan, I went home one evening after track practice and asked my mom if that Thursday night I could go watch a high school girls' game with my coach. She said sure. And just like that, I had permission. I couldn't wait to tell my coach the good news. Who knew it would be so easy?

Thursday night rolled around, and I felt like I was getting ready for a date. He came to my house and picked me up. I felt butterflies in my stomach as I got into his car with him. He was smiling from ear to ear. He seemed nervous and excited just like me. Our conversation was kept very light on the thirty-minute drive to the game. We sat up high in the bleachers, out of the way. We watched the game, but we both were thinking other thoughts the whole time. I knew he had plans to be with me, and I was anxious about it. It had been so long since we had been alone. Halftime came and we both looked at each other, and without giving the obvious reason as to why, we decided to leave the game. We would listen to it on the radio so I could tell my parents what happened in the game, but our purpose of going to this game was not actually to see the game.

We got in the car, and immediately I felt a shift in the atmosphere. Something seemed a little bit off. I still was smiling and trying to talk to him, but very quickly he shut down and an angry face replaced what had been a happy face just minutes before. We sat in silence on the drive back, and then instead of driving toward my house, he took a different turn.

"Did you know you can take this old country road to get to your house?" I shook my head no. My butterflies had turned into fear as we drove down this dark side road that was showing fewer and fewer houses. I didn't know where I was anymore.

If my coach wasn't showing so much anger in his face, then I might've been more excited about the possibility of being lost with him in his car in the middle of nowhere. But his face made me very scared. I knew that look. And I hated, absolutely *hated* when he got angry.

I could no longer see any houses, and he started driving slower and slower, until finally, we stopped. I couldn't even look in his direction. I was terrified of him at that moment. He told me to get in the back, so I turned and started to crawl back there. I was not going to tell him no. Not when he was so angry. I just wished I knew what I had done that made him so angry all of a sudden.

I crawled to the back and he had the seat laid down, so it was just a flat area to sit. And he got out of his car and walked back and got in there with me. With a spirit that seemed nothing short of the devil, he began to use force to pull my clothes off. He would put all of his weight on me as he pushed and pulled to get my clothes off. I couldn't understand his aggressiveness. If he had asked me to take my clothes off, then I would've done it for him, surely he knew that. But he seemed so angry with me. He pulled my shirt up, and when he did, he left my shirt where my arms were still in the sleeves and the front of the shirt was covering my entire head. Then he pulled my sports bra up and tied my wrists together so that I couldn't move and because of my shirt, I couldn't see.

It was dark, but even though my face was covered, I could make out a small light. All I could think was that it could've been was a light from a camera.

With force, he lifted my legs and bent my knees up to my chest. I was ready for the force and the pain that was coming next. Memories of this were in my head, and I was ready, or so I thought I was. With a power like he was punishing me, he shoved his penis into my butt as deep and aggressive as he could. I yelled out in pain.

"Shut up!" he yelled back at me.

I hurt so bad that I thought I was going to pee on myself. I tried so hard not to make any sounds as he worked me over in such a mean and violent way. As he got done, he went up to the front of the car and yelled at me to get dressed, that he needed to get me home.

I lay there, in so much pain and in shock of what just happened. I had my pants around my ankles and my shirt was still up over my head with my hands tied with my sports bra. I struggled to break free, but within a minute or two I was able to. My eyes had to adjust to the light, and I noticed that it was indeed a camera with a light on it that was sitting on the center console. I put my clothes on, and when I was done, my coach grabbed the camera and turned it off and then put it away in a bag he had under his feet. I crawled back up front with him and sat in the passenger seat.

I still had tears on my face. He gave me a wipe to wash my cheeks off, and he put his hand on my thigh in a soft caring way and looked at me.

"I'm so glad we got to spend one last night together, All-Star. You'll always be my girl."

We drove off, and within ten minutes, we were pulling into the driveway of my country house. We didn't say anything during the drive, and then when he stopped the car, he asked me if I was okay. I forced a smile and said yes.

"See you at school tomorrow," he said, and I walked into the house while he drove away. My mom was in the living room when I walked in, and she asked how the game was.

"Oh, it was good. I am glad I went."

I went to the bathroom and then changed into pajamas and went on to bed, since it was a school night. I expected more questions from my mom in the morning, but they never came. And the next day at school, my coach acted completely normal. He still talked to me and was kind and flirty. My mind spun with confusion.

Even though I was fourteen years old, and about to enter high school, I was still very much a kid, a very hurt kid. God knew that my coach had brutally butt-raped me that night because it was a control thing. Whether it was because of my relationship with a boyfriend, or because I was going away to high school, or just because he wanted to show his control over me, there was nothing at all that I did wrong. God knew that I was once again hurt and manipulated and made to feel dirty and used, and it broke God's heart. This was not the purpose of why God made me. He made me in His image. He made me because He already loved me and He wanted to have a relationship with me. And this man was hurting His child and putting a gap between God and me.

God also knew all that my coach had gone through as a child. He knew what choices my coach had made as a result of the trauma he had faced growing up, and He knew that my coach hurt, but none of that made it okay for him to hurt another one of God's children. God was sickened and saddened that His people would hurt each other in this way. This is not the world He wanted. His heart broke as He held my heart in His hands, and He wanted so bad to flush out all the bad and fill me with His goodness completely. But that had to be my choice, not His. He knew that someday I would make that choice. He knew someday that I would allow Him to flush out all the bad and make me like new, but He also knew that it would be a long, hard road until I reached that point. That, however, did not mean He was going to leave me. Not even for a second. No matter my choice, He would stay.

> It is the Lord who goes before you. He will
> be with you; he will not leave you or forsake
> you. Do not fear or be dismayed.
> —Deuteronomy 31:8

CHAPTER 12

As my eighth-grade year was coming to a close, I was excited about my future, about high school, about basketball, and about boys, but I was not at all excited about leaving my coach. His desire for me had become such a huge part of my life, and no matter the pain he had caused, I still felt like I needed him.

Track season ended in the late spring. I made it to state in the mile run, the four by four, and long jump. And as my time in grade school came to a close, I prepared for my graduation day. The very last day of school, my coach invited me to his classroom during a time when he knew his students wouldn't be in there. He met me as soon as I walked in the door, and he hugged me so close, and so dear.

"I'm going to miss seeing you so much," he said to me. I thought for sure he was going to kiss me at that moment, but he didn't. He wiped away tears as he talked.

"You have been so special to me and I know that I can always trust you," he said. Just like at the state championship game, I didn't have any words to say back to him. I didn't cry. I didn't speak. I just listened as he seemed completely heartbroken that I was moving on. But I was certain this did not mean our relationship was over. Just that it would be different.

"Can you come to my graduation? It would mean a lot to me," I told him.

"Yes, of course. I wouldn't miss it."

I smiled and thanked him. We hugged again, and then I left his classroom and met up with my class out on the playground. Tears started to well up at that point, as I thought about what my future would look like and if my coach would still be in it. He seemed to love me so much that I believed that he would still stay connected with me.

Graduation night came quickly. My family plus many of my extended family showed up to see me graduate. But the whole night I was scanning the room, looking for my coach. As the ceremony was over and everyone was hugging and congratulating, I was still hoping that he would show up, just like he promised. But he never did. My heart was disappointed and hurt.

That summer, I was already playing on the high school summer basketball team and was the starting point guard for the varsity team. Jealousy among teammates was beginning, but I didn't care. My goals were being accomplished. My freshman year, I started every single game of varsity and was the second-leading scorer. I made the second all-state team and had several other accomplishments, including placing fourth in state in the three-point competition. Division-1 letters were pouring in, and my dreams of basketball continued.

I spent hours upon hours in the gym. It was where my soul longed to be. The smell of the gym, the sound of the ball flying through the net was my biggest comfort. I didn't think much about my coach, except that I missed him. I would wonder if he missed me, or if he had another girl sitting behind his desk. I would assure myself that he only loved me. No one else.

My coach finally made it to a game my freshman year. It was the sectional semifinal in postseason, and it was arguably the best game I'd played the entire year. I scored twenty-some points and was interviewed by the news when it was over. I was so proud for him to see me do so well, but he didn't stay afterward to talk to me.

A few months later, when the grade schools started to gather at our high school track for their track meets, I got permission from my teachers to go out and watch the track meets, hoping that I would see people I knew. I was especially hoping to see my coach, and I did. I was once again filled with butterflies and believed he would be so excited to see me and so proud of how well I was doing. But as usual, I was disappointed by his response to me. He was nice and polite, but he seemed to have more important things to do than to talk to me. I took the hint pretty quickly and tried to keep my high school swag and headed back to class. But my thoughts were still confused about what to feel. I thought that since I was getting older, my coach would like me more because I was becoming more of a woman.

It's easy to see now that my coach's lust was not for women, but for little girls. I am glad that my mind would've never comprehended that at a young age, and it's even hard to comprehend now. But I will forever be grateful that my mind couldn't comprehend how someone's mind could think in that sick way.

During my freshman year, I spent a lot of time trying to figure out who I was, where I fit in. In the beginning I would spend time with different friend groups. My school was large, with over four hundred students in my freshman class, so I had the opportunity to seek out exactly who I wanted to spend my time with. Really, the only place that felt right was in the basketball gym. Typically my time spent in the gym was alone, with just the sound of the ball and the squeak of my shoes. It was my safe haven, and where I found my purpose. I could envision my dreams and my future. I knew God had given me the love of basketball for a reason.

My favorite people to be around were my parents. They were the only ones I truly trusted and who I felt the most comfortable with. I still had my best friend from grade school, but she was going to a different school and I didn't get to see her much.

I dated a guy all through high school who was very good to me and who made high school a lot of fun. He was great about taking me on special dates and making me feel very special. We dated for three and a half years before I broke up with him. He had some qualities that were red flags to me, and I knew that those qualities were things that I didn't want to have in my future husband.

My sophomore year of high school, I had a very successful basketball season, and I was beginning to receive college letters from places like Duke University, Minnesota and Ohio State, and Indiana University, just to name a few. My dreams of where I could go seemed endless. I played in national tournaments with my AAU basketball team and traveled all over the nation. I played against college teams and was invited to many schools to visit. It was a fun adventure. A few weeks before school was going to start my junior year, I was playing basketball with a couple of guys in my backyard when I went up for a routine left-handed layup, and on the way up, I heard a loud pop in my right knee.

I sat on the ground and grabbed my knee and grimaced for a second. I decided that since I had a summer league game that night, I probably shouldn't scrimmage much more with the guys, and I tried to get up and walk back inside the house. My knee immediately swelled up, and no matter how hard I tried, I could not straighten my knee out.

My parents were out of town, and so I couldn't call them to see what they thought I should do. They were going to be back that evening when my league play was done. I rested up until it was time for my game. I met the carpool at our high school and I told my coach that I had hurt my knee. She promised to look at it when we got to the arena. I could walk fine but couldn't straighten my leg, and when I would try, it would hurt terribly.

We got to the arena, and my team began to shoot and warm up. I asked the coach again to look at my knee. My coach was not someone who knew much about knees, so she put some tape around the bottom of my kneecap and said that I should be ok. I went out to warm up with my team and I could shoot and I could run, but not without a lot of pain. One of my teammates came over and simply said, "I hope it's not a torn ACL." I knew there was no way it was something that serious.

I started the game, and despite not being able to straighten my leg past a forty-five-degree angle, I was still able to score outside of the arc. It wasn't until the second half that my coach pulled me from the game and said, "You can't even run right."

I was a bit confused by her comment. Was she just now noticing this? I went home and called my parents on their cell phone and told them that I hurt my knee. When they came home, they were obviously very worried. I explained that I couldn't straighten my knee, and I propped my knee up on the coffee table and showed my parents that my knee was stuck at a forty-five-degree angle. My dad came up and looked at my knee and said, "Just straighten it." I told him that I couldn't. He was very worried about my knee, but he couldn't seem to understand that I was trying very hard to straighten it, but that my knee was stuck. As my knee was propped up, he decided to try and push down on my knee to force it to straighten. I yelled out in pain as he tried to push down my knee to force it straight, but even still, my knee would not straighten.

Over the next few days, I saw a doctor and was told I needed an MRI, but even the doctor was frustrated at me for not straightening my leg. He thought I was being difficult. The MRI was scheduled for the end of the week, but in the meantime, I had to try and get my leg straight, or they wouldn't be able to do the MRI. So during practice, I would lie on my stomach on the bleachers and let my leg hang off the end. Slowly, my knee would straighten a tiny bit more each day. By the time I went for an MRI,

I could straighten my knee to a twenty-five-degree angle. I was afraid it wouldn't be enough, but they were able to still do the MRI. A few days later, we went to see a doctor in St. Louis, Missouri, who was also the sports doctor of the St. Louis Rams and the St. Louis Blues.

I remember being in the room as he came in and checked my knee. Then he would walk out and look at the MRI results and pictures again. And then come back and check my knee. Finally he sat down and scratched his head with his glasses and said that I had torn my anterior cruciate ligament, more famously known as the ACL.

My dad and I started to silently cry right away. My mom didn't know what this diagnosis meant, but she could tell from my reaction and my dad's reaction that it must not be good. Two days later, I had surgery and began the rehabilitation process. What was supposed to take a minimum of six months to recover from, I worked ridiculously hard and convinced the doctor that I was ready to play ball at just two and a half months after surgery. Within the first two weeks of being released, during an open scrimmage to the public, I went in for a routine pull-up, and my other knee popped three times. As I lay on the floor, I knew what had just happened. I tried to get up and walk, but this time my knee slid all around as I put pressure on it, and I was carried off the floor.

After the second torn ACL, the colleges stopped calling me and stopped sending letters. I had just a handful of Division-1 schools still interested. During the spring of my junior year, I signed with a Division-1 school in Kansas City. I was back playing basketball my senior year of high school, only to tear my left ACL again just eleven games into the season.

The last game of my high school career was during our holiday tournament after Christmas. We were 11–0 and playing like we could finish the season up at state. I was at the top of the key, and with a jab step to the left and a quick crossover to the right, I drove into the lane. The defense collapsed in the paint to stop my drive to the basket, but they were a step too slow and hit me from the side. Right away, I felt my knee slide to the right, letting out a loud pop. I stayed on my feet but limped to the sideline. A foul had been called, and I needed to throw the ball inbound. Thoughts were racing through my head.

Please, Lord. Please tell me that my ACL didn't just tear again. Please. This can't be happening.

I stayed in the game. My knee ached some, but it wasn't horrible. I decided to act like I was fine. I threw the ball inbounds and tried to slowly run back onto the court. Immediately my knee would slide out of place with each step. I was trying my hardest to play it off. I had no idea that my dad was sitting in the crowd, and he knew my ACL was torn. My teammates continued to pass me the ball, wanting me to set up a play, but I knew I couldn't move. I tried to give them the indication to not throw me the ball, but they weren't getting the hint. By this time, my dad was behind the coach's bench, telling my coach I was hurt.

At the next dead ball, my coach subbed me out and I walked to the bench. At the end of the bench was my dad and our team physical therapist. We went out to the lobby area, and I tried to run, but my knee wouldn't stay in place. Immediately my dad phoned my knee doctor and my college coach. Because we were in the middle of a tournament, I had hopes that I could somehow figure out a way to see my doctor and get back by the next game. So midgame, we left.

I met my doctor at the hospital in between surgeries that he was doing on other patients. He did the ACL test on my knee, and it was most definitely torn. Calling both my college coach and my high school coach was really hard. I was officially done with my high school career. I got word on my way home from the doctor that we had lost the game, and our perfect season was over. I was a very heartbroken seventeen-year-old who was about to have her third reconstructive knee surgery.

I went on to college at Southern Illinois University and was on the women's basketball team. I was the starting point guard as a freshman until my knee gave out again, and I was officially told by the knee surgeon after my sixth knee surgery that I will never again be able to play basketball.

Basketball had been the only thing that gave me peace. When basketball was gone, I noticed that I started getting nightmares that didn't make sense to me. The head coach of the university decided to keep me on the team by becoming a student assistant coach. This way, I still kept my full-ride scholarship and I was able to help with team plays, recruiting, scouting, and guard play. It was very informative but also very stressful. The year after I left, our coach was fired because of her emotional abuse toward us. It was a very hard experience. I called home to my parents four or five times a day. I severely missed home. I would often drive home after a college class at 5:00 p.m. and get home a little after six, just in time for supper. Then I would stay awake as long as I could. Being around my parents seemed to be the recharge that I needed. Then I would wake up at four thirty in the morning and leave the house by five o'clock to get to the basketball arena by six for practice.

My senior year of college, I messaged on Facebook a friend of mine from high school. He had been a year below me in school. He was also always in the basketball gym just like me. Usually he was on one side of the gym and I was on the other. But I hadn't talked to him since high school. I knew he was a strong Christian back in high school, but I had heard nothing about him since then. He had actually just gone through what he calls a rebellious period, and he was praying to God about finding a future wife who would love him and love the Lord. I kind of had always known he had a crush on me in high school, but I was dating someone else.

When I messaged him, I sort of had the thought in my mind of seeing if he was boyfriend worthy. We caught up quickly and decided to get together for dessert at Applebee's a few days later. The rest is history, I guess you would say. I knew that I liked him, and I liked all of his qualities, especially his big heart. I knew he would take care of me and would someday be a good daddy. So three months into dating, when he asked me to marry him, I said yes.

We wanted to get married right away, but logistically it didn't make sense since we were both still in college with no jobs. We planned to get married in a little over a year. May 23, 2009 was the date. Matt was the only person I dated who knew how to make me laugh, whether I was mad or sad or hurt. He made my days so much happier.

Eighty days exactly before our wedding date, I came up with this brilliant idea. I told my sweet, loving fiancé that it would be great if we didn't kiss again until our wedding day. It would make our wedding day that much more special. He wasn't as on board as I was. I remember that first night when he walked me to the door, he literally started physically shaking as I made him leave with no kiss. But it got easier. For me anyway. It was a neat thing for us to do together to fast, so to speak, in that area leading up to our wedding day.

My husband had no idea of my abuse as a child. In fact, I wasn't certain of it either at this point. I had asked my coach to actually sing at my wedding, and he told me no. But I was still under the belief that he was a good guy.

I graduated from college in December of 2008 with a bachelor's in Special Education, and in May of 2009, I married the man that God had planned all along for me.

Our wedding day was beautiful. It went off without a hitch. God's heart was beaming as he saw two of his children fall in love and marry. I remember walking down the aisle in tears about the thought of no longer being my mom and dad's little girl. Walking toward my husband at the end of the aisle, I knew I loved him, but I also knew that I wasn't "in love" with him. He is an amazing man, and I had no doubt he would be an amazing husband and daddy. During a special song that was being sung at our wedding, he pulled me aside and asked if he could pray for us. And he said the most beautiful prayer. He prayed for God to no longer use us only as individuals, but as a couple. As two becoming one. That our marriage would be encouraging for others to see and that our love would somehow show others the love of Christ. That I would know every single day of my life that I am loved and cherished by him. And that he will always be there for me.

And in that one single moment, I knew I was instantly madly and deeply in love with him. It makes me sad that my husband thought I was a virgin the night we got married, when in actuality, I have no idea how many men I had been with. And my brain was still very fuzzy on it all. However, when we did have sex that night, I most definitely was brought back to all the pain that I had felt as a child. I stuffed the feeling as quickly as I could.

We left for our cruise early the next morning. We had an amazing time. We slept a lot. We ate a lot. And we laid out by the beach or the pool a lot. Other than tearing my ACL in the ocean in Jamaica, it was a good trip. I'm sad to say, though, that during my honeymoon, I usually cried at least once a day because of homesickness from my parents. I started noticing that it would be hard to trust this amazing new husband of mine, even though I had no reason not to trust him. Something inside me was stirring in fear, and I still didn't understand it.

I was a special education teacher for two years at a high school before becoming pregnant with our first child. He was born on June 7, 2011. It was a long and painful birth. I experienced back labor the entire time and decided after twenty-four hours that I would go ahead and get an epidural. Thirty minutes later, he was born.

I remember when the doctor laid him on my chest, feeling his little tiny breath against my skin. I laid there and loved to feel his breath going in and out. I felt like God had just breathed life into my son's lungs for the first time, and I couldn't get enough of feeling his little tiny breath.

With tears, I held him, and eventually, when it was just me and him in the room, I quietly sang him the songs that I had sung to him all during my pregnancy. And then I shared with him about this man named Jesus. Even though I knew my son wouldn't understand what I was saying, I wanted to be the first one to share with him about who Jesus is. That is a moment I will never forget. My son was born at 11:47 at night, and even though it had been a twenty-four-hour labor, I was wide awake. We were taken to a postpartum room, and my mom and husband both slept soundly. I, however, sat in my hospital bed, just staring at my beautiful little newborn son, promising him the world.

I enjoyed being home taking care of my sweet little boy. It was my dream to be a stay-at-home mom. I had prayed probably thousands of prayers asking for this very thing. I was certain that there was nothing else in the whole world that I would want to do or that God would want me to do than to be a stay-at-home mom. I already had plans of homeschooling my children. Even though I still wasn't remembering the pain from my past, my gut told me that schools weren't safe, and I wasn't going to send my kids there.

Almost exactly two years later it was time for baby number 2. After a very exciting end of a pregnancy, at three in the morning on June 21, 2013, my water broke. I had been having contractions every fifteen minutes for two days. But it wouldn't progress into real labor.

I tried jumping jacks and squats and all you can think of, but the baby wasn't coming. I decided that night to just sleep as much as I could, and sure enough, at 3:00 a.m., my water broke. To the hospital we went, and my sweet little girl was born. Right after her delivery, my midwife's eyes got real big in fear as she looked at me and then at my husband. I didn't know what was going on. It wasn't until we knew for sure that my little girl was healthy that my midwife showed me her umbilical cord. It had a very tight knot right in the middle of it. All my midwife could say was, "She is a miracle baby." I was in tears and so thankful that my baby girl had made it through.

In 2014, my husband and I found ourselves in a bit of a financial bind, so we sold our home and started renting a 750-square-foot apartment about thirty minutes away. With a two-and-a-half-year-old and a six-month-old, we found a way to fit in this two-bedroom apartment, and we were going to save up money to someday buy a house again. We just needed to get back on our feet. We felt proud of ourselves for making the sacrifice of moving into a small place. We were certain that this sacrifice would lead to a bright future financially for our little family. It wasn't easy, but we were sure it would pay off.

Being a stay-at-home mom was enjoyable and priceless, with an apartment full of laughter, the pitter-patter of little feet, snotty kisses, and many bear hugs. It was also challenging having to find time for self-care as well as taking care of my two kids and husband. Financially we maybe weren't where we had hoped, but as far as my family goes, I was living my dream. I had always wanted a large family and to stay home with the kids to love on them and be there for them. I did a lot of research and tried my hardest to do everything right for my kids. I would feed them only homemade organic baby food. We used cloth diapers, and I exclusively nursed. I was overprotective when it came to who they were allowed to be around and worried constantly that somebody was going to come and hurt them. I was already planning to homeschool once the kiddos got school age.

I talked to God often about how badly I needed to have a large family. How I needed to be home with my kids and that my life needed to consist of taking care of my babies. Daily, I would give God all the reasons why I needed these things. I didn't want to mess with the outside world. I didn't take time to understand my reasoning for it. I just knew that it was the desire of my heart. Staying home with a houseful of kids was heaven on earth to me.

Every day, no matter how hard I tried to stop it, I would think about my grade-school coach. But my thoughts were still abnormally positive when it came to him. I remembered how kind he was to me and how special I felt with him.

In January of that year, I had been on a social media site when I came across a picture taken by a mom I knew. She posted the picture and explained that it was a picture of a painting her daughter had made. I was very impressed, considering the little girl who painted it was only in sixth grade. The mom went on to write that her daughter has enjoyed all of her individual painting instruction from a specific teacher after school. This specific teacher she was talking about was my old grade-school coach.

And at that moment, my entire world crashed.

This huge shift in my mind was not a surprise to God, as He always knew this day would come. He knew that so many of my quirks and tendencies and fears and worries traced back to the trauma that happened to me as a child. For so long, my mind had protected me from remembering the truth. The truth about my coach. And the truth about what happened to me. There isn't a time in anyone's life when it is "best" to deal with past garbage. It's never convenient. However, the sooner you can find restoration and healing, the sooner you can learn more truths, like the truth of who you really are.

I had been standing when I read the post about the little girl, and the world literally started spinning. I sat down in my recliner and became lost in my mind as memories that I had forgotten about for so long started coming. I remembered "making love" to my coach and being forced to "make love" to other men. I remembered the white country house. I remembered everything and everyone who was a part of it. And instantly, I knew that this little girl who was spending time after school with my coach working on art needed to be helped. I knew exactly what it was like to be alone with my coach in his classroom, and at that moment I felt intense fear and anxiety like I had never felt before. I ran to the bathroom and threw up.

I cannot even describe the darkness that engulfed my life. It was such an obvious shift that I could almost hear Satan's laughter. I was back to my original confused state of mind, like when I was young. The memories in my mind were as clear as if they happened the day before. I remembered smells and the feeling of having gross hands on me. I was lost at how to move forward. I was stuck between knowing I needed to say something to make sure this blonde-haired little sixth-grade girl was safe and also knowing that no one would believe me.

For days, I rolled around with the memories in my mind. I would spend my days stuffing myself with grotesque amounts of food and then immediately throwing it up. I had the heaviest pain down deep in my gut that I couldn't get rid of no matter how hard I tried. Even though I was still functioning as a mom to my two sweet babies and as a wife to the love of my life, there was an obvious dark cloud hovering over me.

I reached out to a friend of mine who I knew had been sexually abused as a child, to see if she could help me make sense of what was going on in my head. I struggled putting into words the images in my mind. This is nothing that I had ever done before. She was so patient with me, but she also agreed with me that it was very important to make sure this little girl was safe. Since my coach was still teaching, sometimes coaching, was an elder of the largest church in the area, and was in a Christian band, he was obviously trusted by many and was around kids often.

It felt like each day I was being hit with new memories. I felt like I had just become aware of an infection on my arm, but when I went to get the infection out, it became obvious that it had actually been there a very long time and had gone deep into my skin and into my bones and throughout my whole body. Each time I would try to face a small amount of the past, it would seem to drag me further and further down. My heart hurt constantly, and no matter how hard I tried, I couldn't find any peace.

At that time, I felt like God was light-years away. I couldn't hear Him or feel Him, and it was the scariest feeling in all the world. So much evil seemed to be overtaking my mind, and I couldn't find God to help me through it. I began to question God and where He was when I was young and where He was at that moment. Nothing was making sense. And despite all of the horrific memories that were coming to me, I still felt a very strong bond with my coach. I could justify in my heart every terrible thing he did. I believed he didn't mean to hurt me. That he loved me, but that he made mistakes. I wasn't angry at him or anyone else.

Weeks went by, and I started seeing a counselor. My bingeing and purging was becoming a very constant thing in my life. I hurt so bad that I went back to cutting. When my husband found the cuts, he told me that if I did it again, then he was going to have me admitted into a mental hospital. What had been a normal, dependable life had all just gone out the window. The darkness was overtaking my life, and I no longer could breathe.

After seeing a counselor for a few months and trying really hard to justify what happened when I was young and that surely this little girl I saw on social media was safe, I finally decided that an anonymous tip to the local Department of Children and Family Services (DCFS) could potentially save this little girl from being hurt. So after a lot of prayers, I decided to go through with it. Within a week, I received word that my teacher was investigated and nothing was found.

This was how he was investigated: The DCFS went to the school where he taught, and they talked to the little girl and asked if anybody had ever hurt her. The little girl said no, and so then the DCFS went and talked with my coach and explained that he had been investigated and that nothing was found.

I was completely heartbroken. I knew that in sixth grade if I had been asked if my coach had hurt me, I would've said no. The mind games had been too great at that point as a sixth grader, and there was no way I would turn my coach in. I became convinced, once that investigation came back with nothing, that God was leading me to go forward to the police and press charges against my coach for what happened to me as a kid. I knew that there was no evidence to prove it, except I was certain that he still would have child porn in his house. I could even tell the police exactly where to look.

My husband and I sat down and discussed the pros and cons of going forward. We knew that if I went forward, it could be hard on our family because there would be many who wouldn't believe me. My coach had done an amazing job showing to people that he was trustworthy and wouldn't do anything to hurt their kids. So we knew that there would be lots of people who would be upset at us for turning him in; however, we both felt that if we helped just one girl in this process, then it would be worth it. I was scared out of my mind. I had so many ideas forced in my head about never ever going to the police when I was a child that my fears were crippling, but I was feeling enough of a pull from God to follow through with it that I decided to go ahead and press charges. I set up a meeting with a police officer I knew I could trust. I had discussed with my parents some of what happened to me as a child within this period. I kept the details very vague, as they seemed to be very distressed about the news. But the night before I went to the police, I told my parents what I felt God was leading me to do. That I needed to do my part to make sure my coach didn't hurt anyone else. I could tell that my parents were hesitant for fear that I would be ostracized and ridiculed for doing this, but they supported me and my decision, which was great to hear.

I didn't sleep a wink that night, and first thing in the morning, my husband was able to watch my kiddos and I made the thirty-minute drive to meet with my police-officer friend. The whole way there, I was shaking. Terrified, to say the least. I would be sharing the biggest secret of my life and details that made my skin crawl. I didn't understand what the process would be, but I did know that what I was doing was the right thing. And that gave me peace.

I was around fifteen minutes away from the place I was meeting the police officer when I got a call from my mom. She said that she and my dad had talked about it and decided it would really be best if I didn't press charges. That it would be too hard on our family and it would end up just making me look bad. That it was too long ago and nothing would come of it except destroying my name. I told my mom thank you, but that I still felt

God leading me to follow through with it. Even if my name was destroyed, if one girl was saved, it would be worth it.

I drove for a bit longer and received another phone call from my mom saying that she didn't want it to get to this point, but she really did not want me going through with this. I told her I would think about it and pray about it very hard before I make a decision. She said that sometimes we get things stuck in our head thinking it's God telling us to do something, when in actuality they're just our own thoughts, not God's. And that she knew my dad was against it too, and if anyone was in touch with God, it's Dad. So if Dad thinks it is a bad idea, then it is a bad idea.

My mind was racing at this point. She went on to also explain to me that the police officer I was about to talk to was not somebody I could trust. That she knew things about him and that he was not a man that I could trust with this information.

I was trying hard to make my own decision, but I couldn't push my mom's comments out of my mind. I didn't know what to do anymore. I had made the appointment with the police officer and I didn't want to just not show up, so I continued driving toward the place I was going to meet him. I knew my mom was just telling me that the police officer wasn't someone I could trust because she was trying to deter me from talking to him. He was a great guy, and I knew I could fully trust him and know that he was only trying to help me and help anyone at risk of getting hurt.

The whole way, I was praying. My prayers mainly consisted of tears, but I wanted so desperately to do the right thing. I didn't want anyone to be hurt. But my parents were telling me it was a bad decision. That it was pointless because nothing would be done anyway.

I put my phone on silent once I pulled into the parking lot, stuck my phone in my pocket, and headed on into the building. My counselor was waiting for me, and she was able to calm my fears the minutes before the police officer got there. I was shaking and nervous and scared. I wanted to be strong, but in actuality, I felt like a nine-year-old little girl who was telling on her basketball coach. The coach she had loved all these years, and still did love, as passionately as a nine-year-old could. It wasn't a love like what I had for my husband, but a different kind of love, and now I was about to destroy that. So much of me was screaming *"No!"* So much of me wanted to still be that nine-year-old girl who wished someone would listen to her and hold her and let her cry. But at this point, I was twenty-eight years old, and I was the one who needed to save another little girl.

The police officer arrived, and I sat down with him and my counselor. I had a ball in my hands, as it was still the one thing that would help me stay less anxious. We talked for a long time, and I was able to express my fears and concerns, and he was able to explain what the process might look like. Obviously there were no guarantees, but he was very proud of me for taking this step. And honestly, I was very proud of myself. I felt like something good was going to be able to come from this pain.

We were about to actually start the process when I glanced down at my phone to see several missed calls from my dad and a text that said I needed to call him ASAP. I asked the police officer to give me a second, and I gave my dad a call. I knew that dad would be understanding. That he would encourage me to do what I felt I needed to do. At least, that was what he had told me the day before. However, when I got on the phone with him, he seemed more agitated than I expected. My dad is a very laid-back, levelheaded person, so for him to seem anxious and a bit agitated, it definitely alarmed me. He said that he had been to the police station looking for me. I told him that we didn't meet at the police station.

"Your mom called me, Rachel, and she really doesn't want you to do this."

"I know, Dad, she called me too, but what if I keep children from being hurt by doing this? Wouldn't that make it all worth it?"

"Honestly, kiddo, I wish that that is how the system worked, but you will end up being the one put on trial. People will question you and your whole world will change. Your mom and I don't want that for you."

My eyes instantly welled up with tears. Why did I feel so certain on the inside that God was telling me to do this? When I had first felt my world crumble from the memories, it seemed like God was so far away from me, but I didn't feel that distance from Him anymore. I knew this was right. I just knew it. That was until the call from my dad. What if he's right about the system? What if it's hopeless and this wasn't the right thing to do? I felt so defeated and worthless. I felt crushed that my voice wouldn't matter and the pain from my childhood would not be something I could use to fight this evil crime against children and to help other little girls who are being hurt.

When I got off the phone, through my tears, I told the officer that my parents didn't want me doing this. I explained some of my parents' fears. But all I could do other than that was cry. My emptiness came back, and I no longer had a purpose. I told the police officer that I couldn't go through with it. He understood, and he told me that if I change my mind, I should let him know.

A few weeks went by, and I tried the best I could to make sense of my life and my past, but I was still in a cloud of darkness. Nothing seemed to lift the cloud for me. I was still very much present with my kids, but I quickly began falling into a depression and constantly felt an overwhelming heaviness in my spirit. I fought and fought to get the feeling to go away, but the only thing I could find that would sometimes help was to binge and purge. But even that wasn't very effective. At least then I had a physical, tangible thing I could be doing that seemed to help with the pain in my gut.

It was the end of May at this point, and the kids had been dying to be outside to play. Our apartment had a small yard to the side of it, so we spent a lot of time out there playing. If I couldn't help other kids, then I at least wanted to be a good mom to my kids. So I tried my hardest to escape the dark thoughts and the black cloud that loomed over me and tried to be an interactive, loving mother. We were about to go in for lunch when I saw a man walking toward our yard. My kids naively kept playing and having fun, without a care in the world. My world froze as I saw that the man walking toward me was my coach. I couldn't move. He kept walking, and then with a smile on his face, he picked up my eleven-month-old daughter and walked into our apartment as I stood there completely frozen. I was finally able to move and I rushed into the apartment after him, and my son quickly followed.

CHAPTER 13

I walked into the apartment, searching desperately for my daughter. My thoughts had frozen in fear until I found out where she was. My eyes took a second to adjust from the sunshine outside to the darkness inside of the apartment. My coach had carried my daughter into the living room. Instantly, I slowed down as I got closer to them. I don't know why, but I felt like any sudden movements could be harmful to the situation. I still didn't know why my coach had come to my apartment and why he just picked up my daughter and walked into my place as if he lived there. All I could think of was how to get my daughter back into my arms. It felt like an eternity, but it was only probably a few seconds before he put her down on the carpet and she crawled to her toys without a care in the world.

I was finally able to breathe, but only for a second, as I saw his eyes looking straight at me. I knew at that moment that he must've known. That had to be why he came. He must have known that I called the Department of Children and Family Services about him. And he must be mad. He had just been smiling at the kids, but now he was looking at me, and his face spoke volumes to me.

"It's good to see you." He said this with a tone of voice that was flat and emotionless.

"You too," I said. Not knowing how else to handle this situation. I could feel my mind going back to that nine-year-old girl who would do anything to please her coach, who would appease him in any way just so he wouldn't be mad at her.

"I know people, Rachel," he said. "If you talk any more at all, then you and your family will be hurt." He stepped closer and closer to me as he talked, until I was against the wall in my living room and he was pressing against me.

He continued, "I know men who will hurt you so bad that you'll wish you had never talked." I nodded to show I understood and to show that I wouldn't talk. He put his face really close to mine, and at the same time, he quickly grabbed me between my legs. Fear shot through my body with the feeling of his hand forcefully grabbing me. Memories flooded my mind from my childhood, and at that moment, I was reliving in my mind all the pain of my past. My mind had left, and my body remained. When I came back to the present, I could tell he noticed. He still had power over me. Nothing had changed. He smiled real big at me.

"You look beautiful, by the way," he said, and then he slowly rubbed his hand up the rest of my body, and then, as quickly as he came, he left out the back door.

I crumbled to the floor, with a deer-in-the-headlights look on my face. I was confused about what just happened. Did he really just come into my house? One thing I knew for sure, I was not going to be talking about him to the police anymore. I would protect my family first and foremost, and I believed him completely when he said he would send mean men to hurt us. I remembered so many mean men that had been at that white house. I knew he was being for real, and I would not take that chance. Not for anything.

I gathered myself together as best I could and decided that it would be best to stay inside the apartment for the rest of the day. I also chose to not tell my husband what had happened. It had become a theme in my life to try and tell people I love that something bad had happened, and then it always ended up being more of a mess than before. And more hurtful than before. It wasn't fair to my husband to group him into that category, but I had so many situations in my past that led me to believe this would be true of everyone.

Another week went by, and somehow I was beginning to feel a little bit more at ease about things. I no longer questioned what the right thing to do was. My parents were certain that pressing charges would be the wrong thing to do, and then having my coach show up and explain what would happen if I talked any more, my questions were answered. The best thing to do would be to stay quiet and protect everyone.

My bingeing and purging issues were still very much a problem; anxiety and a dark cloud hovering over me were still very much a thing, too. Despite knowing what I would and wouldn't do, there hadn't been any healing from the past.

Sunday morning of the following week, we went to church and then ate out with my parents. My kids loved going to this hole-in-the-wall restaurant where they could have all the cottage cheese and tomatoes and grapes that they wanted. It was the beginning of June, and we were talking about how both my son and daughter had birthdays coming up. I couldn't wait to celebrate with my kiddos. I had been planning a big third birthday for my son and an intimate family celebration for my daughter's first birthday.

That afternoon, I was trying all I could to keep my mind positive and out of the darkness that seemed to always be right there. I had begun working out, hoping that exercise would help me get out of the funk I was in. That afternoon, I took my bike and decided to go for a long ride around town and down to a beautiful river just on the outskirts of town.

My ride there was wonderful. Peaceful. It was exactly what I needed. Until I saw a large black pickup truck driving up behind me. I pulled to the side of the country road and stopped. Leaning on one leg with the bike propped up, I waited for the truck to go by so I could get back to riding. But the truck seemed to go slower and slower until it pulled up right next to me. I couldn't tell at first who it was, but by instinct, I was shaking already. Then I saw, and once again my whole body froze. My coach got out of the passenger side of the truck, and the person driving was his brother. The mean large man from when I was a kid. I wanted to cry. I wanted to run. But all I could do was freeze.

How did they know that I was here? Have they been watching me? I didn't understand why he was back if I had followed his instructions and not talked about him to anyone. I had followed his rule, so it didn't make sense to me that he was back.

My coach got out of the truck and smiled at me. But it wasn't a smile that seemed like it had a purpose or an agenda. It seemed genuine.

"Hey, girl."

In a crazy attempt to make this moment seem halfway normal, I tried to smile back at him and said, "Hey."

"I haven't been able to stop thinking about you," he said.

For a moment, I was back at that nine-year-old state of excitement, knowing that I was once again found desirable in my coach's eyes. This seemed to be the piece that I was always missing in my life. And yet, my adult mind knew that this moment together with him wasn't right. Just like every other moment with him hadn't been right. I had no response to his comment, but I'm certain he could see the wheels turning in my mind.

"Ever since I saw you last week, I couldn't get you off my mind. Do you ever think about me?"

In all actuality, the honest answer was yes. But it felt wrong to say that to him. I just hung my head in hopes he couldn't read my mind. He reached down and held my hand in his like he used to when I was young. He pointed to his two favorite freckles on my right hand. And then he stepped closer to me.

"Hey, how are things with you and your husband?"

I was a bit shocked by this question. But I knew the right answer, and I also knew that this moment with my coach was most definitely wrong.

"Things are good with us. I love him dearly." This was the first time I ever said anything to my coach that contradicted his feelings, and it felt very scary. I wasn't certain of what his response would be.

He talked more, and I listened and occasionally nodded or shook my head, but the exact memory of what was said after that isn't clear. I held strong in standing up for my marriage, but it felt weird doing that to my coach and not understanding what his reason for asking me was. When I continued to nod in response to loving my husband, I could see the smile he originally had turn to anger. The next several minutes, on the side of the road, I was hit over and over again. I'm not certain who was hitting me and what they were hitting me with. I closed my eyes and hoped after each hit that it would be the last. Finally, it was over, and they were in their truck, driving away after telling me to keep my mouth shut. When I finally was able to gather myself, I got back on my bike and rode straight back to my house. I was out of breath and desperate to be home. Tears were stinging my eyes. I wasn't sure it if was from the emotional drama that came from telling my coach that I didn't love him, or if the tears were from the pain in my back and side and arm. It had been so long since I had been hurt in that way. My mind was struggling with staying in the moment. So many flashes began coming back from my childhood of being hit and kicked and thrown. Of being held down and my having my hair pulled. I never had marks back then that would be seen by others. They were always hidden under my clothes, and if there were any marks from this encounter, then they would be hidden too. I just had to make sure my husband didn't see.

I felt a huge amount of anxiety in feeling like I needed to keep all of this a secret. That I was protecting my family by keeping it a secret. That I was doing the right thing by dealing with it on my own.

The next day my stomach, side, and back were all black with deep bruises. It hurt to move and to even sleep, let alone to try to care for two little kids. I had pulled inward anyway, from all the darkness that overwhelmed me, but to hide my bruises, I isolated myself even more. My feelings of fear were overtaking me. My questions about my coach's reason for that Sunday afternoon rang in my head constantly. Was he going to leave me alone now? Would he come back again? If so, what would I do? Maybe he would leave me alone now that he knew I wouldn't talk and that I didn't want to be with him and I wanted to be with my husband.

Urges of wanting to run started to overtake my mind and body. I didn't know why or what the feeling was from, but I would have thoughts of needing to pack up and leave. It was my defense mechanism. It was another thing that left me very scared.

A week or more later, it was a Thursday morning, and I was driving to a nearby town to work out at the YMCA where my husband worked. I was meeting a close friend there to work out. We had been doing this for a month or so, and I absolutely loved the time with her. We would laugh more than work out, but it was exactly what I needed.

Our workout lasted about an hour and half, and I then hopped in the car and headed back home. My dad had come over to the apartment to watch my kiddos for me while I worked out. It was a normal drive, and I remember distinctly how blue the sky was that day. Summer was beginning, and the temperatures were rising, which was something I always looked forward to each year. I wanted the summer to be a good one. I wanted to have wonderful, magical memories with my kids and husband. The beginning of the year had been terrible. Absolutely terrible, with the darkness that had showed up out of nowhere. But I was determined at that moment to make the change. To stuff my feelings of pain and darkness back down so that I could enjoy my life with my family. Living in the past was painful. It wasn't helping me at all.

I had made it almost halfway home when I drove through a small town. I had almost made it out of there when I saw my coach's white truck parked at a bank parking lot. It was facing the main road. I passed by it and quickly looked in the rearview mirror and saw that the truck was now following behind me. The speed limit was still 35 mph, and I struggled to stay that speed. Fear set in, as well as a feeling of failure and compliance to the situation. My mind automatically went to the spot of knowing that I would need to deal with whatever this encounter was going to entail. The thought of ignoring him was not even an option in my mind.

What concerned me even more was looking through the rearview mirror and seeing that there were two heads in the truck that was following so close behind me. Once I was out of the small town, the speed limit jumped up to 55 mph, and so I began to speed up. But as I did, the truck started to pass me. As I drove, they acted like they were going to run me off the road. The truck was going from beside me to behind me and speeding up and slowing down. Then they came up right beside me and rolled down the passenger window. My coach was sitting in the passenger side, and his brother was driving, just like the last time, except they were in my coach's truck this time.

"Pull over," I could hear my coach say, and he pointed to the side of the road. Then they slowed down and got back behind me. Without so much as even slightly second-guessing his directions, I right away began to slow down and eventually stopped on the side of the road. They pulled in behind me, and within seconds, my coach was at the passenger door, asking me to unlock the doors so he could get in. And I did. Once again, I never even thought of the option of not doing it.

"Start driving and on the next road, turn right," he told me. I did as he said, and I noticed that his brother was following right behind me. We drove down this country road that didn't have a single house in sight. Once we were far enough away from the main road, my coach asked me to pull over to the side and to pop my car hood. I followed his instructions, and then he went on to tell me to get out of the car.

My hands were sweating. I felt like I needed to run and not stop. But I knew that wasn't an option. I just needed to talk to him or whatever it was he wanted, and then I could get home and move on. I was trying to logically make sense of what was happening. I was taken out of my car and walked over to the side of the white truck. The hood of my car and the hood of the truck were up, and doors were open. I assume this was to make it look like we were having car trouble instead of the plan that they actually had in mind. As I was walked over to the white truck, I was met with my coach's brother, who threw me into the side of the truck. I was kicked, and my face was forced down into the side of the truck. I couldn't see anything, and at first I started to fight. I hated my coach's brother. He was so big and so strong. I couldn't move, but I desperately wanted free from his grip. I couldn't breathe with how hard he was pushing himself against me.

"Piece of trash."

"This is what happens when you talk."

"You are gross and disgusting. Nothing but a piece of trash."

My head was hurting from the force holding it against the truck. I didn't understand why I was being punished. I did what my coach said. I had stopped talking. Why was he doing this to me?

I hated my coach's brother, and I assumed it was him who was behind this, but then my coach came close to me.

"This is exactly what you deserve. You're a worthless piece of trash."

And with that comment, I completely stopped fighting. They continued to pull down my sport shorts and underwear and had sex with me while my face stayed shoved into the side of the truck. I needed to breathe, but their bodies being forced so hard against mine made it impossible.

I thought I was going to pass out, but at that point, I no longer cared. When they both finished with me, I fell to the ground. Dirt started flying all around me. I don't know if it was being thrown at me or if it was being kicked up on me. The words of how I was worthless and trash and gross kept coming from their mouths. I lay there scared to even open my eyes, and when I stopped hearing them or feeling dirt landing on me, I slowly opened my eyes to see what was going on. No sooner did I open my eyes did I see my coach standing directly above my head.

He was the person I had always strived to impress and to get affection from. The one I trusted from a young age. I had always believed he really did love me, even though he made several mistakes. But I looked up at him with obvious hurt in my eyes. My body seemed to be in a form of shock as I lay there feeling nothing, except wanting so desperately for my coach to save me. To help me up and say he was sorry. Surely he didn't mean those things about me. But as I zeroed in on his face, I didn't see his smile, but his serious, emotionless face.

"You really are nothing but a piece of trash." And then he spit down at me, and then he walked away. They both got in the truck and drove away as I lay on the ground.

I didn't take the time to cry or think or anything. I pulled up my shorts and began to right away work things to where no one would figure out what just happened. It had become instinct to hide. Especially since the real me truly was nothing but trash.

I had dirt all over me. It was in my hair, and I had spit and dirt on my face. I smelled of sex and just knew that when I got home, my dad would be able to tell. I found baby wipes in the car and did my best to clean myself up to where I could cover up what had happened.

I drove home quickly, thinking constantly of how I needed to cover up what happened. When I got home, the kids were ready for a nap, so it was a perfect distraction for me. I thanked my dad, and he headed out after telling me how the kids did for him. He never noticed a thing. I got the kids down for a nap, and I was hurting so badly and feeling really crummy, so I tried to lie down for a nap too. No matter how hard I tried, I couldn't even shut my eyes. Each time I would close my eyes, I would see my coach standing over me and spitting on me. In what I considered a weak moment, I contacted the counselor I had been seeing, and I told her that someone hurt me. She asked me who and I told her my coach and his brother.

That day felt like it was twenty days wrapped up in one. It just lasted forever. After sharing with my counselor, she begged me to go to the hospital, and I wouldn't do it. If I went to the hospital, then that would mean I would have to tell my husband and probably my parents too. There was no way I was willing to go through that pain on top of what I had already dealt with. I couldn't do it.

She convinced me to at least come and see her. I told her I had my kids, and we contacted a mutual friend who came and picked up my kids and took them with her to her church's vacation bible school. Once I was finally alone with my counselor, I did my best to talk through what happened to me earlier in the day, and at that moment I started shaking uncontrollably. After several hours of talking through things, she explained that I had to tell my husband. That he had to know and that I had to tell the police, and I had to go to the hospital. None of those things I wanted to do. I didn't see the point in any of them. I didn't plan to press charges. I knew that would just get me in trouble. But after lots of discussions, I decided I could tell my husband. He worked until seven that night, and so I called him and had him come and sit with me and the counselor so we could tell him together.

My mind was back to its nine-year-old state. I felt like I was in trouble and was hurting everybody. I felt like a nuisance, and honestly, I felt like a piece of trash. Matt came, and he knew something was up. He had never been called into my counselor's office before, so it was apparent that I had a big issue to share with him.

He came into her office with a deer-in-the-headlights look on his face. He was trying to brace himself for whatever news was coming. He had no idea that it would be as bad as it was. I'll never forget the look on his face when he heard the news. He instantly went into anger and then tears. His eyebrows became so heavy and angered that he looked like a totally different person. He hugged me and assured me he wasn't mad at me, but that I needed to talk to the police and I needed to go to the hospital. I understood that logically all those things made sense, but in my mind, they were all things that I couldn't do. What if my coach found out? I had to protect my family. I had to keep this quiet, and going to the police or the hospital wouldn't be keeping it quiet.

No matter my fears and feelings of not at all wanting to go to the hospital or talking to the police, my husband and my counselor were able to coax me into at least trying the hospital. I complied, and we went to the local hospital. I had to tell the doctors and nurses over and over what I remembered happening. I was angry that I was having to do this. I just wanted to go home and go to bed and act like it never happened. I waited and waited for things to get done. It was three o'clock in the morning, and I was getting very frustrated that no one was listening to me. I finally asked everyone in my hospital room to get out so I could have a moment to myself. I fought off the huge desire to just scream out in frustration. I wasn't as frustrated at what happened to me earlier in the day as I was at the punishment that was coming because of it. I was watching my whole life fall apart before my eyes. I couldn't handle it all, and at that moment I had the huge desire to run. The hospital room I was in was set up where there was another door that led to a bathroom and then out into a hallway. Quietly, I walked through those doors and found myself in a different hallway of the hospital, and there was no one around. I finally felt a sense of control and decided this was my chance to run.

I made my way down hallways and through doors until I found myself outside. As quickly as I could, I started running. I didn't know where I was going. My main goal was to get to my kids and then figure out the rest after that. As I started running toward the road, I was instantly filled with fear. A fear that froze me in my tracks. I had a terrible feeling that I would be found by my coach or his brother. Flashes of memories started filling my mind. What if they took me back to the white house? What if I was sold? I felt helpless, as I didn't have any control inside of the hospital and I didn't have any control outside on my own either. I stood there in shock and fear and uncertainty. At that moment, I wanted more than anything to just not be alive anymore.

About that time, my husband came sprinting outside the hospital, followed by several nurses, and my counselor. I stood frozen as they ran up to me. My husband wrapped me in his arms, but I couldn't feel anything. Nothing but fear. The decision was made to do a rape kit. The doctor who did the rape kit was appalled at how injured I was from the force of what my coach and his brother did to me. I was humiliated. With each moment, I became more and more numb. I was checking out mentally and emotionally.

Before we left, I was given drugs to help me not get any STDs, as well as drugs for infection. They offered me the Plan B pill to make sure that I would not get pregnant from the assault. I looked at my husband, knowing what his feelings on this would be. We politely declined the Plan B pill. That is just another reason why my husband and I are so perfect for each other. We knew without a shadow of a doubt how we felt about such a sensitive issue. If I ended up pregnant from the assault, we would love the baby all the same. It's not the baby's fault for what happened, and we weren't going to end the life of a child that God planned to be born.

My husband and I didn't end up leaving the hospital till six o'clock in the morning. Our kids stayed with a close family friend that night. It had been a hard night on them, which made my heart hurt even more. My husband and I didn't say much. I had talked to a police officer, who took the rape kit with him, at the hospital, but he was giving me time to decide if I wanted to press charges or not. My husband felt very strongly that I either press charges or we would move.

Once again, I felt very little control. Neither option was what I wanted, but the choice to fight it was not even there. I sat in silence for a while, and then eventually told him that I couldn't press charges. He said, "Okay, then we have to move." That next day, we drove up to my husband's parents' house. My husband had already discussed with them what had happened, but they were very kind to not bring it up with me. The next weekend we drove up and stayed a few days with his family, and during that time, my husband was offered a job at a car dealership as a car salesman. Just like that, we were moving an hour and a half north.

I was frustrated. I didn't want to move. I wanted my normal life back. I wanted to stay by my friends and near the counselor who had helped me so much and near my parents and my church.

Nothing in me wanted to move, but nothing in me had a choice. Anytime I would argue, my husband would just say that we didn't have to move. I would get excited, but then he would remind me that if we didn't move, then I had to press charges.

We made arrangements to live with my husband's family until we could find a house to rent. We broke the news to my family that we were moving. And we began to pack. In a matter of two weeks, we were ready to move and my husband was ready to start his new job. We all lived in a state of numbness, but wanting desperately to find normality in our days again. There was one thing, though, that was still weighing heavily on my mind. I was beginning to feel the earliest signs of being pregnant. I'd always been able to tell before I've even had a missed period that I was pregnant, and I was definitely feeling the signs. I waited day after day, and finally, once my period was officially late, I decided to buy a pregnancy test.

My husband and I sat in our living room prior to me taking the test. He assured me that no matter what, whether I was pregnant or not, that he would always be there for me and that the baby would be loved and cherished the same as our other kids. I nervously got up and walked to the bathroom. I peed on the test stick, and immediately the test showed a plus sign. I was pregnant.

I walked out of the bathroom and broke the news to my husband that it was positive. At that moment, I was completely overwhelmed with emotion. For the first time since my coach had reentered my life, I broke down crying. My husband came up to me, and once again he wrapped his arms around me. And this time I melted into his arms. My tears weren't from being upset at being pregnant. I already loved the baby that was being made inside of me. I wasn't disappointed with the news. I was just overwhelmed. I was more nervous about how my husband would handle it or how others would handle the news. I already felt a very strong feeling of protection toward the child inside of me, hoping that he or she wouldn't be affected or treated any differently because of my life struggles. Another thing that was important was that there was still a chance that the baby could be my husband's.

It's incredible how quickly a life can change. Just like that, we were growing into a family of five and were moving upstate, starting a new job and still in need of a house to live in. What made it even more difficult was that I once again felt light-years away from God. And that to me was the worst feeling in the world.

> "For I know the plans I have for you," declares
> the Lord, "plans to prosper you and not to
> harm you, to give you hope and a future."
> Jeremiah 29:11

CHAPTER 14

We made the move up north, and I struggled a lot with guilt and shame from what happened with my coach. I knew it had been my fault. I knew something was wrong with me to have put myself in that situation. To allow something like that to happen. So far everyone was being great about the fact that I was pregnant, but I still worried a lot about how the delivery room would be on the day the baby was born. I felt a strong protectiveness toward the little peanut that God was molding and making within me. I knew that the first thing people were going to look at was whether or not the baby looked like my husband or not. My heart would sink every time I would think about it. As I started to plan where I was going to deliver the baby. I thought very seriously about doing it at my home. I knew many who had done that before, but my main reason was because I didn't want anybody near me. I wanted to shut the world out completely. For quite a while, I chose to not see a doctor. I had come to the brilliant decision that I would just carry the baby in my womb for the rest of my life because the unknown of how the baby would be treated was too much to bear. I carried too much guilt, thinking how my mistakes would hurt my child so greatly.

At the beginning of my pregnancy, I battled a lot with nausea. This made it much easier for me to hide that I was purposefully throwing up food. The food felt disgusting in my stomach, and so getting it out was much easier. I also began hiding the fact that I had received some text messages from my coach.

I couldn't understand the thoughts going through my mind. I couldn't figure out why I still desired for my coach to be happy with me. Or why I felt like I just had to do what he said and then everything would be okay. The thought of disobeying him never even crossed my mind.

He messaged a few days after we moved up north. We were still staying with my husband's family, and when I got the message I right away contacted my old counselor. I knew what she would say. I knew she wouldn't want me to respond. But no matter how hard I tried, the small nine-year-old inside of me still wanted to believe the good in him. So when he told me that he was sorry and that he did it all because his brother wanted him to, I believed him. He also told me he needed help from me. He needed me to send him some pictures of myself. And he finished by saying, "You know how I like them."

I was sick over the thought of sending him pictures of myself. I didn't want to, but I also still felt like I needed to do what he asked. I hadn't heard back from my counselor yet, so I went ahead and did what my coach had asked. My counselor was very upset with me. I can see how frustrating it must've been for her to work so hard to help me, find healing for me, and fight for me, only to have me turn around and follow my coach's orders. She had enough at that point and completely stopped talking to me. She stopped answering any phone calls and blocked me on her phone. I felt so alone in the darkness. I didn't know how to live. I wanted a normal life, and yet I still worked really hard to protect everyone around me, including my coach. I hated myself because I felt like I always made wrong decisions, but I also felt like any decision I made would be wrong in some way or another. That someone would get hurt, no matter what choice I made. I always tried to make my decisions based on how to keep everyone else safe, even if it meant I wasn't. It felt better for me to be hurt than to see someone I love be hurt. And maybe, in some weird way, it felt right to be hurt. It was the normal I knew, and without it, I was lost.

Something I learned to do as a child was to separate my two worlds. I wasn't schizophrenic, I simply disassociated. I learned how to shut off the bad world from the good world. It was a blessing from God to have the ability to do that. It gave me the chance to still succeed in life in so many ways. A full-ride college scholarship for basketball, a bachelor's degree, and even an amazing husband and kids. Because I was so good at separating the two worlds, I was able to keep so much a secret. This served me well in survival mode as a child, as my brain was still underdeveloped and couldn't handle the trauma I was faced with. But as an adult, disassociating was no longer serving me in a positive way. At the time, I didn't know I was disassociating or what disassociating was, let alone how to stop it.

For over a month, we lived with my husband's family. We went on with life as normal. I was struggling so much with guilt for what had happened, with shame, and with hatred toward myself. I felt every bit of the blame for the circumstances we were in. I felt like I deserved the bad memories, the flashbacks, and the nightmares. That they were my punishment. When the memories would come, I would grant them the power of destroying me again at that moment instead of stopping them. I would allow the darkness to grow. It felt right to have the pain be so constant. It felt justified for how terrible of a person I was. Because of all the hurt I caused my family. I believed I deserved nothing but pain. When people would try to help me, I would feel like I was accepting their help, but in actuality I only pushed them away. And then it would seem fitting to have another person walk away and leave my life. It was what I deserved after all. I even tried to push away my husband.

"Rachel, please just tell me what happened. Give me the details. I want to know. I want to be here for you." My husband had sat me down and said these words with tears pooling in his eyes. The only thing I could feel at that moment was anger. Intense anger. What I didn't realize at that time was the anger came because I instantly was reliving my past when I had tried to tell people the details. I had tried to explain and had trusted people, only to be told it was all in my head. This moment was triggering all those memories and all those feelings, and I became completely overwhelmed and shut him off. I knew he wouldn't understand. A loud voice inside my head was screaming, "No!" And it was telling me to run. That this conversation wasn't safe. That nobody can help me and I was too far gone. That I didn't deserve help or happiness.

In tears of my own, I lashed out at my husband, declaring firmly that I did not want to tell him about it. That I did not want to talk about it. *Ever!*

He was obviously frustrated and hurt, but he respected my feelings, and we were able to pretend that everything was okay between us. We played our roles as mom and dad and husband and wife, but the walls were up between us.

My husband's new job selling cars was tiring and stressful for him, but he amazed all of us with how good he was at being a salesman. He was working very hard, always striving to be better. Most evenings I would find him reading either on how to be a better salesman or his Bible. His car sales were better than anybody else's, and it was just his first month. Because of his hard work, we were able to rent a house that would fit our growing family. It was a two-story home, plus a basement, built in 1901. It had beautiful woodwork and tons of character. Watching my husband's determination, I became envious of his drive. I remembered the drive I used to have, but at that moment, I just sat wallowing in my own pity party. I hardly ever left the house. I was dealing with morning sickness from the pregnancy. I was still overwhelmed with guilt and shame, and even though at times our life felt fairly normal, there was still always the elephant in the room of the issues I wasn't willing to talk about.

I would hold my Bible in my hands and would want so badly to open it up and feel the precious words of my God down deep in my soul. I longed for His comfort and His peace. But no matter how hard I tried, I couldn't open my Bible. I couldn't read His words. I couldn't pray to Him. I couldn't feel His comfort or peace or presence at all. Hopelessness was settling in.

Not long after we moved up north, I got word that my mom's bladder cancer had returned, and this time the only treatment possible was to remove her bladder completely. I begged my husband to let us move back home. I wanted to be there for my mom. To help her during this time, but my husband firmly said no. It was one of the only yelling fights we've ever had as I begged him to let me go home, but he was firm with his answer. The guilt inside of me had grown even more, knowing that my mistakes had hurt my family so much. That it forced us to move, took my kids away from the people they were friends with, and kept me from being there for my mom during her fight with cancer. My rap sheet was getting worse and worse in my mind.

On October 20, my mom went in for surgery to have her bladder removed. It was a very difficult surgery and an even more difficult recovery. We waited for hours to hear how she was doing and whether or not there was any cancer left while they were in there. We had a hospital room filled with family and a handful of preachers from all around the area who were there for my mom and dad. The day was long and stressful and scary.

Finally, we got word over the intercom for our family to go to a side room to meet with the doctor.

We were led to a room not far from the surgery waiting area. It had a large conference table in the center, with many chairs, but none of us could calm our nerves enough to sit. We stood waiting for the doctor to enter. Everyone was holding their breath, waiting for the news on how my mom was doing. Finally, the doctor walked in, and with a straight face and zero expression, he informed us that my mom had made it through the surgery and was in recovery. And that they didn't find any additional cancer while they were in there. We all breathed for the first time that day, and with tears of joy, we celebrated. Mom was going to be okay.

I quickly grabbed my phone to share the good news, and without even thinking, the first person I started to text was my mom. I caught myself halfway through the text and couldn't help but sit down and cry. She's always the first person I would share good news with, and it hit me just how hard it would be to not have her in my life. I was so thankful that she made it through the surgery. The prayers now were shifting to her recovery because it was going to be difficult and long.

Mom spent a week in the hospital and battled a lot of pain and overcame several obstacles. We were so proud of how well she was doing. She was going to need to learn a new way of life, but she was handling it so well. Only four short weeks later, she was doing great and had become fairly accustomed to her new life, when she tripped and fell while she was playing with my kids. She landed on her left wrist and knew immediately it was broken. What we quickly realized was that it wasn't just broken, it was shattered. To be hit with two major health struggles so close together, my mom was devastated. So were we. At this point, I was thirty-six weeks pregnant and getting closer and closer to having our third baby. My mom had been such a big part of my other births, that not having her there for my third baby's birth made me very sad.

Within the next few weeks, my mom had major wrist surgery and started physical therapy. Her pain in her wrist was almost unbearable, and the painkillers were making her feel worse. Depression had started setting in as well. Not only was she dealing with a new way of life with her bladder being removed, she was also dealing with constant excruciating pain from her recovering wrist. I tried to be there for her as much as I could.

I was driving back home to see my parents again and to have my thirty-eight-week doctor's appointment. I had hoped that the doctor would give me good news that I was soon to have the baby. I had planned on having an all-natural, drug-free birth. I was at my parents' house, and I was working through contractions not long after my doctor's appointment. They were coming often, but they weren't extremely intense yet. We were about forty minutes from the hospital and a snowstorm was just starting to hit, so we decided to go ahead and drive to the hospital. My mom was still in a lot of pain and was taking pain pills to help, but she decided she was going to come with us to the hospital.

When I arrived at the hospital I was four centimeters, and they said that if I progressed within the next hour, I would be admitted. After making a lot of laps around the labor and delivery floor, I was checked again and had progressed to five centimeters. The entire evening I worked through contractions that were always three minutes apart, and amazingly enough, they were never too hard to handle. With my other deliveries, the pain would get so intense so quickly and for so long that I always caved for an epidural at about six or seven centimeters. This time I was able to keep myself in control, and I made it through each contraction simply by praying and breathing.

By nine thirty the next morning, we were blessed with a sweet baby boy who was exactly seven pounds, seven ounces. He was perfect. A beautiful blessing from God. He definitely had a different look to him. He had different color hair than my other two kids. He had fairer skin. My other two kids had black hair when they were born and darker skin, but this baby had strawberry blonde hair and fair skin. Which is exactly how my husband looked in his baby pictures. We were in love with the newest member of our family, and our other two kids were extremely excited to have a baby brother to play with. I felt very blessed and at peace.

Part of the peace could've also been the fact that at the end of my pregnancy, my coach had stopped contacting me. He had continued to play mind games with me and wanted pictures and other things, and I was so relieved and thankful that once my pregnancy had progressed, he had left me alone. So I sat there in the hospital room with a healthy baby, and I truly felt like I was getting my life back.

By surprise, over the course of the next few weeks, we were presented with an amazing opportunity for my husband to take a different job closer to where we used to live. Because I hadn't heard from my coach in several months and life was finally feeling peaceful, we felt safe and comfortable going back. We were certain this was the right choice for our family. When we heard that my husband had for sure gotten the job, we were celebrating. It felt like God was taking away my punishment. That He was allowing me a chance to go back home. I had some red flags in my mind about the thought of being closer to my coach, but I didn't want that fear to keep my family from doing something that would be good for us. I wanted so badly for this to be the start of something good for us.

When our youngest was just two weeks old, we moved back to what felt like home. I was excited and hopeful that things could start becoming normal again. My bingeing and purging had gotten better toward the end of the pregnancy and had virtually stopped at this point. I was going through the struggles of memories and regrets and not feeling God, as well as hormonal changes from having a baby, not to mention being a stay-at-home mom to three kids who were three years old and younger. I had become very good at finding ways to separate myself emotionally. My mind was often filled with darkness and worry, but on the outside, I worked very hard to stay focused on my children and their needs.

During this time, my husband had started preaching at a small church near us. I was struggling more and more with God and where He was, but my husband had turned his pain into something that could be used by God. His passion for people was obvious, and he devoured the Bible and would listen to several sermons a day. He couldn't get enough of God and His grace and goodness. I desperately desired for that relationship with God. I envied my husband for his closeness with God, and I would try as hard as I could to cry out to God, but I still couldn't. I couldn't get past all the mistakes in my life.

We had been living in our new house for a few months when I started trying a new diet to help me get off my baby weight. I was bigger than I had ever been, and I felt disgusting both inside and out. For a week I didn't eat much food at all. It worked well, but I couldn't keep my energy up to take care of my kids on such little food. Then I started eating again and went back to purging what I ate. Before I knew it, I was throwing up everything I ate but trying to keep enough food in my system to keep me functioning for my kids. This felt like something that I could control in my life when I felt so much chaos everywhere else. I was very careful and obsessive about it, especially knowing the importance of having enough in my body so I could continue to nurse my baby boy. Purging seemed to help me with my anxiety and the pain in my gut, as well as help me lose weight and feel better about myself. I was amazed at how quickly the weight started coming off.

In June, we started planning for our two older kids' birthdays. In the middle of June, I drove to the town where my coach lived to pick up a birthday cake that was made by someone in there. I still thought of my coach often, and I decided that while I was there I was going to drive by his house. I don't know what I was hoping for. It was summer break, and I knew there would be a chance that he would be home. Part of me wanted to see him and hope that I would see him miserable and sad. Another part of my wanted to throw eggs at his house. And another part of me wanted him to tell me that he was sorry for all that he had done.

I first drove down the road that went behind his house and then turned on the road that went in front of it. I didn't see him, so I decided to drive around one more time. The second time, he came outside and looked at me. I drove down to the end of the road and contemplated what to do. I wanted so desperately to somehow make things right with him. My life was in shambles, and I couldn't seem to function with how things were. Next thing I knew, he was getting in his white truck and coming in my direction. I decided to pull into the parking lot at the high school that was just down the road from where he lived. No one else was parked there. I decided I wasn't going to get out of my car and I would stay right there where we were easily seen by people. I kept my doors locked but rolled down my window as he pulled up. He got out of his truck and walked up to my driver's-side window.

The conversation lasted only a few minutes, but in it, he did apologize. He cried and felt terrible for everything that had happened. He explained that hurting people was not the man that he wanted to be. He asked me to forgive him, and I told him that I did. I knew that there was good in him. I knew that this was not what he wanted to be doing. It wasn't the real coach I knew. He really did love me.

"You look great, by the way," he said. I blushed and said thank you. It was a lot different from the trash he had called me the last time I saw him. I then went on and drove back home. I felt like things were finally more settled between me and him.

Over the next few weeks, I continued my bad eating habits and was dropping pounds quickly. I was getting a lot of positive comments from people. People were amazed at how fast I was dropping my baby weight.

It was exciting for me to accomplish something positive, even if I was sort of cheating the process.

It was only a few weeks after I had seen my coach when a knock came on my back door. I opened the door and was shocked to see my coach standing there. He was in tears. I let him in, and right away I could tell that he was really hurting. He had large crocodile tears in his eyes and was struggling to even stand up. He apologized for coming over unannounced. I told him it was fine and I asked him what was wrong.

"Rachel, I'm in trouble. Big trouble," he said. I'm pretty sure my eyes looked like saucers. He went on to explain that he needed my help. He needed help getting him out of a bad situation with some bad men. He wanted out of this gang of guys who were hurting people, but he needed a certain amount of money to get out. Way more money than he had, and he didn't know how to get so much money.

Looking back at this time and remembering my thought process, my heart breaks. I had not received the help I needed to be able to think like the adult I was. My coach knew good and well what he was doing and how to get me to respond the way he needed me to. A typical adult would know that this man needed help from someone other than me. That doing what he said wasn't the right answer. I wish I could explain why I thought I was doing a brave and heroic thing by helping him. I'm sure a part of me was glad that my coach needed me again. That I was worth something again to him. This seemed to be what I thought I needed to be an actual person of value.

A few nights later, when my household was completely asleep, I left our house in the middle of the night and walked to a business close by. In the parking lot was a car with a man in it, waiting to pick me up. Fear was rising in my heart. My heart was screaming, "No!" But my mind was telling my heart that this was the only way. There was no choice. This was where I belonged.

I was driven to a nearby hotel that was positioned near a truck stop. For the next two hours, I serviced three men, just as I used to do as a little girl. I felt so much disgust and pain and shame. I wasn't shown any gratitude or respect. Nobody was nice. They didn't even pretend to try and make me feel comfortable. At the beginning of the night, I was convinced that this was what I deserved. But by the end of my stay there, I could confidently say that no human deserved to be treated this way, not even me. This was not what I wanted for my life; even if I deserved pain and shame, this was still too much.

After about two hours, I was driven back to the business near my house, and I walked back home. My house was still sound asleep. I went into the bathroom to wash away all the filth that had become a part of me. No matter how much I scrubbed, the filth remained. Crawling into bed next to my husband, I wanted so badly to tell him. I wanted him to go beat up every man who had hurt me, but my mind knew I couldn't tell him. I couldn't tell anyone.

I hoped that maybe the fact that I was paying my dues, receiving so much punishment, that maybe God would allow me to someday soon find freedom. Complete freedom. Not only from the life of sin, but also from the thoughts of sin and the feelings of sin.

Two or three nights a week I was picked up in that parking lot. I was introduced to a world that I didn't know existed. I knew about the world I had been in as a child and the men I had encountered at the white house. Somehow I had believed that the white house was the only place that this stuff happened. That couldn't be further from the truth. I entered a world, unknowingly, that was a sex trade. No matter how much I wanted out of this world, it wasn't an option.

About a month later, a man showed up at my door during the middle of the day. I answered the door, unsure of who this man was. He didn't come into the house but simply stood on my back porch and explained that on Sunday afternoon I had a new place I needed to go. He explained what town and what road to turn down and that they would be watching for me to lead me the rest of the way to this hidden location.

To say I was numb and in a fog is an understatement. Physically, my body was skin and bones and weak. Emotionally, I was empty and in survival mode. Spiritually, I was lost. I was in robot mode. I tried as hard as I could to keep myself appearing good to others. Those around me knew I was struggling some. That I was losing weight. That I constantly seemed tired and out of it. That I had a sad look in my eyes. But nobody knew the horror that was taking place behind the scenes. I would hear concerns about my weight and that I needed to start eating more. Losing weight was the least of my worries.

Sunday afternoon came, and I asked my husband if it would be okay for me to go and spend some time alone, just me and God. He knew how much I was struggling and that I was searching desperately for help, for God. This seemed like a normal request to him, and he was okay with it.

I pulled out of the driveway and followed the instructions I was given. When I reached the street where I was told to pull down, a car was waiting for me, and someone motioned for me to follow them. So I did. It wasn't that far into the country that I saw a camper parked on a piece of land. Nothing about the camper looked unusual or suspicious. It just like a typical camper. We pulled around to behind the camper and parked. I wasn't certain at this point if anyone was even there.

The man got out of his car, and he seemed no different than someone who was getting out to go into the grocery store.

"Hey, how are you doing?" he said with a smile on his face. He didn't look mean or scary. I was really surprised by how nice he was being. But I still didn't trust him.

"I'm good," I replied. "How are you?"

It wasn't really a question that I expected a response to, which was good because he didn't give me a response. He opened the door to the camper and motioned for me to go in.

Because of his nice demeanor, my defenses weren't high. I hadn't disassociated. Walking into the camper, I noticed a lot of equipment that made it look like a photography studio. It seemed bigger inside than I had expected. And there were at least five guys and a girl already inside. They were nice and joking around and being friendly to everyone. I stood back and watched. They weren't hurting the woman. She seemed to actually be friends with all of the men there and was laughing and talking with them. I was beyond confused, and slightly hopeful that this situation was going to be better than I had thought. I had gotten used to truckers who stunk and were mean and rough. These people seemed like people I would sit next to in church or at a restaurant. The camper was very clean and smelled nice. Everything up until this point was comfortable and good.

Eventually, they stopped their conversation and acknowledged I was there. Still it wasn't mean. I wasn't understanding what was going on. They asked if I wanted to sit down, and I shook my head no. They offered me a drink and some other things, but I kept saying no, and then without seeing it coming, someone from behind grabbed me and quickly put some sort of bag over my head.

> When you go through deep waters, I will be with you.
> —Isaiah 43:2

CHAPTER 15

My head covered
My brain screaming
Everything was dark
I wished to be dreaming

Was it two men
Or was it three?
How many were holding me down?
How many were on top of me?

My head still covered and barely breathing
Someone grabbed me from behind
Hands around my neck, he said
"You are going to be mine."

Everything was black
But I closed my eyes anyway
I knew how to escape this place
To take my mind where I wasn't afraid

Sunny skies, kids laughing
Through these thoughts I could escape
Singing songs with smiles and joy
With these thoughts I was safe

Yet something hurt so deeply
Like holes being blown into my anatomy
I tried to think of swimming pools and hayrides
Of my house, my friends, my family

How long until it's over?
How long till my punishment is complete?
How long until my body is given back to me?
How long till I can be free?

I left the camper that day with marks around my neck from the bag and bruises on my arms and legs from being held down. I knew better than to let my guard down. I should've known that even though the people were acting nice, that they wouldn't be that way to me. No. I was just property to them. They saw me as nothing. Except maybe money.

I drove home in pain, and I was still going back and forth from my pretend life of joy and happiness in my mind to the brutal reality of what just happened. My anxious heart seemed more concerned with how to keep it a secret than the fact that I just went through another living hell. As my car got closer to home, I almost gave way to tears. What kind of mother am I that comes home covered in the smell and germs of so many men?

I was embarrassed to walk in the door, believing that the last few hours were written all over my face and my body. It was a Sunday afternoon, so my kids were napping, and if I were lucky, my husband would be napping too. I had originally told my husband that I was going out to get some time alone with God. And as I sat in my car, I closed my eyes wishing so badly that somehow God could fill me with His Spirit and peace. That somehow I would feel better despite what just happened.

I took some deep breaths, checked myself in the mirror, and then decided to walk on into the house. In my mind, I looked like I had been crying. Like I had been through a war, and even though my husband wasn't napping, he was completely enthralled with a sports game on TV, that he didn't notice anything unusual about me. He asked how my quiet time was and where I went. I made up a place and told him it was nice. That it was exactly what I needed.

This double life went on for a long time. I wanted badly to find freedom, but the cost of freedom seemed to be too much. It either meant taking the chance that these evil men would hurt my family, or trying to stand up for myself by telling people the truth about what has been going on. Both ways seemed to leave me hurting others, and with how things were now, I was the only one getting hurt. At least that's how I saw it. It seemed safer this way. It seemed almost right. It's terrible that Satan can convince you to stay in darkness by scaring you into believing that the pain of getting out of the darkness would be more than you can handle. I was believing Satan's lies. I was used to living two lives as a kid, and it had become the norm for me. Living this way now was hard and scary, but in a sense, it was playing out how I believed I deserved it.

Sunday afternoons became a common thing. Almost weekly, I would go to the same location. On weekend nights I would often hear outside the rev of the engines of men's trucks. It was the call for me to go outside and meet whoever it was. With my house asleep I could easily sneak out.

I've heard people question this simply because they can't imagine that my husband would have slept through all of it. They can't comprehend that he didn't notice I was gone or that he didn't hear the revving of engines. And that's their choice if they don't want to believe it, but it's the truth. My husband knows he's a very heavy sleeper and can sleep through pretty much anything. He always has. Also, there would be times when I'd end up sleeping in my kids' rooms or in the living room, trying to deal with my nightmares. He was never concerned that I wasn't lying next to him when he rolled over. It just meant that I was somewhere else in the house. You also have to understand that there was nothing inside of him that would've thought I was sneaking out. It never crossed his mind to even be worried about. I know it's hard for some people to understand, but I'm not going to change the truth simply because people have trouble grasping it. This is just how it was.

I would struggle through the days leading up to the weekend with nightmares and flashbacks. I was scared. No, *scared* is not a strong enough word. I was terrified.

Remember how I had been through several knee surgeries in my life? Well, I remember the nerves in the days leading up to each surgery. This felt similar, except I wasn't put to sleep, and afterward I had to act like nothing hurt or like nothing was done to me. I had been hurt so deeply that I learned to not only shut off my brain during the pain, but during the time in between. If you would've looked in my eyes, and I mean really looked, I was nothing but a shell.

Still to this day, hearing the revving of truck engines can cause me to go into "fight or flight, freeze or fold" mode. Hearing that noise always meant something bad was coming. Often, when I would go outside to meet the men after hearing their engines, it would be to give them sex or whatever else gross sexual pleasure they desired. I learned even as a little girl how to perform in such a way to get it done the fastest. Even if it meant acting like I enjoyed what was happening or what I was doing for them. Sometimes the men would get more aroused if I put up a fight, and I usually could tell who those men were because they were much more violent in their actions.

I was in robot mode and couldn't seem to find a sliver of light anywhere. I still struggled with praying and reading my Bible. But I would often cry out to God with the simple words "Help! Please, please help me!" I had gotten to a point where I no longer could cry. I couldn't feel much of anything. But anytime I was able to mutter the words or even think the words asking God for help, the tears would start falling uncontrollably.

I didn't know what else to do. My children were growing up. My husband was slowly pulling away from me. And I was in a prison of pain and shame that I didn't know how to get rid of. Not to mention I wasn't eating, and what I did eat, I threw back up.

My eating habits had gotten so out of control, and I was so good at hiding it that no one knew anything was up. Every morning I would not eat breakfast, or if I did, I would have massive amounts of cereal. And once my husband went to work, I would go into the bathroom and throw it up. We didn't have much money at the time, so finding food to binge on became a creative process for me. Foods that I would binge on would be things like entire containers of chocolate bark, containers of icing, cereal, pasta, or peanut butter. And I would binge with this food multiple times a day and finish by throwing them up. Or I would just go the entire day without eating and plan to never eat again, only to binge the entire next day. I was a mess.

In the evenings, when I would sit down with my family for dinner, I would eat a normal amount, or maybe a tad on the side of eating too much. And then I became a master at finding ways to get my husband preoccupied for one minute so I could run to the bathroom and throw it up.

I would suggest things like maybe he should vacuum, or wash the dishes, or take the kids outside to play, or run up to the store to get something we needed.

In the times when I couldn't think of anything that would make sense to ask him to do, then I would find an excuse to go outside myself. Where we lived, we had a detached garage, and in our garage we had a black bunny that my oldest son had received for his birthday. If I couldn't get my husband out of the house, then I would say that I needed to go feed the bunny or clean her cage. So I would grab some paper towels and head out to the garage. In the garage was a window that the glass had been broken out of. That was not my doing, I promise. But I would go over to the window and would stick my head out and throw up. Then I would use the paper towels to clean myself up. I could do it quickly and easily, and my husband had no idea. Then I would go ahead and take care of the bunny while I was out there. It's terrible how engulfed you become in a sin and the lengths you would go to protect the sin from being found out. The amount of stress I added to my life by having this coping mechanism was awful. But I still didn't feel like I could stop.

On occasion, I would find myself in a situation where I had eaten more than I felt was appropriate and I wouldn't have an excuse to get away and throw up. In those moments, the anxiety would build to extreme levels, and I would feel myself getting angry and extremely irritable. I needed to get the food out of me and I didn't know how to do it, so anger would take over. Sometimes that anger would show itself by simply getting quiet, and sometimes it would be a snappy remark to my husband or the kids.

I was so addicted to the high of bingeing and purging, that living without it seemed to be impossible. Not to mention the fact that I was melting away faster than I ever could've imagined. There was a thrift store that was walking distance from our house, and I would often have to go over to buy pants that fit because my pants would be falling off my waist. I couldn't believe it when a size zero actually fit me.

I started hearing more and more people expressing concern over my dramatic weight loss. People would ask if I was sick. Some would comment and say how great I looked and they wanted to know my secret. For a long time, my mom seemed proud of me for the weight I had lost and how thin I was looking, but then there came a point where she started to get scared. When I walked through her house one day and I couldn't keep my size 2 pants up, she noticed and started to cry. She told me that I had to gain some weight and that I looked sick. The concern and worry were written all over her face. I felt the anxiety building in my chest as I promised to try and gain weight, but in my mind, I wanted to explain why I was losing weight. And what was happening to me multiple times a week that was destroying me so much more than just weight loss. But I knew that telling her the truth was not an option.

A good friend of mine, whom I had originally reached out to when I started having memories of what my coach did to me as a child, had come by my house and noticed large bruises on my arms. Bruises that resembled the hand of a large man grabbing ahold of my wrists. Along with other deep bruises. She asked me what the bruises were from, and I told her I couldn't remember. I tried my hardest to change the subject or come up with something to explain where the bruises might've come from, but my friend was pushy, and she was concerned.

"Who is hurting you?" she asked.

I would play dumb and act like I had no idea what she was talking about. She would go on to ask more specific questions that involved my coach's name, and from my reaction, she knew that I was being hurt again. Out of fear and anger and helplessness, she left my house in tears.

I look back and remember her genuine concern, but at the time, I was furious that my secret was found out. I had become so scared of what would happen if the truth was found out, and I would do anything to keep that from happening. I have no idea if they were my own fears, or if they were fears instilled in me by the perpetrators, but the fear was real, and it was strong.

I know that God sent me this woman as an angel. He put her in my path and gave her the eyes to see the truth so that the process toward my healing and my freedom could begin. I want so badly to go back to that moment and wrap my arms around her, tell her everything, and allow her to help me.

She left my house that afternoon in tears and claiming that she couldn't do this anymore, and for over an hour I didn't hear from her. My mind worked in odd ways. That hour felt like an eternity as I waited to hear that she still loved me and still cared for me. Even though I couldn't fathom the thought of the truth getting out, it hurt just as much to think that since I couldn't share the truth, I would lose a friend. Someone who loved me enough to care. The war was raging within me. How do I get her not to leave me like my old counselor had?

Finally, after a long dreadful hour, I heard from her through a text, saying that she couldn't stand by and watch me get hurt. And that I needed to tell her what was going on. Through text, I went on to try and tell her in the most positive way possible that yes, I was being hurt, but that it was okay. That I had it all under control and that I was pretty sure they wouldn't bother me again.

She felt very strongly that I needed to tell my dad what has been happening. My dad was the preacher at our local church, where I went and where my friend went. Not only that, but my friend's husband was an elder at the church. I can't imagine the distress she felt every Sunday morning, knowing what she knew and having to react to my family as if she was clueless. This was not an easy thing for her to do, and every Sunday became miserable for her and also for me. I worked very hard at church to make it seem like she was okay, and that I was okay, and that everyone was okay, and that everything was going to be okay. It was emotionally exhausting. Not to mention miserable.

At this point, my husband had been hired as a part-time preacher for a small country church about thirty minutes away. The church was so small that they didn't have any youth or activities for youth. So my husband and I decided that even though he was preaching somewhere else, it would be good for me and the kids to still attend my parents' church, where the kids would have lots of involvement in youth activities and such. However, even though it seemed wise at the time, that time apart from my husband just made our situation and communication even worse.

One terrible evening, when I heard the engines rev up outside my house, I once again headed out to do what it was that these disgusting men wanted me to do. This time was different, however. This time, I was taken to one of the large sheds that were near my house. Inside of the shed was probably five or six men. I still get shaky and lose my breath thinking about the realization of what was going to happen that night. They weren't there to have sex with me or to do anything sexual. They were there to torture me and to brand me.

The demonic presence around these men was obvious. The chill in the building and the looks in their eyes showed nothing but evil and darkness. The joy they got from my screams and the fight that they had over who could use the blade on me was disgusting. Lying on a cold and dirty concrete floor, looking up at these men who seemed to be straight from hell, I found myself believing I was the same as them. I must be. For all that I was allowing and doing and working so hard to keep a secret, I lay there watching their eyes and faces and wondered if others saw the same demonic look in me. And that scared me more than anything that night.

They went ahead and branded me, but they also had fun using the blade to carve a word in me that, at the time, I didn't know the meaning of. The word was *trick*.

The next day, what I had hoped was a nightmare was made very real when I had to work hard to hide the bruises and two carvings. Not only that, the carvings were already starting to look infected. The day went on, and I got more and more nervous as the carvings got redder and redder. I finally contacted my friend and told her that everything was fine, but I needed some advice. I explained that I had two words carved into me the night before and I was scared that they were infected. After doing my best to keep her calm, I sent her a picture of the one I was most worried about, and she was mortified.

"Does that say *trick*?" she asked.

I said that yes, it said trick, but I didn't even know what that meant. She thought for sure I was lying that I didn't know what it meant, but honestly I didn't. But when I found out that a *trick* is an easy woman that sleeps with lots of men, my heart dropped. My heart dropped out of embarrassment and shame because the men were right. I was nothing more than a trick.

The way I was manipulated and played fit perfectly with my personality, both as a kid and as an adult. I was harder on myself than I was on anyone else. I've always been that way. Despite the situation, I couldn't help but believe these men when they told me that I was nothing but trash and dumb, and easy, and even a trick. I would go to church on Sunday mornings, claiming to love God and all He stands for, but on Sunday afternoon, I would be in robot mode following Satan and everything he wanted me to do. The guilt with that is something I still struggle with, and I often have to remind myself that anything I did that was wrong, I have to lay it down at the foot of the cross, and I can't pick it back up ever again. Not only must I remember that God has already forgiven me, but also that I need to forgive myself.

In desperation, I started trying to reach out more and more. I reached out to another friend I knew from my childhood who was a strong Christian woman, and I also reached out some to my husband. I reached out to my husband only in the sense that I started explaining to him that I wasn't doing well. That I needed help. That I was hurting so badly and struggling so greatly each and every day that I really did need to find a counselor. I also admitted to him that I had some eating issues. I wasn't certain that my issues could be defined as an eating disorder because I didn't think I was thin enough for that, but I did admit to having some issues.

My husband is amazing, and he agreed to let me try and find a counselor. Despite the fact that we didn't have the extra money, we were able to make it work, and I started seeing a counselor whom I prayed could help me. The worst part about counseling was that each time I tried someone new, it took me a little bit of time to trust them enough to even start talking. Then if I got to the point where I felt like I trusted them enough to tell them my story, I couldn't get the words out anyway. Usually I spent between one to three sessions with a counselor before giving up on them. For one reason or another, they weren't the right fit for me.

I was recently studying about people who have been traumatized and read that there have been studies where images of a person's brain were captured while they were in a flashback. There were many eye-opening discoveries with this study, but there was one in particular that really stuck out at me. The same spot on the brain that indicates a person has had a stroke and has lost all verbal skills also lights up when a person is going through a flashback. I've always tried to explain to those helping me and even counselors that I can't get the words out, and it would be frustrating to most people. But this study showed me the exact reason why I struggled so much to form the words.

Explaining to my husband the struggle I had with finding the right counselor wasn't easy, but he was good about letting me try out someone new, hoping this time would be someone I was comfortable with. During this time, my husband was still preaching, and he grew extremely passionate about God. And most of all, about God's grace. He would often sit down next to me and proudly and profoundly try and speak to me about what new thing he had learned that day about God. Or he would recommend that I listen to a certain sermon or read a certain book. And I would try. I would always start, but my mind couldn't stay on all the fluffy words about God's grace or strength or wisdom when I was in this deep, dark pit, crying out to my God for help and I could see no signs of hope anywhere around me.

I distinctly remember one night after the kids had gone to bed, I was sitting in bed trying to read one of those many books that my husband had recommended. My husband then walked in and asked if he could tell me what he just realized about God. As a Christian, can I really say no to that question? Can I really say, "No, sweetie. That sounds like something that I don't want to hear about. But thanks for asking."

I obviously said yes, and I even silently said to myself to try and open my heart and listen. That maybe I can get something from his new revelation. Lord knows I wanted to. My sweet, darling husband sat next to me on our bed and proceeded to speak in such a way that sounded almost word for word as the sermon he had just been listening to. And I say sermon, I mean, sermon. And I mean that I felt as if my husband was sitting on our bed preaching at me. I knew my husband was right with everything he was saying, and I really did love his passion for God. Honestly, I was also jealous that my husband was so close to God, while I couldn't see God or feel God at all anymore.

But as I sat there on our bed, the frustration started to build inside of me. My husband was preaching to me about grace. About God's grace. About how we are forgiven and free by grace, not because we are good, but because God is good. Not because we deserve it, and not because it guarantees we won't mess up again. Only because of how great our God is.

So my husband was saying these things to me with tears of joy flowing down his face. I mean, this man was seriously blubbering. He seemed completely taken aback by the love of God and the real truth behind His grace. I'm sorry, but all I could do was roll my eyes. I mean, seriously? I know that my husband was clueless about the struggles I was in at that moment, but he did know enough to know that God and I were on the outs.

And that I was hurting and I was in a pit. That daily I was dealing with a deep pain inside of me that would not go away. That I had been hurt so horrifically as a child, the memories still haunted me. And he was going to sit on our bed and cry huge crocodile tears about grace?

It seemed demeaning to me that he would do that. And in frustration, I stopped my husband short from finishing his passionate speech on our amazing God, and I told him that I didn't want to hear about it. That I didn't want to hear about God's grace or God's goodness. "I don't want to hear about how great things are going for you and God and how you are growing by leaps and bounds in your faith. I don't want to hear all those things as I sit in the same spot, deep down in the pit, finding little to no hope in this God who seems to be pouring into you and caring very little about me."

My husband was hurt, and he was mad. And when I was done ranting to him, I rolled over and tried to close my eyes and go to sleep, but I knew deep down in my heart that what I had just done was wrong. I knew that I should've been happy for my husband. That I should've tried harder to see things like he was seeing it. I knew I was wrong, but somehow the frustration stayed with me. I couldn't let go of how my husband seemed completely clueless at the pain I was in. I saw him as only working to grow himself in Christ and leaving me behind to fend for myself. And it made me angry and sad.

> They have silenced me in the pit and have
> placed a stone on me. Waters flowed over my
> head; I said, "I am cut off!" I called on Your
> name, O Lord, out of the lowest pit.
> —Lamentations 3:53–55

"Help! Please, God, help me!"

The cry for help to my Lord was almost always in my heart. I knew He was the only way out, but why was it so hard to find Him? Why was it so hard to feel Him or to see Him working? The days were long, but the weeks were short during this time in my life. Time was flying faster than I could realize, and I was lost in this mess of slavery and bondage with no understanding of how anything was ever going to change.

I didn't understand the little miracles that were taking place at that time, the small miracles that were leading me toward complete restoration and healing. At the time it felt like dead ends, one after the other. But in actuality, they were stairs leading up out of the pit.

My close friend who had been trying to help me confided in her husband, who was the elder at our church. He was deeply disturbed by the information and felt led to discuss it with some elders of the church, and even more so, he wanted to bring this all to the attention of my dad. This news was devastating to me. I tried through texts and visits to convince them to not share this information with my dad. That I was an adult and if I wanted him to know, I should be the one to tell him. I was angry that they saw it as their place to interfere like this.

I see now how ridiculous my thoughts were. I wanted my friend to be there for me, to let me lean on her during this difficult time, but I didn't want her help with getting me out of the life that was killing me. I just wanted her to hold me and tell me that everything would be okay.

My friend and a few elders met with my dad over the course of several months, trying to explain to him what was going on. The other good Christian friend that was helping me also cornered my dad in the grocery store and explained the same things to him.

My "flight or fight, freeze or fold" mode went into high gear as I found out my dad was informed of the life I had been leading. You have to better understand my relationship with my dad to know why this was so difficult for me.

I was a daddy's girl. I had my dad wrapped around my finger from the moment I was born. My dad was my biggest fan. He had been a preacher since he was eighteen, so that was all I knew of him, a Godly man. I adored him. I respected him, and I was proud to call him my dad.

My dad had sat through these meetings with the people trying to help me, and right away he contacted me. He told me what was said to him. And he asked me if this information was true. Once again, filled with shame, I told my dad that this was not true.

Right away, my dad believed me. He said that because of the abuse that had taken place when I was a kid, I was struggling and my mind and soul were hurting. I could see the pain in my dad's eyes as we talked about it. He asked me how I was doing, and I told him that I wasn't doing good. Not at all.

How does a father handle this? There are perfect scenarios where a father says and does everything exactly right, but when you throw in emotions and hurts and being human, doing and saying everything perfectly is impossible. I wish my dad would've seen past my mask that day. I wish he wouldn't have asked me if it was true or not, but just started taking action in helping me. The only words of advice that he could give me was that I just needed to get over it. That there was no other choice than to get over it. Otherwise, my life was going to be miserable.

Tears came at those words because I so desperately wanted to simply get over it. I didn't want to be in this pit, or to feel this way, or to be stuck in this prison. I was crying out for help in the only ways I knew how, but no matter how hard I tried to convince my brain and my heart to simply "get over it," it never worked. Not even for a second.

I couldn't figure out what was wrong with me. What was my problem? So many people have dealt with abuse as a child, and they get over it. But not only couldn't I get over it, but I somehow ended up back in it. This is not how a Christian handles this. Something had to be wrong with me. I wanted so badly to just "get over it." But at the bottom of the pit, I still sat.

I felt alone and lost. No one understood what was happening. No one understood how to help me. Some wanted to fix the problem. Some wanted to act like it wasn't really there. And what I desperately wanted was for someone to come meet me in the pit. Someone to remind me that I'm worth more than what was happening and that I am loved. That God hasn't left me, and that I am not alone.

In frustration and feeling like their hands were tied, my friend needed space from the situation. She couldn't stand by and watch me get hurt while nothing was getting done to stop it. I found a counselor around this time whom I actually liked. I began to go to her, and slowly I started telling her my story. It was hard for her to comprehend the problem in the bits and pieces that I was telling her, but I was fearful that if I told her too much, she would leave. That she would throw her hands up in the air and say that she couldn't help me. I didn't know what information to share and what information to hold back. Not to mention, I was very ignorant of all that was happening to me and my mind, and explaining it to others seemed impossible. I would try to explain things in the most logical way, but nothing that I was experiencing was logical. I felt so alone, which I'm certain is exactly what the ring of men hurting me wanted.

I heard a quote once that said something along the lines of the fact that you can't make sense of evil. When your mind doesn't think in an evil way, when you think in a normal, loving, logical way, you can't comprehend evil. I try to believe that the reason so many people turned a blind eye to my abuse as a child was because their minds couldn't comprehend the evil. They couldn't begin to believe that a man would do something evil like that to a child. Unfortunately, the incomprehensible still happens, whether we understand it or not. Evil exists. Satan is running rampant. And so many are sitting back in an unbelieving state of shock and denial. I couldn't make sense of the evil happening to me, and I couldn't explain it well to others. It was a very lonely place to be.

The process of dealing with the pain of what was going on in my life was all pretty much done alone. I think one of the reasons why I struggled so much was because I had numbed myself, but not completely. I had the Holy Spirit living inside of me and that light, was still burning, even if it was faint. I battled a lot with right and wrong, with what God was doing and how I must be such a disappointment to Him. I felt the war raging within me between God and Satan, and it felt like it was Satan who was winning most of the time.

The Holy Spirit still burning ever so faintly within me also allowed me the chance to fully take in the brokenness that I saw while I was at these brothels. I would see girl after girl with a completely lifeless look on their face. They were empty. They had been so deeply hurt that their minds and souls had gone into hiding. Jesus was not somebody they knew. Hope was not something they knew.

I would go home feeling so much guilt for not helping those girls in some way. Some of the girls I saw were just like me, and some were women who didn't speak English and seemed to be from another country. Some were younger girls who I assumed either ran away from home or were kidnapped. But I wanted to take each and every one of those girls home with me. The Holy Spirit would bring up a fight in me for those girls. Sometimes I would fight, but usually I was then either tortured and punished or drugged to shut me up. The demonic presence around these people was obvious.

I believe that while I was going through this hell, God opened my eyes to one girl in particular. Of course, it was hard to miss this girl because she was most definitely a fighter. Her name was Kaitlyn.

I met Kaitlyn during one of my many visits to the camper out in the country. I'm not sure the exact spelling of her name or if Kaitlyn was even her real name, but that was the name she told me. Girls were brought in and out of the camper often. Some were brainwashed and programmed to follow rules. They could go home in between because their minds were controlled by their owners. This was the case with me. Whether by fear or coercion or force, there didn't appear to be a choice. No matter how much we wanted to go against what they were telling us to do, physically and mentally we couldn't. That's hard for people on the outside to grasp, but it's the truth and it's real. We could lead what almost seemed like normal lives on the outside. The only sign of the other world would be the emptiness in their eyes. And possibly the bruises and brandings on their skin. There were also girls who were brainwashed and programmed but were kept in a shack or a shed at all times. Those girls seemed to be the runaways or the girls that didn't have a family. Their hours of "working" would be ridiculous, and it seemed they were moved around often.

It's been explained that human trafficking has grown so much bigger than drug trafficking because you don't have to replenish your supply. With drugs, you always have the problem of needing to get more drugs. But when you are selling a body, you have the ability to sell it over and over again and still receive the same amount of money. Eventually the body wears out, but the average lifespan of a woman in trafficking is seven years. That's seven years of turning tricks multiple times a day and bringing in a lot of money. It's sick and sad, but again, it's reality.

I was doing "work" one day and was being hurt pretty badly. I couldn't tell you how many men were hurting me at that time and what their purpose was other than to get pleasure from my screams. I knew that getting them off me was not an option, but I couldn't take the pain. I started begging them to give me some drugs. To please just knock me out. I couldn't handle the pain anymore, but I knew my pleas for help were useless. Then somewhere, I started hearing another girl screaming. I was almost sick from the pain I was in, and I assumed they were hurting her somewhere nearby too. I just remember feeling helpless. But I then realized that this other girl wasn't in fact being tortured or hurt. She was actually telling the "$%@# face men" to get off me. Next thing I knew, she was kicking and punching these naked men right where it hurts. For a brief moment, we were able to make eye contact, and she smiled this warrior-princess smile that I will never forget.

She wasn't a very big girl. Maybe five feet, six inches at the most, and she had long blonde hair. Her eyes were sad, but they still had fight in them. I'm not certain how long she had been at the camper, but she still had hope; she still had a reason to get free and to fight back. And apparently she wasn't just going to fight for herself—she was going to fight for all of us.

That day, she fought for me. And what it ended up getting her was a seat right next to me for the next hour or so. But she wasn't going to let those animals win, even if day in and day out they would continue to beat her down. Each time I went back, we would try to find each other. The men picked up on the fact that we cared for each other, and they used that against us a lot. I was the one who was free to go home. She would've given anything to have that option. She said she would've never come back. I honestly had never thought about that being an option. Looking back, I'm guessing she hadn't been abused and used as a child to where she lost her sense of having options, which was probably why she was such a fighter. She still had a strength that I had lost many years earlier as a child. One thing that did enter my mind a lot, though, was that I needed to get her free.

We got very little time to talk, but as best we could, we would try to come up with a plan to get her out of that hell. I would pretend to be brave like her. I wanted her to think I was strong just like her. But I knew I really wasn't. What human in their right mind would be at this place simply because they were told to? Granted, my thoughts were skewed because of the abuse all through my childhood, which is often the case with trafficked adult victims. And I felt like this was what I had to do to protect my family. I still felt like a coward, and I knew I didn't have a stitch of bravery and courage like Kaitlyn did.

It took us a while, but we finally got a plan figured out to try and get her to escape. On a Friday evening, I was going to drive to the field that surrounded the camper, close to where she was staying. She knew the schedule of these men front and back, so she knew the exact right time that she could make a run for it. I was going to be waiting for her with my car headlights off at just a small run from the shack she stayed in. We had it all planned out. I didn't fully know how she planned to escape the shack, but I knew if anyone could do it, she could. She had explained to me that she didn't know times at night based on a clock, but on the rotation of men. So when the men were making a switch with some of the girls, she was going to make a run for it. And I would be ready.

I was terrified. I still get extremely emotional and sick thinking about it to this time. I was completely scared out of my mind, for myself and for her. If we got caught, it could be deadly. She had a chance during one of our conversations early on to tell me just a little bit about herself, and I knew she was from Indiana and she had a family. Her family life had been messed up, and so she ran away. She felt responsible for everything that happened to her and how she got into the sex trade world, but she wasn't going to quit fighting until she was free and on her way back home. I was excited for her. She was a brilliant girl, and she truly had an amazing future ahead of her.

I sat in my car, anxiously waiting for her. I kept my eyes peeled off in the distance for her. I would often think that I would see her, but it would be my eyes playing tricks on me. I waited and waited for over two hours. I didn't want to leave, but I also knew that my husband would start to worry about where I was. I had told him I was meeting with a friend for the evening. I felt sick. I was worried that they had caught her trying to escape and hurt her. Or that they had caught wind of our plan and decided to ship her off. I didn't know what to do. I waited for as long as I felt like I could, and then I reluctantly drove away. I had never felt so sick.

I wasn't supposed to be "working" until Sunday, so from Friday night through Sunday, I was a nervous wreck. I didn't sleep a wink. I needed to know what happened. I needed to know if she was okay.

Sunday came, and I made another excuse to my husband as to why I needed some time alone. I drove to the locations where Kaitlyn was and where I was supposed to "work." When I got there, I went straight to the shack where Kaitlyn would sleep. She wasn't there. I went into the camper, and lying on the couch was Kaitlyn. She had been beaten to a pulp. I went over to her. She was in terrible shape, to where I wasn't even certain if she was breathing at first. Thank God she was. I knew she needed to go to the hospital. I was terrified that if she didn't get medical attention, then she would die. I was so scared.

Some men came into the camper, and they were some of the biggest jerks there. I hated them, and after I heard them talk about Kaitlyn, I hated them even more. I begged them to let me take her to the hospital. That she was going to die. But they didn't care at all. I wanted to take her home with me. At that moment, I felt like the worst human being on the planet, completely helpless to the situation. I didn't know what to do to help her. I tried to think of what she would've done if she were in my shoes, but my brain isn't brave and strong like hers.

That was the last time that I ever saw Kaitlyn. She was not there the next week when I came back, and I was told by one of the other girls that she had died a few days after I last saw her. For a long time, I believed that she had died like I was told. I remember just how bad she looked. But more recently I have started to have hope that maybe they lied. Maybe she was still alive. Maybe she had been hurt and then sold, and they wanted us to believe she was dead.

I don't know what the truth is, but at this moment, I choose to believe she is still out there and she needs me to find her and rescue her. And this time, I will do it right. My hope is that in the process of searching for her, we will also rescue many other girls as well. She deserves rescuing, as does every man, woman, or child who is stuck in the sex trade industry.

After hearing that Kaitlyn had died, I became very despondent and down. I understood my life to be a waste and that everyone would be better off without me around. I would be saving everyone just by simply ending my life. On many occasions, I would take drives on my own and feel my consciousness telling me to hit the next telephone pole.

Functioning as a mother to three kids that were four years old and under was hard enough on its own. I was getting very little sleep, and my eating habits were getting worse and worse. On multiple occasions, I would throw up blood during one of my routine binge-and-purge moments. It would terrify me. I would see my children running around the house in laughter and joy, seemingly oblivious to the nightmare that was happening to their mother. And at that moment, I had wanted so badly to stop this hell. To jump out of the pit and never go back. I would try again and again to cry out to God, but it seemed like His answer required more from me than I was willing to give. Hadn't I been giving enough? Did He really want me to give up more? I was frustrated. I know now that my thinking during this time was all wrong, but it was the way the brainwashing worked. God had not asked me to be captive and a slave. That was not His doing. The slavery was from Satan and having terrible thoughts of myself and my worth seemed to fuel Satan's power. Unbeknownst to me, it was about to get worse.

I had been in the kitchen when the back door flung open, and in walked two men. Two large and mean men. I yelled out to my kids to go to my room and shut the door. Praise God they did what they were told. These two men proceeded to beat me and rape me in my own home, and when they were done, they proudly proclaimed, "Welcome to your new owner."

They left, and I gathered myself together. The fear running through my body was intense. What happened with my coach? I began trying to go back in my mind to comprehend what was going on. I had been under my coach's control since I was nine, but he must've sold me. I had a moment where my heart ached from the hurt of my coach's decision and the fear that these new men would ask more of me. I hung my head, knowing I was going to have to grin and bear it. I then heard the sound of crying coming from my room and a tiny voice yelling out for mommy.

I jumped up and ran to my bedroom, immediately more aware of the areas that were just beaten on my body. I opened the door to my room, and standing there in tears were all three of my children.

"Are you okay?" I quickly asked.

My oldest responded, "We didn't know where you were and Sissy keeps trying to hug me."

"Aw, honey, I was right in the other room. I'm sorry, sweetie."

We decided that it was a good time for a snack, and we went out to the kitchen to make popcorn, but before I did that, I made sure all of the doors were locked.

My kids were protected that day, and many days, by a legion of angels. They had to have been. How else could you explain that they were not touched or harmed? Psychologically, though, I was starting to see my oldest battle fear and anxiety. And my eyes were starting to open to the fact that even I was able to keep my family physically safe, they were still affected by the fact that their mom was hurting.

I quickly found out that I was right to have feared this change in ownership. Things definitely got worse. The only positive thing was that the events were less frequent, but when they happened, they were beyond the normal realm of being sold. That sounds like an oxymoron, but the evilness was upped to an even more extreme level.

There was a particular place that I struggle remembering the exact location of. I'm not sure if that is because I wasn't shown exactly where it was while we were going there or what, but this place was horrendous. Absolutely horrendous. I've gone back and forth on whether or not this was something to even share in my book, and I've leaned toward leaving out the details of what went on in this building, but the number of men being served and the way they were served was similar to something you would expect with livestock. Meaning we were treated worse than most animals in America. We were truly the "nothings" that we were often told we were.

I would see my new counselor once a week, and I was hesitant to explain to her just how much danger I was in. She was so sweet and she was disgusted at all that I told her, but she eventually figured out that these events that I was talking about were actually recent. That my routines and schedules were so well known to my new owner that I was often followed and hurt when I was driving alone. I was constantly in fear who was around me, of who was watching me. During one of my trips to see her at her office for one of my counseling appointments, I was followed. She begged me to call the cops, and I used my usual line that everything was okay. That I had this all under control. And that I was pretty sure that these men were done with me at this point. I was so scared of the ramifications of getting the police involved. I was beyond terrified of the police and the reaction of my owner if I were to go to the police.

She knew better, and she told me that if I wasn't willing to call the police, she was going to have to stop seeing me. That it was starting to put her in danger as well and she couldn't continue to allow this.

I begged her not to leave me. I started making any and every promise I could think of to try and get her to stay by me. But it didn't matter. I was crushed and alone. I hated myself for trusting someone else. I knew better than to allow someone in that much.

I took some time away from counselors. God was most definitely working during this time, but it was all behind the scenes. What I was seeing was hopelessness.

Through what could've only been a voice from God, I felt the idea to contact someone from my past. There was a lady that my parents had me see one time when I was around twelve years old. It was after I had tried to reach out about someone hurting me. The school had recommended that I see a counselor, and this was the only counselor my parents trusted. I remember sitting in her office as a child and hearing her ask if someone had hurt me, and I told her no. I wanted to get in contact with this lady now so that I could explain that I really had been hurt as a child. A part of me was angry at her for not pushing harder when I was little. My intentions were mainly to shout out in frustration that she was just one more person who didn't protect me.

I reached out to her and just explained that I felt the need to tell her that when I sat in her office as a child and I told her that no one had hurt me, I had lied. That I had been hurt. I'm not sure what I had expected from her, maybe that she wouldn't believe me, or that she wouldn't care.

But she not only believed me, she also wanted to start counseling me. She had retired recently, so she wasn't technically a counselor anymore, but she wanted to me with me more as friends and it would be free.

This was definitely a God thing. This lady had known me since I was nine years old, and this made explaining things to her so much easier. I went over to her house, and I was very careful about what I told her. I was afraid that my story would run her off like it did the last counselor. But she seemed to be more in the know about sex trafficking, and she was able to help me to gain some strength.

She started by making sure I got to see a doctor. My health wasn't great from all the abuse, malnourishment, and stress. I had been dealing with a constant headache for about six months, and no matter what medicine I took, the headache never went away. When we met with the doctor, we were able to get me some of the help I needed medically. My counselor also helped me to be strong enough to not follow orders a few times, when they wanted me to meet a man somewhere. I was still very much frightened and worried, but I was feeling somewhat stronger and less alone.

Then in February of 2015, on the first birthday of our third child, I found out that I was pregnant again. Knowing that I hadn't been with anyone except my husband for the last few months, it made me very happy that I could say for certain that this pregnancy was definitely from my husband. I was ecstatic. I was a bit happier about it than my husband. This would be four kids in five years. It took a day or so, but he then became excited too. I wanted to make sure that this pregnancy was different. I wanted to find joy in every moment of it. In a way, it felt like God was blessing me for finally getting strong enough to stop obeying orders from my owner. I felt like this was going to be the start of a new life.

A few weeks after I found out that I was pregnant, our landlord came to us and said that they had other plans for the house they had been renting to us. We needed to find another place to live. At the time, it felt like a terrible situation to be in, but God was still working.

Weeping may endure for a night, but
joy cometh in the morning.

—Psalm 30:5

CHAPTER 16

I was just six weeks pregnant when we were told we needed to find a new place to live.

What in the world are you doing now, God? Now we are losing our home. Is this the plan you are choosing for us because I'm going to be honest here, God, this plan really sucks.

I wasn't necessarily feeling anger, but hopelessness. I had started to break away from the traffickers, but I was still very much living in fear. I had kept from obeying their demands, and I was shocked that my counselor had been right, they didn't follow through with any of their threats. We had remained safe.

I desperately wanted a normal life, free of fear and free of guilt. Each night I would struggle with hearing the revving engines outside of my house and feeling fear that if I didn't go outside, the punishment would be so much worse. But I stayed put in my bed. I would eventually fall asleep, only to be overtaken with nightmares of past experiences and fears for my future. I'd wake up sweating and scared. Feeling so alone and unsure of whether or not I was doing the right thing. Hearing that we were losing our home, I felt like it was just one more thing that was keeping me from having a normal life.

It didn't cross my mind that God was working, that there was a way that God was going to use this. I just felt like I once again needed to figure out a way to protect my family, and now that meant even finding them a home. My hope and my faith in God were strong, but only in what He could do for others, not with what He would do for me. I knew I was different. I was a lower class or less of a person. I was trash. I had to be, or why else wasn't God working in my life or caring about what was happening to me?

At this point, I was still seeing this new counselor, and we were continuing to make headway. I could feel myself getting stronger. I could feel myself finding God more and more with each day. Each day was hard. Each day I was scared. Especially with not knowing who was going to show up and if they would hurt me. A few times, I was threatened and hit and told to be at the camper or else. But I didn't go. The fear of what my punishment would be for not listening to them was terrifying.

The Lord had been doing little things along the way that set us up to where I was going to find restoration. During the time that my husband was growing a lot in Christ, he became really close to his boss at work. They began having Bible studies together, and they talked a lot about God and faith and grace. The stories my husband would tell me after coming home from work, about what his boss had seen and experienced during trips to Haiti or India, were mind-blowing to me. It was very hard to hear stories of how God performed miracles and delivered people from demons. It seemed completely impossible. It was more proof to me that God loved others more than me. But there was something deep down inside of me that longed for the kind of faith my husband's boss had. To be able to believe that God could do something miraculous in my life. Whatever it was that this man had, whatever he knew, I wanted it.

So when we thought about which town to choose when looking for a house, we definitely wanted one close to where my husband worked, but even more than that, we wanted to be in a town that would help us grow closer to God. We realized that the town where my husband's boss lived was the perfect place for us. My husband loved the idea of living closer to his boss because of the relationship they had formed. So we started searching for rentals in that town. We made just one phone call, we were referred to one house, we went and saw the house just one time, and just one day later, we signed the papers to start renting it. Within just two days of learning we needed to look for a new home, we were able to find the perfect house, with a wonderful neighborhood, in our price range, and big enough to fit our family. We were amazed at the timing.

Something deep down inside once again told me that possibly this was God orchestrating some things for us. A glimmer of hope showed up inside of my heart. Just maybe, God was still there and was still working. I wasn't going to get my hopes up too high, but there was a glimmer of hope.

The move was exciting for our family. Our kids were the same age as the neighbor's kids and quickly became really good friends even before the move. Preparing for the move was very hard on me. I was constantly in fear of what would happen if my owner got to me. I hadn't been listening to orders, and I knew it was just a matter of time before he made me pay for it. But what scared me more was if he were to find out that I was pregnant. I knew of girls who were given abortions and then fixed to never have kids again. I would do anything to make sure the baby inside of me remained safe. Just like I was doing everything I could to keep my other kids safe too.

With my mind trapped in fear over the what ifs, I was also battling morning sickness really badly and basically felt like death warmed over. I'm sure my poor health from all I had been through played a big part in that. I explained it as all day sickness instead of just morning sickness. I was also very tired and fatigued easily. So to be able to get our entire house packed up in just three weeks, it seemed impossible. My husband worked, so the packing was put on my shoulders, and I pretty much just threw my hands up in the air right from the very beginning.

I went through everyone's clothes and donated what we didn't need and organized and packed what I could. Without knowing if we were having a boy or a girl, I had to hang on to both sets of baby clothes just in case. I felt like I had made some headway, but come moving day, I realized that I was very much mistaken.

We didn't have a moving truck, but just pickup trucks from friends. They loaded up all the big stuff, and then somehow left behind was a ton of little things that had not been packed up. Toys and diapers and papers and pillows, and the list goes on and on. So then we got trash bags and just started filling them up with all the miscellaneous stuff. There was absolutely no rhyme or reason to any of it. So by midnight we were finally moved in, but we had trash bags of random things lying all over the place. It took several months to finally go through all the bags. I felt a deep desire within me to become organized, but the desire wasn't strong enough to combat my morning sickness, so nothing changed in that area.

We were preparing for the upcoming school year, and I'm sure it's no surprise to hear that I wanted to homeschool. I was terrified of schools and leaving my kids alone with someone else. I had felt the desire to homeschool for years, so with my oldest starting kindergarten in the fall, I began to research curricula and ideas for kindergarteners. My son was very excited about doing school at home and having the freedom to do more of what he wanted. I was excited to get to be a part of his educational journey and to see him learn and grow. What I also knew was that my due date for our fourth baby was October 26, which was right in the middle of the school year. I knew I needed to plan ahead because I wasn't going to feel like doing much prep work in the last few weeks of pregnancy. I also had hoped that homeschooling was going to be just what I needed to keep myself involved mentally and emotionally, to where my fears and what ifs would start to subside. That my mind wouldn't constantly be thinking about who could stop by today. But instead "What is on the agenda for school today?" My child's education meant a lot to me, and I wanted him to have a fun and meaningful year of kindergarten.

During an ultrasound about halfway through my pregnancy, I found out that I was having another girl. I was excited to call my husband and share the news with him that God had blessed us with two boys and two girls. It felt absolutely perfect.

As my pregnant belly began to show, I didn't receive near as many drop-ins or threats. A big part of me began to think that this fourth child was what I needed to completely get me out of trafficking, that they were going to leave me alone for good.

My spirits were getting higher as I enjoyed the peace of knowing I was safe. I still struggled with prayer, but in short moments I was able to speak out to God for guidance and listen for His response. I could feel Him in my life a little more than I used to. I remember one time in particular around this time when God made it very clear to me what it was that He wanted me to do. And feeling Him in that way again was the best feeling in the world.

As a family, we had been attending the small country church where my husband was preaching every Sunday morning and Sunday night. It was a church that had experienced highs and lows in attendance, and for the last decade or so, it had endured a very low attendance. No matter the number that walked in the door each week, though, they continued to stay open. My husband was passionate about the Lord and about spreading the Gospel to everyone he met. And he enjoyed preaching very much.

The moment came when my husband then got a phone call from another church that was interested in him trying out as their preacher. At first, I felt a whole lot of pride in knowing that my husband was being asked to potentially be the preacher of this larger church. It wasn't a huge church but it was quite a bit bigger than the church we were currently attending.

We went that first Sunday for my husband to preach, and we enjoyed a potluck afterward and visiting with the congregation. It was very hard for me to walk in that church, though. I had a strong feeling that I was pretending by being there. To be there as if I was a preacher's wife, when in actuality, I was trash. The mental war began the moment we walked into the building, as I felt dirty and was certain was obvious to everyone else. I just knew they were going to be able to tell all of the terrible things I had done in my past just by looking at me. I worked hard to fight those demeaning words in my mind, reminding myself that I was there to support my husband, who was doing great work for the Lord. Hopefully my dirt wouldn't affect what great things God was doing in my husband's life.

My husband had a very strong, passionate sermon, and his eagerness to preach the Word became something that this church grabbed hold of. This church had been through quite a bit as of recently, and they needed a fresh start. They were hoping for a young family like ours and a passionate preacher, which my husband definitely was. We had several conversations with the leaders of the church, and for the next week, both my husband and I believed that this was an obvious answer from God. That God would most definitely want us to take this church as our next ministry.

Two weeks later, we went back again, and even though the shame and feeling of unworthiness were still there for me, I was surprised when I felt a strong feeling in my heart that this was not where God wanted our family to go, which didn't make sense to me. My husband had another great sermon, and we enjoyed another great conversation with the members of the church. You could see their excitement in the thought of us becoming their preacher's family. And through it all, I tried to quiet the voice in my heart that was telling me that this wasn't the place where God wanted us. I was certain I was hearing this voice wrong. That it was probably just my past coming through again, believing that I shouldn't be a preacher's wife.

We once again drove home, and my husband even more so felt strongly about saying yes to this church. This time I didn't say quite as much, and my husband noticed. I told him that I didn't know what it was, but something didn't feel right.

Now, please note that for the last three years, I had been nothing but a shell of a person. No spirit, no life to me. I had completely stopped sharing my opinions and using my voice with my husband. He knew my struggles with God. So when I said that I was not feeling right about it, it instantly made him defensive. And I didn't blame him one bit because the worst part was that I didn't have a reason to tell him. On paper, it looked like it was an answered prayer. I had no idea why my gut was saying something different than his. And it honestly made us both frustrated.

I began to worry that maybe it was Satan putting doubt in my mind. But in the best way I could, I started to pray. I still struggled with prayer, so more than anything, I tried to listen. And I tried to understand. I was ready to be a preacher's wife if that was what God wanted from me. What I kept believing was that there was no way God would not want us taking this church, or doing His work in that way. Maybe it was Satan trying to mess up God's plan.

But I kept listening, and finally on the following Wednesday, I was able to write down on a notepad why I felt God was telling me that this was not the right move for our family. It finally made sense. It was as if the Lord gave me the gut feeling first, and a few days later He gave me the reason why.

For the first time in a long time, I felt the need to do something for myself. And saying no to this church was something I desperately needed. Prior to this, at that small country church, while my husband preached in the auditorium, the kids and I would go back into a small room. We called it children's church, but honestly, I spent most of the time trying to keep the kids quiet so that the people in the auditorium couldn't hear them. We would do a lesson, but mind you, my kids were four, two, and one at that point. It got to where I dreaded Sundays, and so did the kids because we would be put in that small room with nothing to play with and basically had to stay quiet. It was a sacrifice I was willing to make for my husband to be able to preach, but I didn't realize how much it took out of me. Or maybe I should say, how much it kept me from being filled the way I needed to be.

Even before this church, I was at my parents' church, and for the last ten years or so, I was working with the children during the service. I hadn't had a chance to consistently sit through a church service, hear the sermon, and be spiritually fed. And maybe part of that was on purpose. Maybe it was easier to be the one sacrificing my time so that I couldn't truly be challenged by a sermon. Either way, God was making it clear to me that I needed to be fed. And not only that, but I needed my husband to be the one to feed me. I saw clearly how passionate he was about helping people and sharing with them the good news of Jesus, but he didn't seem to see the pain I was in. Somehow he continued to miss my struggles, the fact that I was in slavery, that I was badly hurting and I struggled even to wake up each morning. I wanted and needed my husband to choose me, not his ministry as a preacher for a church. I needed him to choose me and to choose his kids. And there was one more thing that God revealed to me. God wanted us to start attending a new church. Not my parents' church and not the church where my husband was currently the minister. But a church just a few minutes from where we lived. It was the church associated with the preschool that our oldest son had attended, and I felt very strongly that God wanted us to start attending that church.

So after I had written down a lot of the thoughts God had placed on my heart, I texted my parents and asked if they could watch my kids for the evening so that my husband and I could go out on a date. They agreed, and I messaged my husband next and asked him if he'd be willing to have a date night with me. I told him that I finally figured out why God gave me that gut feeling and I wanted to share it with him.

At this point, my husband was pretty aggravated at me. He struggled with understanding why I was now putting my foot down and using my voice. He honestly believed that I was trying to keep him from doing what God wanted him to do, and it made him angry, which I completely understood. I knew I had to be very careful with how I delivered my reasons, and I knew I needed God to lead.

When my husband picked me up for the date, I told him that I would like to go sit at the park and talk. He was quiet but agreed. When we parked, I took several deep breaths and then told him that I would like to pray. This was probably the first time I had prayed out loud with him in years. So when I took his hand and started praying, I think it really took him back.

"Dear Lord, I am so broken right now and so lost. I know that what I am about to share with my husband might not make sense, but God, please help him to see my heart. Help him to understand what I'm feeling and I pray that together we can do exactly what it is that You want us to do. In Jesus's name, amen."

I was literally trembling with emotion at this point. It was hard to breathe, and my eyes were pooled with tears. I was going to use my voice, and I was going to say that I am worth fighting for. Both of those things had become so foreign to me. I wasn't certain that I really was worth fighting for, but God was telling me at that moment that I was, and I believed Him.

Through tears and sometimes actual sobs, I explained to my husband that I couldn't be a preacher's wife right now. That I couldn't help him lead a church. That I couldn't give to others in that way when I so desperately needed to be fed myself. That I needed and wanted a relationship with God and I was just starting to see a glimpse of hope in my future with Him. That I need Him as much as I need my next breath. I told my husband how sorry I was for getting in the way of him doing this ministry, but I needed him to choose me and the kids right now. *We* needed him. *We* needed him to minister to us and lead us and equip us.

By this point, my husband was bawling too, and he agreed wholeheartedly with me. He hadn't heard me use my voice in so long that he was beginning to think that maybe I didn't want him to succeed as a preacher, or that maybe I didn't think he was good enough. And that really wasn't it. But for three days, all I had was the gut feeling and no answers. It was an amazing moment to truly feel God lead us in a direction. We didn't understand all the whys to it, but we had a peace that surpassed all understanding.

My husband was supposed to have his final trial sermon the upcoming Sunday, and he said that he would go ahead and let the church know that he wouldn't be accepting the position. His next question for me was "Then where do we go to church?" And I was thrilled to be able to tell him exactly what God had spoken to my heart.

Together, as a family, we started to attend this new church. I had no idea why God chose this church at the time because our town had a dozen or more churches in it. But God knew exactly what He was doing. He was putting us around an army of believers who were ready for battle. And that was exactly what we needed.

This is how we've come to understand and experience love: Christ sacrificed His life for us. This is why we ought to live sacrificially for our fellow believers, and not just be out for ourselves. If you see some brother or sister in need and have the means to do something about it but turn a cold shoulder and do nothing, what happens to God's love? It disappears. And you made it disappear.
—1 John 3:16

The transition into this new church was very eye-opening to me and my husband. I was still very broken and going each Sunday, and seeing the faith that these believers had at this new church was changing my thought process on God completely. They weren't afraid to go forward and ask for prayer. They didn't put on this front that they had it all together. It was no secret that the Christians in that building were living their life for God, and no, it wasn't easy or perfect, but they didn't hide their struggles. Together as a church family, they fought their battles.

Whatever these people had, I desperately wanted it. I needed it. I needed God back in my life, but I didn't know how to do it. I didn't know how to find their hope and their peace. How did their faith look so much different than mine?

We were entering the summer months, and I made my first attempt at seeking guidance from someone in the church whom I had watched and admired. What I didn't take into account was this woman's schedule. She had so much going on in her life already with five kids, plus work and church. So when I came up to her and asked she would be my mentor, she gasped and quickly responded with "Now?"

It was obviously not the right time to be asking this, with summer camps and her kids needing to be in all different places and going in all different directions. My husband laughed at me when he heard that I had asked her to be my mentor. He said that usually a mentor just kind of happens after you form a relationship with someone. I just wanted help so desperately, waiting for a relationship to form didn't seem possible. In my heart, I felt the same sense of shame. I couldn't get the thought out of my head that it was because something was wrong with me. It was as if I could see God just of reach and no matter how hard I tried, I couldn't get any closer. I was certain that these Christians could see the dirt of my life all over me. They seemed to have such a close relationship with God that I was convinced God would open their eyes to who I really am, and then my chance of seeing guidance would be gone.

During this time, my husband started to be approached by people in the community who believed he would be a great addition to a local car dealership. After hearing all the pros and cons and after my husband and I prayed, we tried to then just listen to our hearts to see if this was the path that God wanted us to take.

I had always been under the belief that no matter what you are doing or what choices you make, you can always be serving God. God doesn't have one particular path you had to take. For example, I never once considered where God would want me to go to college. I never once thought to ask God if basketball was even something He wanted me to play after high school. It was what I wanted, and so it would be the path that I would take, and I would bring faith and God with me along my journey. That's just how I understood life.

But at this point, I started to believe that maybe there was a destiny for me, a purpose. Maybe I was supposed to be doing something in particular for God. But if this were the case, then what in the world was God asking me to do?

Instantly, at this question, my heart leaped into my throat. I knew what God wanted me to do. He wanted me to be honest. He wanted me to tell my husband and my parents the truth of what was going on. He wanted me to give the control to Him, by no longer living a secret life of pain. He wanted me to be vulnerable and to trust Him and His people to bring me to freedom. True freedom.

The sacrifice that it would take to get to that freedom was too much in my eyes. I didn't like this plan or this purpose that God was seemingly asking me to do. There was no way I was going to risk my marriage, which would also risk my relationship with my kids. There was no way I could tell those I love the most the truth about my life. This would cause me to lose everything that I cherished the most. And I wasn't willing to do it. I had to try things in a different way. God's way was too hard.

If you go against the grain, you get splinters, regardless of which neighborhood you're from, what your parents taught you, what school you attended. But if you embrace the way God does things, there are wonderful payoffs.
—Romans 2:9

Steven Furtick preaches for Elevation Church, and he taught me a lot in one of his sermons where he explained that God's presence is guaranteed. God will be with me even if I don't go to the places He wants me to go to. God will be with me even if I don't follow the plans He wants me to follow. God will be with me even if I don't do the things He has prepared for me to do. He will always be with me. His presence is not conditional; however, His promises are optional. There are conditions with how we experience His promises. How far I want to go is up to me when it comes to His promises. His peace, and His joy, and His grace is there, but it's conditioned on my faithfulness. So when I chose a college and I chose to be on a basketball team, I was making those choices off what I wanted, and God was with me through it all. He never left my side. However, the peace and the joy during those four years of college was definitely not there.

God is always there and will always love us no matter what. Only the freedom and joy that comes from following His plans and giving up control to Him is conditional on whether or not we truly trust Him and follow Him. How far I want to go with God is completely up to me. It isn't about dragging God along with me wherever I want to go. As if I'm a good Christian by simply letting Him be in my life. But it's actually giving Him my life and fully committing to where God wants me to go and what God wants me to do. It's living in the purpose that God has for my life. Another powerful quote from Steven Furtick's sermon that seemed to stop me in my tracks was "The problem is that most of us have shrunk our lives down to the size of our own personal interests." Basketball was my interest for so long, and I never allowed God's purpose for my life to trump that interest. It was time for me to finally let God lead.

After we spent a lot of time praying and seeking God's guidance, we felt that without a doubt that this new job was the next step God wanted us to take. He wanted my husband to switch jobs. It was going to be more time away from home and more stress, but he would have the potential for advancement and would be able to provide much easier for our family financially. But even with all that aside, it felt right. It felt like this was God's plan for us, and we were excited to be within His plan.

The next month went by, and this time I felt like God was pushing me to seek guidance from our preacher in the church. It was always a blessing to be a preacher's kid growing up, but honestly, having my dad as my leader was sometimes also hard. I didn't realize that it had been hard until I had the chance to seek guidance from something that I didn't feel like I had to protect emotionally.

I originally texted our preacher to see if I could ask him some questions. He was quick to reply with an enthusiastic yes. He made me feel comfortable enough to share with him in the next text that I had been hurt as a child and that I was hurt by several men for their profit. I then explained that I was frustrated that I couldn't get past the hurt, that images and memories were almost constantly on my mind. I explained that I still struggled with a strong feeling of guilt from all that I've done. I felt bad for not protecting others. I felt that I had betrayed my family. That I was an embarrassment. I didn't mention anything to him about the events in recent years. Honestly, at this point, part of my mind was working really hard to convince myself that it was all in my head, that maybe I was just crazy. No matter how hard I tried, I would always remember the truth when I looked down and saw where I was carved or where I was burned. I wish so badly that it had all been in my head, but the nightmare was real. I just wasn't ready to share that part with my new preacher yet.

I was still very hopeful that my days of being trafficked were over and that my number one battle was finding peace and joy and acceptance from God. After I gave a summary of my struggles to the preacher in a long text, he responded immediately that this was a subject we needed to discuss in person. We made plans to meet up the next evening when my husband was off work so he could be home with the kids during our meeting.

I was nervous and uncertain about what the preacher would think of me after he heard some of my past. But there was nothing judgmental in his voice. He was hurting for me. He hurt for my parents and their pain of finding out that I was hurt as a child. He hurt for my husband and kids. I begged him for guidance toward how to have the relationship with God that I should have. I wanted to have a checklist of things I should do to gain this relationship, but of course, that is not how things work.

In that meeting, we decided that he would reach out to a woman in our church who was just starting to mentor younger women. She had recently overcome cancer and felt like her calling from God was to be a heart and an ear to listen to young women in hard situations. In fact, it was the mother of the woman I had originally asked to be my mentor at the beginning of the summer. I was hesitant at first because I knew this woman only from what others had told me. And there was absolutely no relationship between us at that point, so I wasn't certain if this would work. I was afraid to let her know all of the truth for fear that it would be too much for her to handle. I felt a need to protect her emotionally from my story.

I was a few months away from having our fourth baby, and during those last months, I met with this woman often and was slowly telling her what I thought was enough for her to know. Each time we met, I felt stronger. I felt empowered and motivated to keep fighting and keep working on my relationship with God. She shared some of her life with me and allowed me to see what struggles she had in the past and how God worked out miracles along her journey. She taught me a lot about hope and how important hope is in our life. I would go home and write down anything that I remembered her saying, just so I could remind myself of it when the darkness would start to rise in me again. And the darkness always came back. I would go on spurts of feeling hope and faith, and then it would be replaced with fear and emptiness. I would try to explain to my new mentor about the darkness and the pain and the fears, but it was hard for her to understand when she only knew a small portion of my story.

On October 19, my husband and I went to the hospital to be induced. The baby had been doing lots of flips in my stomach, so once we finally got her head down, we weren't going to risk her flipping again, and we went ahead with an induction at thirty-nine weeks. By midnight I was in full-blown labor, and by morning I was ready to push. However, with it being my fourth baby, I didn't even have to push. She basically fell out on her own. The end of the delivery was scary, as her heart rate would drop to very scary levels, to where we wouldn't see any heartbeat at all at times. We were so thankful when she was finally here and to get word that she was healthy. Just like our other kiddos, she had the most adorable dimples and the sweetest eyes you could ever imagine.

I was thrilled to have my baby girl in my arms; however, there was also an instant fear. I was no longer pregnant, and in the past, that meant that my owner would be back knocking on my door, telling me to get back to making him money. I tried to keep the hope and faith that this time would be different and that surely no one would want a thirty-year-old woman who had four kids. But it had only been one month since I had the baby when I was confronted at a gas station by my old coach.

Still confused and still fighting the feelings that maybe he had changed, he showed me his phone. He had pulled up a porn site, and when he showed it to me, I was sick to see that there was a video of me there. He showed it to me quickly and then made it very clear that this video would be the end of me. It would take away my husband and my kids and basically everything that I was holding on to so tightly. I was speechless, and he walked off back to his car. I got back in my van and hung my head in horror.

My children were in the back, asking me a million questions. I couldn't process what they were asking at all because at this point I had a million questions of my own. One big question was that I thought my old coach had sold me to someone else, so why was he saying these things? Another question was how many people had seen this video and were there more? But one of my biggest questions was for God: *What is it that I'm supposed to do now?*

Jonah was furious. He lost his temper. He yelled
at God, "God! I knew it—when I was back
home, I knew this was going to happen."
—Jonah 4:1-2a

CHAPTER 17

My coach showing up at the gas station gave me that strong, very familiar feeling of worthlessness. The thoughts in my head were constant.

I will never get out.
I've done so many terrible things that I deserve this life, this torture, this pain.
If those videos get out, then everyone I love will know the dark things I've done.
I will lose everything.
I have no chance of ever being free.
I am still a piece of trash, and if I'm not careful, then everyone I love will find that out.

The dark cloud had come down on my life again, and instantly I went back to believing all of Satan's lies about my worth, all the lies that were told to me by so many men. Satan was not going to give up his hold on me so easily. He loved that I felt worthless and powerless and helpless.

I look back, and even though at the time it seemed fitting that it was my coach showing up to remind me that I was still owned, it seems odd now because, from my understanding, my coach was no longer my owner. So why was he the one concerned about what I did?

I could spend a lifetime trying to figure out why this ring of men did certain things or what their reason was for each move. But the fact is that it is evil, and you can't make sense of evil. Their dark world will never make sense to me, and for that I am grateful and I praise God.

At the moment, logic didn't cross my mind. I didn't think about the fact that in his threat of exposing me, he would be exposing himself too. I see now that if I would've looked him square in the eyes and said, "Go for it," then he would've been mortified. It would be throwing his plan back in his face. It is an obvious answer to me now, but back then, I was so filled with fear and mindful of the pain I had endured in the past if I didn't listen, so I succumbed to his threats. He had done a number on my confidence, on my mind, and on my feelings toward myself. Seeing him at that gas station, I only felt defeat and shame that were crippling.

I went to church the next Sunday and found that my heart was a little harder, a little frustrated at these Christians around me singing out about freedom, and about being a child of God, and having hope. My eyes were mostly on the people around me raising their hands in praise. I just knew that I was different. I had to be. That I was kidding myself by even pretending to be there and sing the same songs. My life was not valued like theirs. The hope they sang about was not possible for me. I had tried so hard to find the hope, to find the freedom that they were singing about, and I was no closer at this point than I was two years prior.

The frustration continued until it made my blood boil. They were singing about freedom, and they had no idea how many people around them weren't free. And at that moment, I could no longer sit in church. I felt like I was living in a joke.

I stood up and walked to the back, making some excuse or another. I just couldn't sit there anymore. I desperately wanted someone to understand, to care, to grab ahold of me, and to try hugging the hurt away.

This was such a discouraging time for me. I had started to feel God and believed that my time in sex slavery was over. I had begun to believe that my battle was not only in finding peace with my past and recovering from all that I've been through. But then I saw my coach at the gas station and I realized my time in the market was not over. I couldn't help but feel an even bigger sense of despair. I had gotten a taste of God, and then in a split second, it seemed like He was gone.

I felt like I was spinning my wheels trying to keep my head afloat. I felt alone. Lost. I felt that there was no hope for a normal life. That I had no hope in God. During this time, my soul began searching for someone who would maybe know the way to freedom and who could show me this path. I am not sure what led me to this woman at church except that she seemed to be kind. My mentor was still helping me, and we had grown really close. She also had a lot going on in her life and was keeping several family members at her house who were home from being missionaries. I needed more help. I needed someone to help get me free.

I never believed that I could go to my parents and share with them the truth. I never felt that talking to them was even a possibility, and I can't put my finger on the exact reason why. I know that my parents love me dearly, but I could not stomach the thought of explaining to them the trouble that I was in. I didn't believe that they would comprehend how I got to this point and why it was so hard for me to get out. I needed more than love at this point, I guess. I needed someone with fight, and I felt certain that my parents would be happy if I found someone to help me. Getting help was the most important thing. And I do believe that God knew that and that He led my spirit to a particular woman at our church.

I had remembered seeing her often at church and watching her with her family. Her kids and grandkids loved her dearly and they called her Granny, but she looks the furthest thing from a granny. She was a strong woman with a determination in her that I've not ever seen in anyone before. Her determination is matched with a faith and commitment to the Lord that was just as strong.

During an annual Christmas gathering at our church, she approached me. I'm not sure if she recognized the pain in my eyes or the emptiness. I'm not sure if she even knew that she was impacting me, but she came over to where I was standing and she began to talk to me. She asked questions and started to get to know me. I left church that night wondering if maybe she could help me. If she would see me as worth fighting for. That I was someone who could live in this world and not be in the sex trade.

Over the course of the next few weeks, I started reaching out to this woman. I just made small talk and simple comments and eased my way into a relationship with her. I was aware that my story and my life were complicated and I couldn't just insert myself anywhere. That many people would be scared to death to have anything to do with me and my story, and most people probably wouldn't even believe me. I started by asking her to pray for me and my battle with an eating disorder, and she seemed to gladly be in prayer for me in that. The next time I saw her at my son's rec basketball game, she enveloped me in a big hug, which showed me how much she cared and that she was going to pray for me like she said.

It's hard to explain how someone's life can change so dramatically when others simply love you. When they love you not because of who you are or what you can do for them, but when they love you because they want to. They don't want to change you. They want to love you right where you are.

At this point, I had fallen back into the routine of going and doing what I was told to do by these evil men. Men were showing up in odd places and sometimes even at my house to give me my orders. I was sneaking out again at night and was back to hiding all the pain that I was enduring. I was back to living in a hell on earth. I decided one day to finally send Granny a message to see what she would do if her daughter came to her and told her that someone had been sexually abusing her. Her answer was that she would grab her and hold her and cry with her. That she would be there for her and do what she could to make sure the person who was hurting her was brought to justice.

That was really all that was said by either of us, but she seemed to pick up on the fact that I was hurting because of some kind of abuse. In an effort to be there for me, she decided to see if I would be interested in meeting with her that next night to talk. I said yes. I was embarrassed to explain to my husband that yet another person was coming to try and help me talk through my past abuse. He seemed surprised when I told him that I was reaching out again. He was in the dark about most things, and so he was confused as to why I was needing so much help and affirmation from people. I was in a dark place, but my cry for help was a quiet plea for someone to care.

She came to my house, and we decided to hop in my car and just go for a drive. I was still fairly unfamiliar with our new town, so she had to direct me to good roads to drive on while we talked. She asked some questions, and I tried my best to answer them. I was very thankful for her, but I was also still very closed off and careful. During the drive, she prayed with me and encouraged me. I vividly remember her explaining to me that there is hope past this pain. That God is there and He loves me, and if I need her for anything, she would be there.

She had worked with young kids for most of her career, and she was able to pick up signs of a child being abused. She was able to use some of the experiences that she learned about at her job to help encourage me. One comment that she said was that oftentimes people abuse kids because it's about power. And quickly, without any hesitation, I responded, "Yeah, or it's about money."

Her jaw dropped open, and she loudly proclaimed, "*What?*"

I started to somewhat paint a picture to her about how I was used and abused by a teacher/coach as a child. I was still very careful about what I said, and there must've been something about my demeanor that brought concern to her. I had zero emotion about some of the things I was saying. I mentioned that I was raped as a young child by a coach and videotaped and such, but I explained everything in a factual way instead of an emotional way, and that was concerning to her. She could see that I was no more than a shell of a person. I'm not sure if she fully understood just how badly I was hurting, but without hesitation, she said she wanted to help me. And at that moment, she became my spiritual confidant I could trust and depend on for anything

Over the course of the next month, she would stop by my house often to check on me. Most of the time I was stuck on the couch, evidently with very little desire to live. I don't remember much about our conversations during this time. I'm not certain what things I shared with her, but I do remember her proclaiming that I have finally told the right person. Meaning that she was not going to leave me and that she was not going to let me waste away any more of my life. She wanted me to see that my life was planned by God, and this was not His plan for me. That His plan was to prosper me and not to harm me. And that even though I may not understand what has all happened, God does. And that my story is not too much for God. I had gotten to a point that when Granny was with me, I would cling to her and beg her not to leave me. The safety she seemed to bring with her and her love and support was something that I couldn't help but hold on to and never want to let go of.

She had a large family that she was always doing something with, and she also had her mother, who was recently moved to an assisted living facility because of a recent fall that had broken some bones. Granny also had a job, and she would babysit her grandkids, and she was very involved in our church. So her schedule was jam-packed, and even though I appreciated the time she spent with me, I never wanted to see her go.

Panic would set in when she would start to leave, and as if I was a young child, I would hold on to her and not let her go. Something in her gave me hope and gave me an understanding and a love that I needed, and when she left, I no longer felt safe. I didn't know when the next man would stop by my house and expect me to sell myself again. I had yet to tell Granny that the abuse from my childhood was still going on.

So I made mention at one point that my old coach was still expecting things of me, but I didn't explain very well how he was involved with me. I decided then that I needed to be strong and confront my coach. Granny was giving me glimpses of what I deserved, and a life in slavery was not it. I wanted to get things settled with my coach and make it clear that he needed to leave my life.

I'm certain that explaining this to others seems crazy and stupid. And I'm not sure I could disagree with that, but my abused mind and abused heart was searching through the dark to find any way out, and this seemed like the right thing to do. I lived in a constant state of fear and was often crippled by that fear and by the mind control that was used on me for so many years.

I am unable at this time to explain the events that happened when I confronted my coach. I know that I was hurt, but that three different memories mesh together, and my brain has struggled to separate each memory. I know that this may sound crazy to you because if I were reading this, my first thought would be that it's nuts, but abuse affects the mind in many ways. I am not crazy. I have been hurt, and through God, my brain has gone through a lot to protect me. There are still certain memories that my brain will not allow me to remember. I have proof that something happened, but the exact memories are still being protected in my mind.

Around this time, I started seeing a new counselor. It was a man who came highly recommended by so many of my friends. And he was the first one who could explain to me why my brain was not remembering certain events. He said my brain would dissociate. Basically, in an effort to protect me, my brain would go to autopilot mode. I was there, but not really. So according to my counselor, I may someday remember these forgotten events, but I also may never remember them. There are still moments when new things become revealed to me, and I'm able to put the puzzle pieces together. Even though dissociating is a sign of a strong mind, it is also very frustrating, especially when it comes time to explain to someone why I have bruises. Saying "I don't know" doesn't really fly with people.

Whatever happened with my coach that night, I ended up with bruises that were pretty bad. And when Granny saw them, she became very concerned. She believed that I needed to get some X-rays done, and she felt very strongly that I needed to tell my husband. But I was definitely not up for that. I used my typical response when people want me to tell my husband or my family: "I think it's over now. I really think they won't bother me again. I'm fine."

I felt like I had her somewhat convinced. And so when my husband came home from work that night, I showed him my bruises and said that I had fallen in the bathtub that morning. He believed me, so we went on with the night. We were in the process of making supper when all of a sudden I saw Granny and her husband walking toward our house. My heart stopped. I asked why they were here, and she said that this needed to stop and that my husband needed to know what had happened. That this couldn't continue. I spent a few seconds begging them not to do this. But they wouldn't listen, and they started to walk toward the kitchen where my husband was. I proceeded to grab the keys to our car and tried to get out the front door. But Granny and her husband stopped me. I continued to try and run, but they held on tight to me and wouldn't let me go.

They proceeded to inform my husband that I had been hurt and that I needed help. That we needed to contact the police. All of this was not what I wanted, and it scared me. I had been told from a young age how bad it would be for people to know the truth. And here it was happening. My thoughts were that I was going to jail. And that I was going to lose my husband and my kids. I was terrified and certain that all this was going to happen. And I didn't know how to stop it at this point. I tried to start saying that I made it all up, but they knew that wasn't true.

That night was a blur. I know that I fought them most of the night. That friends came to help. That we did make a police report, and after fighting them all night long, I finally signed the police report. In my mind, I was signing the fact that I was going to jail and losing everything. I believed that with all my heart. I was beyond defeated.

I couldn't see that this was God answering my prayer. That He was coming to my rescue and had sent people to care and to fight for me. All I could think about at this point was all the threats and fears instilled in me by the evil men. I could only think to run. Running was my instinct when things felt out of control. I would either dissociate or run, and on this particular night, I tried to run many times, only to be caught by people who cared immensely for me and my family. They weren't going to let me run. They weren't going to stand by and watch me get hurt. And they weren't going to allow me to be used by evil men for money or anything else ever again. They were declaring a stop to my life in trafficking and the start of my living in freedom.

I'm so glad we didn't know at that time just how hard of a road we had in front of us to guarantee and ensure that freedom. We believed that this would be all that was needed to bring me freedom. But we didn't know just how difficult it is to get free from trafficking. We didn't know that only 1 percent of trafficked victims find freedom. We didn't know that these evil men would not give up fighting to get me back for years to come.

After everyone left, we went to bed. My husband lay next to me in bed, and this was the first night that he slept lightly, making sure that I didn't try to make a run for it. My phone was taken away. And I was not left alone ever. I felt a strong fear that I was going to jail, and so in the middle of the night, I wanted to find my phone to see if I could get ahold of the police officer who did the report. I wanted to see if I could get the report back. But my husband woke up as soon as I got out of bed, and he stopped me. I once again felt hopeless.

I needed the tough love that these people were giving me, but it was beyond difficult to handle, especially with feeling so far from God. The fears that came along with being in the sex trade were terrifying, but the fears of all that had happened over the years and it being brought to the light and taken to the police were petrifying. I felt like once the police heard my story, I would be locked up for sure.

Granny and her daughter, who was a close friend of mine, drove me to the state police office, where I was meeting with a police officer to explain what had happened. I was taken back down a long hallway into a small room with no windows. The door was shut, and I sat down with two male police officers who wanted to know what had happened. They explained to me that they were here to help and not to harm me and that they were sorry I was in this position. They wanted me to feel as comfortable as possible talking to them. That they not only needed to hear my statements, but they also needed to videotape them in order to do their best job to remember all that I said. They said all the right things, but it didn't matter. I couldn't trust them. I was certain once they heard the truth, they would lock me up for sure. I also wasn't convinced that they wouldn't hurt me themselves, even though they promised me they wouldn't. On several occasions, I had met with police officers in similar rooms, only they were in hidden buildings or sheds, and they had video cameras and forced me to do terrible things. I was not certain these men were any different or that they weren't involved with the police officers that had hurt me in the past. So no matter what they said, I couldn't trust them.

I sat in a cold metal chair with my legs pulled up to my chest, and I waited for the moment when I would be handcuffed and taken away. I said very little in explaining things to them. How could I explain to them that I don't remember exactly what happened, that I have three or more memories colliding together and I'm confused about which one is which?

They began asking me questions about my childhood, and those memories were clearer to me than the recent stuff. So I answered them as best I could, feeling more confident in what had happened as a child. And that surely they wouldn't send me to jail for the childhood stuff. And then when it came to talking about what had just happened with my coach, I froze up. I told the officers very little, and finally they said if I just wanted to pursue justice on the childhood stuff, that was fine, and we can refrain from doing anything with the assault that had just happened.

I was thrilled with that idea and agreed. The officer took pictures of my bruises and then walked me down the hallway to where Granny and my friend were waiting. They asked the officer a few questions about how I did, and he assured them that I did a good job and that he would be in touch. We walked out the door and got in the car. By this point, it was probably close to five in the evening and the sun was setting.

I was sitting in the front seat, and they asked me a few questions about what I said. With joy, I explained that the best part was that the officer said I didn't have to anything about the recent assault, just the child stuff. I thought this was wonderful news, that it was an answered prayer. But apparently, I was wrong because Granny and her daughter became very concerned, to the point where they thought they were going to be sick. I didn't realize that without pursuing the adult stuff, the police wouldn't be able to protect me from these evil men currently. That I wouldn't be able to have a reason for a restraining order. That the police wouldn't be able to give me and my family the protection we needed.

After hearing that, my stomach started to feel sick too. We quickly got out of the car and went back into the police station and asked to see the police officer again.

Sitting in that room, trying to make sense of everything that had happened, it was so hard. I kept thinking about the camera in the room. The second guy in the room seemed very critical of me and only sat in the back and wrote on his notepad. I felt like I was on trial and that I was now for sure going to jail. I had a huge desire to run, to leave the whole situation and everyone who loves me. They would be better off without me anyway. I just needed to run. Even if I couldn't take care of myself and didn't have a place to stay or food to eat or anything, it would be okay because that's what I deserved anyway. I just needed to run.

This time with friends fighting for me was the first time I could say that I physically felt the Lord. Somebody who was willing to put their life on the line for me, willing to wrestle me away from the door, preventing me from jumping out of a moving vehicle, can only be described as the love of Christ showing through His people. My fears and concerns lay in the fact that I didn't feel good enough to get that kind of love, that kind of help. That these people would find out the truth about me and I would be left behind. I was just sure of it.

God knew that I was scared, that I felt the blame. And He knew that I needed a support team that would be His hands and feet in order to get me through this. Not a single bit of this was easy, and even though Granny encouraged me by saying that talking to the state police that day would be the hardest part of this journey and that it would start to get better from here, she was very much mistaken. Bless her heart, that's what we all hoped for, but it ended up not being the case. Not by a long shot. We had a long road of recovering and healing and redemption ahead of us. A long road of pain and hurt. Many more trips to police stations. But we also had some huge moments of joy and overcoming and victory ahead of us as well. A roller-coaster ride stood before us.

When I walked through the door of my home that night, my husband stood in the kitchen next to our dining room table that was full of gifts for me. He had felt the need to somehow show me that he supports me and that he is there for me through this. His way of doing that was by going to Wal-Mart and buying me all the dishes and bowls and pots and pans of the

Pioneer Woman line. He then grabbed me and held me and told me how proud he was of me for doing the hard thing. That he was honored to be my husband and was thankful that I was willing to do some difficult things in order to keep our family safe. I wanted so badly to believe him, but I still felt certain that I was going to jail. I was certain that these men would somehow make it look like it was my fault. That I was crazy or guilty. That I was a detriment to society and a terrible Christian. That I was the one hurting people and couldn't be trusted. I just knew that somehow it was all going to fall apart. So resting in my husband's arms that evening didn't feel comforting; it felt wrong. Hearing him say that he was proud of me felt immoral. He couldn't possibly be proud of me if he knew all that I've done.

This feeling actually felt worse than being alone because now I felt like a liar. I felt like I was pretending to be someone who deserved justice and love. But in my heart and head, I knew that it would all end soon. That everyone would leave. I knew better than to think that justice would be served on account of me. I knew the one who would be punished was me.

Trust in the Lord with all your heart, and lean
not on your own understanding; in all your ways
acknowledge Him, and He shall direct your paths.
—Proverbs 3:5–6

CHAPTER 18

Fight

Sometimes I see glimpses of light. And when I do, I drink it in as deeply as I can for fear that the shadows will quickly return. One sound, one smell, one thought has the power to bring back the shadows . . . to where I can't breathe, can't speak, can't cry. All I can do is hurt. I remember the light. I long for it. The warmth, the joy, the peace. Why can't I get to the light? Why won't the shadows leave? I hear crying. Is it me crying? Can't be. I don't have the ability to cry anymore. Maybe it's somebody else crying, someone I've hurt or someone I couldn't save.

It's getting harder to remember the light. Why would I deserve to see the light anyway? The light would just show who I really am. The shadows are getting darker and darker. My heart hurts from loneliness. No one could handle the darkness that lives around me and is now growing inside of me. I am alone and will remain alone. This is no place for someone of the light to come.

I can hardly keep my eyes open. The pain and the darkness and the heaviness in the air just make me want to sleep. Yeah, maybe I can just sleep, sleep and never wake up. But wait! I hear a voice. How can I hear a voice when I'm alone? I hear someone say, "Fight!"

Am I dreaming? Is this voice real? Is someone really telling me to fight? I don't have the strength to move—how am I supposed to fight? The shadows are swallowing me, and each breath is getting harder to take.

"Fight!"

Where is this voice coming from? Is there someone out there who can see me, someone who cares, someone who sees a reason for me to fight?

The shadows are lifting a little. What was black is now grey. Is it hope that's taking away the darkness? Is that the answer? Maybe it's hope plus love, love from whoever is on the other side of the darkness telling me to fight?

My breaths are coming easier. My heart doesn't feel the sharp pain of loneliness. Someone loves me. Someone wants me to fight. The light begins to shine through, but the darkness is holding on. It won't let me go. How do I get to the light and get the darkness to leave? I want so badly to get to the light, to find this person who cares for me, who loves me, who wants me to fight. But I'm scared too. What if that person sees who I really am and sees that I'm not worth fighting for? I can't handle going back in the darkness again. My heart can't feel that pain again of loneliness. But I also can't stay here with the light so close, but the darkness is keeping a tight grip. What am I missing?

"Fight!" I hear it again. The person is still there. I can't believe they are still there. They haven't given up on me yet. Maybe having hope and having love isn't enough. Maybe I also need faith, faith that this person wouldn't tell me to fight for no reason at all, faith that I am worth living in the light, faith that I can have joy and that I can have the freedom and that darkness does not have to reign over me anymore.

"Fight!" The voice is getting louder. The shadows are lifting. I believe. I believe in this voice. I believe in the Maker. I believe my life is not over but just beginning. What seemed impossible and not worth the fight just became possible as I now stand here breathing deeply, feeling whole, and loving every moment standing in the light. I will fight!

The fight for justice continued after the meeting with the police. The police told us to be very cautious and to keep our eyes peeled for any strange behavior. My husband quickly got a security system for our house, and between the time that we made the report and the time that the police made the case known to my coach, we stayed at a friend's house for security reasons. We were carefully watched over by close friends as we waited for the call from the police.

A song that became our anthem during this time, and what was played almost constantly on my phone and my husband's phone was "Psalm 23" by Shane and Shane.

> The Lord is my shepherd I shall not want
> In green pastures he makes me lie down
> He restores my soul and lead me on for His Name
> for his great name

Surely goodness surely mercy
right beside me all my days
and I will dwell in Your house forever
and bless Your Holy name

You prepare a table right before me
in the presence of my enemies
though the arrow flies and the terror of night
is at my door I'll trust you, Lord

surely goodness surely mercy
right beside me all my days
and I will play all in Your house forever
and bless Your Holy name

Even though I walk through the valley of the shadow of death
I will fear no evil
even though I walk through the valley
of the shadow of death
You are on my side
even though I walk through the valley
of the shadow of death
I will fear no evil
even though I walk through the valley
of the shadow of death
You are on my side

Surely goodness Surely mercy
right beside me all my days
and I will dwell in Your house forever
and bless Your Holy name

Well, maybe I should reword that. My husband introduced me to this song, and I grew attached to it and would soak in the words. I would put it on repeat and play it almost all day and all night to the point that my husband grew very tired of this song. Now when I hear this song, it takes me back to the frozen-with-fear feeling I had day in and day out and how much I was longing for the Lord to remove this tribulation we were going through. I did not see how any of this was going to work out. I saw nothing but jail time in my future because that was what was instilled in my mind from a young age. I could hardly put one foot in front of the other, let alone function.

After a couple of days of staying with friends, I was in the living room when my husband and Granny came rushing into the house. I could tell something was up by the look in their eyes. And they said, "They got them. It's over. They have been arrested."

Instantly my instincts popped up, and I took off running for the door. I didn't have time to think why I was running or what I was scared of, but I just started running. Before I could reach the door, I was tackled by my husband and Granny. And I crumbled to the floor in a mess of tears and fear. I didn't know what this meant. I kept picturing my coach in handcuffs and the anger in his eyes, knowing that he was made aware that I had turned him in. I could just imagine how angry he was at me and how I was going to have to make it up to him. I didn't know if he would forgive me for this. And I was terrified what this would mean as far as punishment for me

I can only imagine how confusing it must be to hear my concern for my coach and how he would respond to the police report. I agree that it is not the right way of thinking, but I think it goes to show just how twisted their mind control was and how much of a strong hold they had on me. It breaks my heart to think of how much I gave up in order to keep this man happy. And even in the moment when justice was being served, I could feel nothing but guilt and remorse for what I had done—guilt, remorse, and a huge amount of fear.

The report back from the police said that my coach and his brother were both taken into the police station by handcuffs and were questioned. My understanding is that the state police, the FBI, and the Secret Service went into both homes. The police took them both to the police station for questioning while the Secret Service and FBI raided their houses and pulled every electronic device they found to check for child porn.

We were advised by the state police to proceed to the courthouse and get a restraining order on both my coach and his brother. At this point, I was physically and emotionally a mess. The thought of going into the courthouse in front of a judge and explaining why I needed a restraining order seemed completely impossible. During this time, I had become very quiet and struggled putting my thoughts into words at all, even to those I completely trusted and loved. I just couldn't physically get the words to even come out, so the thought of explaining to a judge what had happened seemed overwhelming and awful.

We hopped in the car quickly and drove to the county courthouse. I walked in and understood what I needed to do. It was just having the ability to actually do it that I was struggling with. I had many people praying and trusting in God that I would be able to speak and would be issued the restraining order.

We had trouble at first trying to figure out where to go in the courthouse to get what we needed. I had friends help with explaining to the judge that I was very nervous and very scared and very traumatized. Thankfully, God softened the judge's heart enough to where I was able to sit in his judge's chambers to discuss my case there instead of in the large courtroom. Through tears and shaking and trembling, I was able to answer his questions and explain somewhat what had happened. He saw my bruises and my fear. He said that he would issue an emergency two-week restraining order on both my coach and his brother. We agreed and signed the papers and left the courthouse feeling like things were moving in the right direction.

We were advised to find an advocate that would help us in the court process. So after the courthouse, we headed to another agency in town that helped women have a voice after being hurt. During the drive there, we were told that both my coach and his brother were released from the police station because the police didn't have anything to charge them with on first sight. They needed to go through all of their electronics and such to look for any child pornography, but from talking to the men and searching their house, they did not find anything that would keep them behind bars for the moment.

This was a huge disappointment and letdown, finding out they were going home. Going through all of this with the police led me to hope that I wouldn't have to fear my coach or his brother anymore. But knowing they were walking free was very disheartening, very discouraging, and very scary.

Over the course of the next couple weeks, I continued to go to counseling and worked on finding peace in everyday living. I continued to talk to the police. I was also being approached by some men while I was at church who made it very clear I was not good enough to be there, that I was nothing but trash, and that the police were never going to take me seriously. These were men that I had seen at the shed where I had been sold on several occasions. They also had paid for me at times. They were a big part of our church and would often be serving communion or were a part of the security team. Seeing them at church and knowing their thoughts of me were strong reminders that I was a person of no worth.

It's unfortunately very common to find traffickers at church. Sometimes these men believe that their trafficking lifestyle is not wrong, and they feel no guilt in living that lifestyle while continuing to proclaim that they are a Christian. Sometimes these men use the cover of being a Christian to abuse others. Don't get me wrong—most people are in church for the right reasons, but there are a small percentage of those who aren't. That small percentage are the ones who abuse the "Christian" name and gain trust simply because they claim to be Christians.

I had a lot of frustration in knowing that these men who hurt me and had been a part of such a sinful act were attending my church. It was discouraging to be served the Lord's Supper by them mainly because I was supposed to be focusing on the sacrifice that Jesus gave for me, but instead, my mind was focused on my worth and place in this world.

During one of the last visits I had with the state police, they started asking questions about the night of the recent assault. They started asking some very specific questions, and I was trying really hard to remember, but the memories were colliding. I started getting really scared about them sending me to jail. I didn't know what to do. Their questions were things that I know now a traumatized victim would have obvious trouble recalling. But at the time, I felt like I was crazy and that they weren't going to believe me. They could tell that I had shut down, and I couldn't go on based on my comments and body language. They apologized and explained that they needed to have these questions answered, but they understood how difficult this was for me. They told me that they believed me, but they needed more information in order to make this a case that would win. They recommended that I get counseling and really work toward recovering from the trauma so that I could be of better help to the police, to help me find my voice. And we did just that. But because of my struggle to explain to the police, the state chief police officer decided they didn't need to speak with me anymore until proof came back from the evidence taken from the homes of my coach and his brother. I could tell by his decision that they probably thought I was crazy, which is what I was always told would happen if I went forward.

I continued working with my counselor. We were trying to recover my mind from so many traumatic events and memories. My mind was working slowly in the process, and it was hard not to get frustrated. I felt like a failure.

I have been told on numerous occasions that the recovery from sex trafficking is long and hard. That you have to be intentional about your recovery and healing every single day and that many don't ever recover. I was informed that there are people who can do nothing but sit in the corner of a room and suck their thumb because their mind can no longer function after the torture they endured. And even though there were moments when hiding in a corner sounds like all I can do, I refused to be that statistic. And even though I understood that the recovery is not easy and it will be a lifelong process, I will not allow myself to sit back and wait for my recovery to get to a certain point before I start doing something about the epidemic going on around us.

During this point, I was numb and following the direction of my husband, Granny, my mentor, and friends. They were pushing me through the deepest valley I had ever been in. Getting out of sex trafficking was even harder than staying in. And I know that sounds backward, but I had to face so many fears and stand up against my biggest demons. I had to say that I was worth more than what these men had done to me, and at that point, I did not think it was true. My support system knew it to be true, and so trusting them, I continued fighting as if I believed I did have worth.

I can only imagine the frustration and fears that my friends and family felt as well. They knew what things needed to be done in order to ensure my safety, but they were not only fighting the criminals and the evil of the world. They were also having to fight me. I could not see what they were seeing. I could not feel what they were feeling. My mind was stuck in fear and couldn't comprehend having faith at that point. Praise God these people didn't allow my reluctance and unwillingness to move forward to stop them from making sure I was doing the right thing. They very easily could've quit. They could've believed that since I seemed to not have any fight left in me that they didn't have a reason to fight either.

I had many counseling sessions and many talks with Granny, and I got to where I trusted her enough that she could tell me what I needed to do, and even though I often disagreed, I would still do it. I'm not saying I always did it with a jolly attitude and without a little kick in the butt, but

I did it. I still struggled believing that she really wasn't going to leave me, that she wouldn't decide that I was too much of a burden and give up or that I was too dirty for her to want to be around. I felt that way not because of how she treated me but because of past experiences with other people because of the mind control and emotional abuse that I had endured for so many years.

All of the people who have helped me were completely clueless when it came to fighting this kind of evil and how to help someone who had been traumatized so much. They didn't know the first thing about what modern-day slavery was or what it looked like or how to get someone out. But they prayed a lot. They looked for answers through God's Word. They kept their focus on always trying to do what Jesus would do, and because of that, as a group, we made a lot of good decisions. It was not easy for them to explain to me what I needed to do legally when I had no fight left in me. But they weren't willing to let me settle for feeling like I'm not worth the fight. Even when I didn't see a reason to fight, they wouldn't let me quit.

Isn't that a perfect example of what a church family should do for each other? When I couldn't stand on my own two feet, when my family was being hit with evil from all sides, our church bonded together and fought back. And in the process, I began to see that maybe I really was worth the fight. And maybe God's plan for me wasn't just to be another statistic.

Two weeks passed quickly, and before I knew it, it was time to head back to the courthouse to try and extend the restraining order on my coach and his brother. The first one was considered just an emergency restraining order. This time, it would be in place for two years, but my coach and his brother would have the option of being there and fighting it. We honestly believed that we would not be put in this position because we had thought at this point that they would both be locked up. But the case was moving slowly, and so we needed to go ahead and move forward with getting the restraining order extended.

My husband could not take off work that day, and so Granny and my minister and a few friends came along to be supportive. I was putting the kids down for a nap when everyone arrived at my house. One of my friends was going to stay and watch the kids while I was gone. No matter what people told me, I was certain that my coach would be at the courthouse. Nobody else believed that he would. That it wouldn't make sense for him to come. But I knew better. I knew he would be there, and because of the thought of facing him, I froze. My fight-or-flight instincts took over, and I ended up having to be dragged out of the house and into the car.

We drove to the county courthouse that was about fifteen to twenty minutes away, and the whole time, I was trying to figure out ways to run. I felt like I was being driven to a place to meet a man and to be hurt. It was too familiar to the times the men dragged me to a car and forced me to do something terrible. Even though I was sitting in a vehicle with people who loved me and were doing what was best for me, my brain was only able to connect a bad memory with that moment. And I was on high alert.

Granny and my friend that was with me in the car were nothing but supportive, reminding me that I needed to do this for the safety of my family and for myself, that I was stronger that I believed, that God would give me the strength and ability to do what I feel was impossible. And also, they reassured me that most likely, my coach would not even be there.

I soaked in their words as best I could. I wanted to believe them. I wanted to believe that I would be able to walk into that courtroom with confidence and strength that would give me the ability to fight for my family's safety. But my heart was racing, and my mind was going back to the last time I saw my coach's face and his anger and hate toward me. It was crippling. I tried to be hopeful that everyone was right and that he wouldn't be there.

We rounded the corner to the county courthouse, and we right away saw my coach's brother walking in. I yelled out, "He's here!"

And I immediately dove onto the floorboard of the car in fear. There was no way I could walk into that building knowing they were in there. I couldn't face them. A few friends went on in and were going to try to explain to the judge that I was here, but I was too scared to face the men who had hurt me. When my friends went into the courtroom, they saw not only my coach and his brother but also a whole army sitting next to them, mostly people from the large church that they attended. The whole side of the courtroom was filled with them.

My friends came out and explained that I needed to go in the courtroom but that, yes, my coach and his brother and their families were in there along with a lot of people from their church. Granny knew that I wouldn't be able to go in the courthouse. She knew that I was frozen in fear, and she promised me that she wouldn't make me go in and face them, understanding that it would be asking too much of me.

The time for our court date was quickly approaching and everyone felt defeated. In that moment, my friend who rode with me there became filled with the Holy Spirit. That's the only way I can describe what happened next. She flipped a switch and decided that we were not going to back down, that this was not going to end with me in the car lying frozen in fear, that this needed to be done, that if I didn't walk into that building and fight for myself and my family, it would look like I had made everything up, that my family would still be constantly fearful, and that I would have to go home to my husband and explain to him that I froze in the car and couldn't get the restraining order.

She got down in my face and told me to sit up and look at her. If you knew this girl, this was completely out of character for her. She has a soft spirit and quiet demeanor most of the time. She wouldn't make me do anything I didn't feel comfortable doing. That's just not her personality. So when she wanted me to sit up and look at her, I did.

"You are doing this!" she told me.

I looked at her and gave her a small glimpse of possibility, and she ran with it. Next thing I knew, we were walking the sidewalk toward the courthouse. At this point, I had my small army surrounding me, and we began walking in together. Along the way, my coach's face kept entering my mind, his anger, how mad he was going to be at me. I felt like once again I was being dragged into a building to be hurt. My mind kept jumping back to past experiences of being held and dragged into places where torture awaited me. In those moments of remembering back, it put the flight mode in me to want to run. I stopped walking but somehow, between both women on either side of me holding on to each arm, I continued moving toward the door. I literally had my heels dragging on the ground, trying to stop, and these women continued moving me forward. I'm not certain where this strength came from for them to do this, but it had to have been a God thing. When I was able to gather myself and see who I was with and remember that I would always be safe with them, I then understand my purpose of being there and begin walking again, but it usually only lasted a second before more memories came flooding back, and I would put the brakes on. I would be surprised if there weren't skid marks from my shoes on the sidewalk leading into the courthouse. I also can't imagine what the people in the courthouse thought of the sight of these two women dragging me inside. I remember Granny and my friend assuring people that everything was okay and that I was just a little nervous. But the sight had to have been something to see.

Naturally, the courtroom that we needed to be in was on the third floor, so not only did they have to drag me into the courthouse, but they also had to drag me up three flights of stairs. Once we reached the third floor, I was then taken into a small room just to the side of the courtroom.

Simply knowing he was in the courtroom and a matter of yards from me, I was terrified. Nothing but a wall separated us. I sat in a corner of that room curled up in a ball. I couldn't believe this was happening.

My small army of support were conversing, trying to figuring out how we were going to do this. One of my friends decided to go explain to the judge that I was there but that I was hiding in a room, scared to face these men. While he went to go explain that to the judge, Granny came over to where I was huddled and wrapped her arms around me. She held me and began to pray. She prayed for strength and for understanding and for peace. She prayed that justice would be served and that our family would become safe. She prayed for my spirit and my soul, my heart and my mind. She prayed and prayed, and by the time my friend came back, he had good news to share.

He gives power to the weak, and
strength to the powerless.

—Isaiah 40:29

CHAPTER 19

My friend came in after speaking to the judge, and his news made the next process possible for me. The judge agreed that I could meet with him in his judge's chambers again and that it would be a meeting with me and him and with my coach's attorney. We also had a lady there from an organization in my town that was acting as my advocate. She was a very nice lady and seemed to care very much about my well-being. However, she didn't provide the voice I needed in this situation.

I ended up agreeing to what is called an order of protection instead of a restraining order. I wasn't certain at the time what the difference was or that the difference was even a big deal. As soon as the meeting was over and the papers were signed, I was allowed to leave out the back door with my support system, and my coach was asked to wait ten minutes before he left the building. We, unfortunately, felt like this had been a battle we did not win.

I came to find out that the order of protection was basically just a piece of paper that said he shouldn't come near me, and if he does, then I would have the right to call the police, but it doesn't mean that he will get arrested for it. If we had gotten the restraining order, then it would've gone on his record that someone had a restraining order on him, and he would have been limited to what public places he was allowed to go. And if he came near me, then he would've automatically been arrested.

As we rushed out the back door of the courthouse to our car, I felt like I had just done one of the hardest things in my life, and it turned out that I wasn't any safer than when I first walked in. I got in the vehicle with Granny and my friend, and we were all quiet. Granny was in tears as we drove home, remembering that she had promised me that I would not have to go in the courthouse if my coach and his brother were there. She felt like she had lied to me, and even though my mind was struggling to process the events that had just happened, I knew better than to think she had lied. That wasn't the case at all. I knew that she didn't want me to have to go through what just took place, but she also understood the big picture. I needed to get that protection from the judge. And both she and my friend felt like I was strong enough to fight for that. I didn't have a way to speak at that point in the car, but I grabbed a hold of her hand and held it, hoping she would realize that it was my way of saying that I wasn't mad at her.

Going home, we felt defeated. We felt like we had done our part, but the legal system had let us down. We talked about how I must still be on alert and that I must still call the police if I see my coach or his brother. This was an obvious response for most people, but calling the police was hard for me. I had several memories of police officers hurting me at the shed or the camper or in a hotel room. Knowing that I wasn't sure which police officer would show up, a good one or a bad one, I couldn't take the risk to call them. I didn't trust them at all. I was told by a counselor that oftentimes, these rings will dress men up as police officers to make the girls scared of police and hesitant to ever call them. In my mind, I could see that making sense, but I still couldn't trust police officers. It still felt too real. Calling the police seemed like an obvious answer to my army, but it was not a possible answer for me.

There were many nights when I would hear engines revving up outside of my house, and in my mind, I knew it was these evil men, and they were mad. I even heard tapping on my window one night. I would tell my husband, and we would try to find the people but never could. We didn't know how to protect ourselves from this evil.

We started considering the possibility of moving. We didn't feel safe, and we had moved before to try and get away from these people. But the more we discussed it, we felt like it was time to stand up and fight, that we finally had an army of people willing to fight with us, and it felt like God was calling us to stay, calling us to learn to use our voice and to fight. Running away didn't seem to be the answer. Leaving our support system seemed unfathomable to me. I didn't want to run again.

Despite many of the steps forward that I had made over the course of the last few months, a big step backward came one morning. It hadn't been long since my husband had gone to work. My mind was on the kids and not on the fact that my front door was unlocked, and in walked two men, two men I knew, one of which was my owner. I was in the living room when the door opened, and they walked in. I immediately felt the mama-bear protection instinct kick in, and I knew that the first thing I had to do was make sure my kids were safe. In my mind, that meant getting the men to stay focused on me, and not on the kids. I had a three-year-old daughter at this point, and I was terrified that she would be hurt.

They walked in and shut the door behind them. And they were smiling, smiles that would make your skin crawl, smiles that were from the deepest parts of hell and as evil as evil can be. I walked toward the back door, keeping my eyes on them the whole time, almost walking completely backward so I knew they were following me. Had they at any moment showed interest in my kids, I would've killed them. I would've gone ape on them and destroyed them piece by piece. I feel certain about that. So as they followed me while I walked backward toward the back door that led to the garage, I felt relief. As they were following me, I knew that meant they were getting farther away from my kids.

In the garage, I was raped. I was tied up and brutally raped. I was reminded what little I was good for and that freedom was not an option. I was brutally punished for not obeying orders for so long. The darkness came over me like a blanket once more. When I thought these men couldn't steal anything else from me, they somehow found a way to take even more. Each time hope would start to return, they were quick to take it away.

My brain checked out. I was nothing but a shell again, and when I wasn't answering my phone, Granny rushed over, and she found me expressionless lying on my daughter's bed. I couldn't move and couldn't talk. Thoughts were not forming in my mind. I wasn't thinking about what I should do next or how I should handle this. There was just nothing. My brain had shut off.

Granny stayed with me and helped make sure my kids were okay while I lay there motionless on the bed. Finally, I was able to sit up and answer some of her questions. I nodded to the question she asked about if someone had come to the house. Before long, she figured out who had come to the house and what had happened. I remember seeing the look on her face. Worse than any pain these men could put me through was seeing the hurt in the face of someone you love. Seeing her hurt and her anger and her feeling of helplessness put me in a state of needing to fix that for her. Seeing her hurt was more than I could handle.

The abuse that had taken place for most of my life had lots of effects on my brain, but making sure that no one else ever got hurt was always a big part of my mindset. No matter what effects it had on me, I couldn't stand to see people hurt even if they were hurting for me and it was because they loved me. I couldn't handle it, and I would do whatever I could to "fix" that pain or hurt.

Seeing Granny in that state snapped me out of my fog, and I started assuring her that everything was okay. She insisted we tell my husband and call the police, and she wanted me to go to the hospital and get a rape kit done. And I firmly said no to all three. I wasn't telling my husband. No way, no how. I could not bear to share with him again that his wife had screwed up. I couldn't see the hurt in his eyes like I was seeing in Granny's eyes. I tried using my words to calm her down and assure her that I was okay and I'll be smarter next time, that it won't happen again.

She walked out to her car, shaking her head, tears in her eyes. She explained to me how serious this was, that I was raped and something needed to be done.

I looked at her and said, "Do you have any idea how many times I have been raped in my life?"

She just hung her head. Being raped is a big deal, but to me, it was not much different than what I had experienced thousands of times before. She tried to still explain to me that it was different now, that they were there to help fight with me, and that we need justice. But I couldn't stand firm that I didn't want to do anything.

"Why is the only time you show some fight when you are trying to protect these creeps and doing all you can not to turn them in?" she asked me through her tears.

I had no answer. I didn't know how to respond because what she said made sense. I could see her point. Why was I working so hard to make sure I didn't turn them in?

She left, and my head began to spin.

How do I fix this? How do I stop hurting people, and how do I fix the hurt that I had just caused?

My thoughts were no longer on the assault that had just happened and instead stayed focused on trying to get my life back to normal, trying to fix everything and appease everyone in that moment. I was instantly terrified that my army was going to leave.

I had to go to my parents' house for a dinner we had planned that evening. My husband was going to meet us there after work. I needed to leave, and I tried to get a hold of Granny on the phone, but she wasn't answering. She texted, "This is crazy, and you're not thinking straight."

She said that she was going to my parents' house, and she was going to tell my husband and my parent's everything.

As many red flags as you could imagine started popping up in my brain. *This can't happen!* I could not let Granny tell my parents and my husband. I had to get a hold of Granny and actually talk to her on the phone. I had to talk her out of this.

Finally, she answered her phone, and she was adamant about going to my parent's house. She told me again, "This is crazy! People don't just come into your house and rape you with your kids in the other room and get away with it! You don't get raped in the morning and go to dinner at your parents' house that night and act like everything is fine! It's not okay! I can't stand to watch it anymore!"

I couldn't explain to her my fears that were rushing my brain. I couldn't put into words the anxiety that was overtaking me. I couldn't find words for it because it all stemmed from years and years of abuse. Someone who had never through what I had gone through would right away tell their husband, their parents, and call the police. They would head right over to the hospital and have a rape kit done and cooperate as much as possible with the police. Reasoning with my mind at that time was impossible.

Granny listened to what few explanations I had to need to wait to tell my family. She promised me that if I didn't tell my husband, she would and that I needed to do it as soon as possible. I promised her that I would. We got quiet for several seconds, and Granny said in tears that she felt like she was going to throw up. I could easily relate because I felt the same way.

Nothing inside of me was angry at the two men that came to my house and assaulted me that morning. Nothing in me was angry at the men involved in this sex trafficking ring, including my coach, and how all of this started with him. My thoughts never went there. I didn't feel pain from what had happened that morning. I didn't physically feel the pain that was obviously inflicted upon me by the men. I didn't feel anything except a strong sense to make life return to normal as if nothing had happened.

A day had passed, and I continued to promise Granny that I would tell my husband but that I needed more time. I was thinking that I would tell him but that I would probably wait a few years until things settled down. It made sense in my head, but I could tell Granny wasn't buying it.

One Sunday evening, I went over to Granny's daughter's house, the one who had driven me to the courthouse earlier and was a good friend. I met there with my friend, my friend's husband who was a leader in our church and a local detective, and Granny.

I sat in their living room, and I was able to convince the girls of my concerns about telling my husband. They began to see some of my anxiety and why it was so hard to tell my husband, but they still didn't have peace about it. My friend's husband, however, would not budge on it.

"Your husband deserves to know," he explained. "If I found out that my wife had been raped in my house and she didn't tell me, I would be furious at her. This is something that you can't keep from your husband. It's not fair to him. And as his friend, I can't look him in the eye and know what I know and not tell him."

I was furious, livid. It felt like I once again didn't have a choice in the matter and I had no control. He was adamant on my husband knowing. I wished in that moment that my friend's husband had never been told. I knew deep down that he was the one making sense and I was not. But the feeling of it all being taken out of my control scared me. I didn't control my anger at this man very well even though he definitely did not deserve my anger. I still felt it, and so I left. I walked out of their house, and I started walking.

It was ten or eleven o'clock at night, and their house was next to a busy highway out in the country. It was close to freezing outside, and I had just decided to give up and start walking.

It still blows my mind that my brain was so against doing the right thing to the point that I was willing to walk away from everyone who was actually trying to help me. I started to get cold, and I needed an answer. I sat down, and in the most awkward way, I asked God for help, for Him to show me what to do. I had become desperate and needed God to intervene but not in the way everyone else was hoping for. I just needed God to help fix everything and not let the truth of all that happened come out. That's what I desperately wanted God to do.

I still can't put my finger on why I was so bullheaded about accepting help and allowing people to hurt for me and with me. I couldn't handle it at all, and that's when my brain would go through all sorts of ideas to keep my biggest fears from happening. It was as if I was hurt by these men, and then I would try to double up my hurt in hopes of keeping anyone else who loved me from hurting—if that even makes sense. Maybe it was me showing that I was deserving of the pain, but no one else was.

Whatever the reason, I wouldn't allow my Christian friends and family to bear the burden with me. And in a way, I pushed them and their help away even though it was what I had prayed for and wanted for so long. I would do anything to try and keep them from feeling the pain and the sorrow with me. And in a sense, I wouldn't allow God even to share the burden with me. I felt like I was the only one deserving of the pain. But isn't that where we often find ourselves when it comes to understanding what Christ did for us on the cross? So often, we hold on to our pains and struggles because we feel like it's what we deserve.

And Jesus Christ is saying, "No, I died for that pain to be taken away from you. I took that pain and that struggle and that sin, and I already paid the price for it when I died on the cross."

But we still hold on to it. We still can't let it go. Does it make us feel like a better person by carrying all the pain and blame on ourselves? Accepting the help or accepting the grace doesn't make sense in our minds because logically it isn't what we feel we deserve.

I didn't even want to give my husband the chance to share in this pain with me. I worked so hard to try and keep others from feeling the pain that I felt. And for what? What was I trying to prove? I want to say that this way of thinking is from the abuse all those years, but maybe it's just from my pride. Maybe it was simply allowing Satan to rule my thoughts and feed me lies. Maybe it's about not wanting to give up that control. Or maybe it's about my feelings of worth and that I didn't feel worthy enough for someone else to hurt on my behalf. Whatever the reason, it was wrong. But at that point, I didn't see the wrong in it.

I found myself a spot to sit on the ground, and I pulled out my phone. In desperation, I pleaded for God to help me, to get me out of this. And the thought came into my mind to call my preacher. To be honest, I thought I could use my preacher in my favor and that he would understand my feelings and make the others understand and respect those feelings.

I called him up. Mind you, it was pretty late at night, and the first thing I said was that I needed his help. I went on to explain the situation and how nobody was listening to me, that my voice once again didn't matter and that they were going to tell my husband even though I didn't want him knowing, that I promised to tell my husband when I was ready, and that it should be my choice as to when and how I tell him, whether people agreed with me or not.

Man, did I feel like I really explained my side of it well? My preacher started responding with how he understood. That it was very important for me to feel like my voice was being heard. He then asked if I would hand the phone over to Granny so he could talk to her.

I had to then explain that I had ran and that I was a ways from the house. You know, I never give preachers enough credit for their smarts, but in this moment, my preacher knew what he was doing. He said that I needed to go back into the house. And I responded with "okay." He promised me that he would explain to Granny why it's important for my voice to be heard, but the only way he would talk to her was if I took my phone to her. Only then would he talk her. He knew better than to hang up with me and expect me to walk back up to the house, so therefore, I had to walk into the house and give Granny the phone.

They talked, and Granny came back understanding a little better my side of it. I was given the green light to hold on to the information if that's what I felt was best, but my friend's husband made it clear that if I didn't tell my husband within the next few weeks, then he would tell him. I gave him a mean glare. Honestly, this man was doing a nice thing by caring enough about me and about my husband to make sure the right thing was done, but all I could see was betrayal.

The next week, I had a scheduled counseling appointment. I was all the time asking Granny to go with me to counseling sessions, and she usually had a lot going on that she couldn't. But on this particular day, she texted and asked what time my counseling appointment was. I told her, and then I asked if she would come with me. I really wanted her to come mainly because I was certain that my counselor would be on my side and that he would agree that it was my choice on whether or not to tell my husband. I just wanted Granny to hear him say those words. Otherwise, I didn't figure she would believe me.

I was excited when she said she would go with me. The drive there, we kept it mostly to small talk about the kids and such. When we got there, I noticed my counselor didn't seem surprised to see Granny there with me. In fact, their greeting almost seemed like they knew each other, and I was a bit taken aback by it. But I assured myself that I was just imagining things.

We went in his office, and I plopped down at my usual spot on his couch, and Granny sat down on the other end of the couch. My counselor had a seat in his chair, and he asked me the same question that he always asked me at the beginning of any session.

"So what would you like to focus on today?"

And as usual, I shrugged my shoulders and said that I didn't care, that whatever he wanted to talk about was fine with me. Always before, he would encourage me to explain my week or recent things that had happened, and we would work through them. He was very knowledgeable about trafficking and about the extreme trauma that I had endured. On this occasion though, he said he actually did have something he wanted to discuss.

He went on to explain that he had received a phone call from my preacher. Red flags went up in my mind right away. I looked at Granny and asked why the preacher would call my counselor. She just kept her eyes down at the ground and didn't answer. With recently confiding in my preacher, I made sure that he promised he would not tell anyone what we had talked about, and I trusted him in that, so when I heard that he had called my counselor, I felt betrayed.

My counselor went on to explain that my preacher called because he was concerned for my safety and that he had explained to my counselor all that had recently happened. My counselor went on to say that he had also talked to Granny on the phone and they had discussed the situation. I looked at her, and she had her head down still. I felt betrayed.

I jumped up from my seat and said I was done and walked out of his office and out of the building, and I was out in the parking lot trying to figure out my next move when my counselor came out. He kindly put his hand on my shoulder and assured me that he understood that I felt betrayed but said that these people loved and cared for me enough to do the right thing even though they knew it would make me mad, that I needed to see past the feeling of betrayal and see the love that they were doing this in.

I wanted to scream. I wanted to scream because I was frustrated that I knew he was right. I was upset, but I also saw how I had put them in such a terrible spot. I went back into his office, and even though I was understanding why Granny and my preacher had done behind my back to do this, I still was hurt and I felt like I couldn't trust them anymore. I could hardly even look at Granny.

She went on to talk and with tears flowing down her face. She explained that ever since the rape, she had not been able to sleep or eat. That tore up her insides because she knew that I desperately wanted to keep this from my husband because I didn't want to see him hurt. But she knew deep down that telling him was the right thing to do, that it was what God was telling her that needed to be done. And she couldn't go against God anymore. She physically and emotionally couldn't handle it anymore. She didn't know how else to get my attention, and she thought that I wouldn't have agreed to go with her to see my counselor if I had known that they had talked.

That session was unbelievably hard because we came up with a game plan on how my husband was going to find out what had happened and to basically fill him in on everything that I had kept from him over the past few years. My husband had been patient with me in knowing that there were a lot of details I wasn't ready to share with him yet. But he assured me that he wanted to know and that he wasn't going to look at me any differently. My husband could've been very upset that some people knew a lot more than him, but God put in him an understanding spirit that allowed him to show me grace in that area, that he was okay with going at my speed as we walked through the healing process.

We explained to my husband that he would be meeting with the preacher and with Granny at a certain time at the church and that they were going to go ahead and explain to him all that he didn't know. After that, my husband was going to drive to see my counselor to process things with him.

I was literally sick the morning that all of this was going to take place. In tears, I looked at my husband, and I was terrified that he wouldn't ever look at me the same again. I tearfully told him that I was scared that he wouldn't love me anymore after he found out the details. And he assured me that that could never happen. He said that he had a pretty good idea based on what he's heard in conversation about what they were going to tell him. We hugged, and he promised me that he wasn't leaving me. Not ever.

I went on to stay at Granny's house with one of her daughters while Granny and the preacher talked. Granny came back to her house and let the preacher and my husband talk for a while after Granny had shared all the information with him. She said that my husband was hurting for me, that he was in tears and was furious with the people who had hurt me, and that he wanted to fight with me. She assured me that it went really well, but I still doubted her words. I was certain that it would click with my husband at some point that he was married to a prostitute and he would want out.

I was embarrassed to even see my husband again. Recently he had gotten an app on my phone that tracked where I was and where he was, and by looking on that app, I could see that he was driving out to Granny's house to see me. This is not at all what I wanted. He was supposed to go talk to the counselor first and then see me. I was too embarrassed to face him. He walked in the front door, and I backed my way into the laundry room. He followed and shut the door behind him.

My head hung down, and I stared at the floor. My husband put his arms around me and told me to look at him in the eyes. I shook my head no with tears streaming down my face. I was too ashamed. This man was more than innocent and pure, and there I was a dirty, filthy mess. I couldn't raise my eyes to look at him. He then took his hands under my chin and raised my head until we were making eye contact.

He softly said, "I love you."

My head dropped down once again in shame. How could this man love me? With all that he just heard, how could he think I was worth loving? He shouldn't love me. He should be mad at me. He should hate me.

He went on talking, "I went into this meeting thinking the worst, and what they told me was even worse than that. But I'm not leaving you. I love you all the same, and I'm sorry that you have gone through this."

At this point, we were both sobbing. A tiny bit of anger filled me. Not at my husband, but at these men. That it was them who caused this pain on our family, that we deserved to have a normal life with stresses that included busy schedules and ornery kids. Not this. My husband didn't deserve this.

In a short time, in Granny's laundry room, we talked, and I was made to understand the importance of telling him everything and that he will never look at me differently. We came up with some new ideas as far as a game plan and keeping me safe. We hugged and cried, and then he headed on to meet with the counselor.

From what my counselor told me, when my husband walked into his office, he sat down on the couch and leaned forward and asked, "How do I make sure this never happens to my wife again?"

And that was one of the best feelings in the world. Not only knowing the love that my husband has for me and the grace he was giving me but also that he was ready to protect me and keep me safe. He wasn't going to spend time feeling bad for himself. He was going to fight to get his family back.

Be kind to one another, tenderhearted, forgiving
one another, even as God in Christ forgave you.
—Ephesians 4:32

CHAPTER 20

My journey since 2014 had been mostly extreme lows, adjusting to a life where my body was no longer my own. Or maybe I should say readjusting because as a child when my coach was around, my body wasn't my own either. I was now at a point of adjustment. My husband knew the truth. He knew everything about me and about what I had done and what I had gone through. I struggled looking him in the eye, knowing he knew the dirt on me. He knew the real me, not just the me that I had chosen to show him in seven years of marriage. The real me. I almost felt indebted to him because I knew that he didn't have to stay with me. He could've said he wanted out of our marriage for many reasons. So a piece of me felt like I owed him something for choosing to stay with me.

Adjusting to a life that was no longer in hiding was awkward and confusing. I had gotten to where I enjoyed my time with my husband prior to his new knowledge and being able to pretend like everything was okay. It was the normalcy of it that kept me going and made me feel like I hadn't lost everything that was good. I loved my time with him, and we were usually laughing and cracking jokes and being goofy.

Now that he knew the truth and he knew that I was hurting and broken, I didn't know how to act around him. When I would show him that I was struggling at that moment, then he would come in and want to hold me, and he would explain all the reasons why it would be okay. That sounds like a dream to some people, but to me, it made me want to scream. I didn't want to hear that everything was going to be okay, and I didn't want to hear all the ways that this nightmare we were in was going to be fixed. I needed him to simply hear me, to sit in the pain and struggle with me and just be there. And oftentimes I needed him not to change the way he acted around me. I still needed him to be goofy and fun.

Needless to say, we got into a rut. We both didn't know how to live this new life together. I felt like he was constantly trying to fix everything when most things weren't fixable. They just needed to be expressed and felt. And he also had a lot of fears around my safety, and in turn, he wanted to keep me locked up in the house all day long. I was trying to get stronger and to find my voice, so staying locked in my house all day with four kids was not going to work. I felt like a prisoner. My husband had cameras up around the house, which was really hard for me because I don't do well with being videotaped or knowing that someone is watching me.

On one occasion, I was over by the video camera in the living room picking up toys, and I bent over to put toys into a bin, and through the camera's speaker, my husband whistled a catcall at me. Apparently, he had been watching me, and he thought it would be funny to whistle at me when I bent over. I walked out of the room and went and cried in private. In a normal situation, that would've been fine, but not in our situation. Knowing he was watching me was hard because it was too similar to other traumatic experiences I had been in. It was difficult to find the balance with my husband. It wasn't fair to him because he deserved to do things like whistle at his wife, which made my guilt even worse.

We struggled finding the right amount of normalcy in our marriage, and the balance of understanding that our marriage wasn't normal at the moment. We'd been hit by the enemy, and things were going to look a bit differently for a while.

I still struggled sharing with my husband as things would come about. It had been instinct and was much easier discussing things with females, but this was hard for my husband to comprehend. He was my protector and my best friend, so to him, he felt like I should be telling him first and telling him the most. But this was not the case.

At this point, since I was still in survival mode, whoever I could feel comfortable talking with and however I was able to do that were all that mattered. I couldn't focus on the fact that my husband was getting his feelings hurt that I told him third about a memory instead of first. This was one of those moments where our marriage had to step outside of normal. Most women who go through the process of healing from trafficking aren't married. They don't have the responsibilities of marriage or the certain biblical rules that need to be obeyed. Many Christian friends would insist that my counselor and the person I should confide in the most should be my husband. But these are people who were only looking at it from an adult marital perspective. They didn't understand that so much of my mind was still stuck at a traumatized nine-year-old girl, that I could not feel comfortable sitting down with my husband explaining to him the details of the abuse I had endured. People may not understand or agree with me, but until you're in my shoes, then you can't judge. And over time, my husband and I have learned the boundaries to balance my struggles of the trafficking world and our marriage. We've learned that there were some things I needed to keep between me and my counselor and spiritual mentors, and some things I needed to come to him first with.

It's not been easy juggling the healing process and the normalcy of life, but we are finally starting to figure it out. And I praise God for that. We both had to learn to use our voice, more so that we could walk through this journey knowing exactly what the other person needed. It was definitely a process, and we accepted a lot of help and advice along the journey. And honestly we still do. We both have a spiritual mentor from our church that helps us grow in this process. And that's been such a gift from God.

Things had gotten quiet from the police for a while. We weren't hearing updates as much. I continued counseling and continued trying to trust people and make strong decisions. It's hard to explain the setbacks along the way. Like when the camper that I used to go to on Sunday afternoons or in the middle of the night pulled out in front of me while I was on my way to get my son from school. (We decided halfway through my oldest son's kindergarten year that he needed the social aspect of school, so we enrolled him into the local Christian school that was attached to the church we attended.) Without thinking, I instinctually followed the camper back out into the country. It was a setup, a trigger, and for about seven minutes, it worked. I had followed him. But then my kids in the back of the van started making a lot of noise, and it brought me out of the fog, and I was able to turn around and go to the school to get my son.

Then as I got home, the camper pulled up in front of my house and rolled down the window. The man driving started mentioning Kaitlyn to me, among other things that were meant to trigger me to go back.

I was able to get a license plate number of the camper so we could track the plate to who the owner was and figured out his name. We then gave the information to the police. I had always known faces of these men. Faces were easy to remember. Faces would often haunt my dreams. But I never knew names. But seeing the camper and the man's face brought my mind back to the past. I remembered that face driving carloads of girls. I remembered the girls he would be transferring would be expressionless. These men had meant this man and camper to be a trigger to get me back, but God used it to help us bring more information together. This man and his presence was meant for harm, but through his boldness of coming to my house, I was able to figure out his name and add it to the investigation.

With his mention of Kaitlyn, it made me really wonder if she was still alive. I felt a very strong desire to try and find her. I had remembered hearing something about Texas, and I didn't have logic in my thinking about the time, but I was going to drive down to Texas to find her. Never mind that it is a huge state, and it would be impossible to find her. I just believed that I would instinctively know where she was.

I began having nightmares that focused a lot on the other girls. I felt guilty for being out and them still being stuck in it. I wanted to find them and try to save them. A couple different times, Granny and I loaded up in her car to drive around and find this shed that I had talked about so much, the shed that had a shack nearby that kept these girls. But no matter how hard I tried, I couldn't remember where it was. After talking to my counselor, we figured out that when I would go to the shed, it was after a trigger, and I would be zoned out. It was as if I was on autopilot and would go straight to the shed. It was that dissociation that I had mentioned earlier as a result of years of trauma. So when I wasn't zoned out, my mind couldn't remember where to go.

After a few weeks of debating whether or not we should try looking for these girls some more, Granny and I came up with an idea. We weren't getting any help from the police, and we felt frustrated and stuck, so we decided to try and figure this out on our own. On a Sunday afternoon, Granny and I loaded up in my car. We decided we were going to find this place. These girls needed someone to care enough to search for them and find them and then to fight for them. Granny was going to lie down in the back seat of my car so that I would almost forget that she was there. And I was going to start driving. No matter how long it would take, I was going to drive, and our hope was that I would get triggered by simply seeing familiar places where I had been hurt in the past and end up going to the shed. Granny had rules for me, like don't drive down any country roads that are dead ends or anything where we couldn't get out. I said okay, knowing that if I did get triggered and zone out, then I wouldn't really have much control over where I go. But nonetheless I told her okay.

We had Granny's husband in the truck driving behind us. He was keeping track of us and had a gun or two in the truck in case we needed it. I don't think anyone was super thrilled about this idea, but we felt desperate to find anybody who was still stuck in this trafficking ring. We couldn't stomach the thought of these girls being hurt somewhere near us while we were not doing something about it.

So I began driving. I yelled back at Granny and said that I felt like I needed to drive back to the last town we had lived in and that I thought I would be triggered there. There were a lot of memories from that town that were very traumatic, so I was pretty certain that when I saw those places where I was hurt, my mind would go back.

As I drove, I was scared. I tried to forget about the fact that Granny was in the back of my van, and I tried to think back to the times when I was driving to the camper or the shed. I thought about Kaitlyn and the trucks' engines revving. I thought about the faces of all the men that had used my body like it belonged to them. Once my mind started going there, there was no going back. My mind kept racing until I felt the need to go to the shed and to meet the men.

My memory of that afternoon is choppy. I can remember some things, but then other things I don't. But Granny in the back seat of my car remembers perfectly what happened.

I had started driving toward the last town that I used to live in, but while driving, I all of sudden slammed on the breaks and did a 180. Granny was on her phone and was texting her husband who was driving behind us. She was lying down flat, so she didn't know for sure what I was doing. She said at one point she felt like we were going pretty fast and she really started getting nervous.

It wasn't but maybe ten minutes later I made a right turn and then I slowed down to turn into a driveway. Granny had told me not to drive down any side country roads that were dead ends and especially not driveways. But my mind wasn't thinking right. Once she realized that I had driven down a driveway, she scrambled up to the front of the car and started yelling at me to stop the car. I guess I was so zoned out that I was not responding to her in anyway and continued driving. She tried throwing water on my face and hitting my arms to get me to snap out of it. Somehow she got me to stop the car, and she reached forward and put the car in park.

We hadn't been in the driveway for more than thirty seconds when a car came around the driveway to meet us. Granny quickly shoved me over to the passenger seat, and she hopped in the front seat and quickly put the car in reverse and started backing out of the driveway.

As we drove off down the road, this car followed us, staying right behind us, and Granny's husband was behind them. I was still zoned out in the passenger seat, and Granny was trying to figure out a way to get this car behind her to stop following us and to not give away her identity to whoever the driver was. As we got on a four-lane highway, the car came around to get beside us, and quickly, she turned to a side street, and her husband driving behind us was able to keep the other car from turning after us.

This was definitely one of those moments when you realize that you're brilliant idea wasn't probably that brilliant after all. However, God kept us safe, and in the process, I was able to show Granny and her husband what driveway to take to get to the shed. And I was able to connect some things in my own brain. I was able to remember how to get their even after I came out of my zone. We looked up on Google Earth the location of where I drove them to, and in the winter, you could see amongst the trees a shed and a shack hidden deep within the trees just like I had described.

The rest of the day, though, I struggled zoning in and out. Something that happens to me after I zone out is I get extremely tired like it's almost impossible to wake me up. I'm a very light sleeper any other time, but when I'm recovering from zoning out, I am so exhausted that I can't even stand. It's an overwhelming and scary feeling.

I went back to Granny's house for a while that day and slept hard. She could hardly wake me up to leave her house hours later. She finally got me home, and I went straight to sleep in my bed, hardly even able to talk. It is the strangest feeling, as if you literally feel your body shutting down completely.

This little escapade is something we can look back on now and feel relieved that it turned out like it did. But we know that it was something we should've never done and will never do again. It came down to the fact that we wanted to save any girls that were left in that shed. We knew we had very little time to get this information to the police so they could get in there and save those girls before the girls were moved again. We started making phone calls and explained everything, but to our disappointment, the police could not do anything to this property to find out if there are in fact girls there. My word was not enough for them to go in there and search the property. This was beyond heartbreaking for me and for everyone else helping.

We ended up moving into a new house. It was in a nice neighborhood next to a park and near several families that we are close friends to. It brought us hope that maybe this could be a new start for us. I was hopeful that these men wouldn't know my new address and that I would be completely left alone. No more strange men showing up at any time. No more surprise visits or cars following me home. No more men walking past my house or around my yard. I was hopeful that everything would be better at our new home. Not ever feeling safe is very hard on the mind and body, so I was hopeful that in our new home, I would feel safe and protected just like anyone should feel in their own home.

My husband decided he wanted even more cameras at our new house, but I used my voice and expressed to him that I didn't want cameras on the inside of the house. I would love to have them outside, but not inside so I that I don't feel like a prisoner being watched at all times.

I did a whole lot better at packing this time around than I did the last time we moved. With this being our eighth move in eight years of marriage, you would think that I would have it down pat. Come moving day, we had a lot of helpers from our church, including volunteers from the church young group. We ordered a dozen pizzas and several liters of soda, and we headed over to the new empty house with excitement.

We had brought a few things over with us in our van on our first trip to the new house, when it was just my husband and me. It was a special moment walking in and having the feeling of being home and being safe. We both felt hopeful that this would be our long-term home, so it was a very exciting time, especially with how much we had moved in the past. After our nostalgic moment of walking around the bar, a quiet house just the two of us, we then started carrying in a few things from the van. During my second or third trip out to the van, a vehicle drove by that I knew. Instantly, my joy was gone. I was back to feeling hopeless and not safe. It was a vehicle of one of the men involved with my coach, and I knew at that moment that they already knew where I was moving to and that I didn't even get thirty minutes of feeling safe in our new house.

I still lacked much fight in me at all. Instead of being angry at these men for not leaving me alone, I felt sad. I felt defeated and overtaken. I felt put in my place. I continued to bring our things into the house from the van, but my light spirit was no longer there. It was back to survival mode, and that meant separating myself mentally just a little bit from all that was going on around me.

As more and more people started coming to help us move, I felt very blessed, but I also started to become overwhelmed. I am somebody who struggles when there is a lot of people around, and then I am unable to keep my eyes on everyone and everything. It is probably from needing to have that feeling of control and awareness of all that is taking place around me. I had become really good at constantly being on alert, but with people coming in and out and moving in all different ways, I started shutting down. I physically started shaking and could no longer help in the organizing and putting-away process. People would ask me questions like, "Where do you want me to put this?"

And I couldn't answer because I honestly didn't know. My mind was reacting as if I was in the middle of a tornado and needing to find safety when in reality, I was amongst my friends and family during a wonderful moment in our lives of buying a home.

The day was a blur of hustle and bustle, and many times, I would feel my eyes well with tears. How many times does a person have to be disappointed? I was serious in my talk with God at this point. How many times do I have to be let down and brought back to the reality that I am enslaved?

My hopes were up at feeling safe in my new home and having a fresh start, and that hope was taken away almost immediately. How many times will I have to know defeat? How many times will I have to feel hopeless before things start to change?

I made it through moving day, and once we had all of our things put away and in place, my heart started to ease some. I started to feel more relaxed in the comfort of our new home, but it still wasn't like I had hoped.

I knew I was still being watched, and I had simply come to accept that at this point.

Near this time, my husband and I decided to take the kids to a nearby city to let them play at different playgrounds and shop at the Lego store and eat at their favorite restaurant. We wanted it to be just a fun family day. During the drive there, I saw one of our Bibles in the car, so I picked it up, and I turned to my husband and said, "Give me a book, chapter, and verse, and I'll read it out loud."

Being the typical goofball that he is, he said, "Habakkuk, chapter 1, verse 3."

I rolled my eyes at him with an ornery smile and said, "Really? Habakkuk?"

He smiled back at me. "I was being a dork. Let me pick a different book."

And I told him that I would go ahead and look it up. I had no idea what was in Habakkuk, and my husband didn't either, but I was sure it had something good to say or else God wouldn't have put it in the Bible. So I went through in my head thinking about the order of the books of the Bible, *Joel, Amos, Obadiah, Jonah, Micah, Nahum, Habakkuk.*

Finally, I found Habakkuk chapter 1. My stomach was in knots at the thought of reading God's Word. I still really struggled with reading the Bible and praying. It was hard to physically do it, and I couldn't explain why. God just felt so far away. Once I found verse 3, I read it out loud for my husband to hear. It said, "Why do you made me look at injustice? Why do you tolerate wrong? Destruction and violence are before me. There is strife and conflict abounds."

My eyes got real big. My husband had jokingly picked a book of the Bible that doesn't get read that much, and somehow that scripture asked the exact question that I was wondering myself. My husband, of course, tried to act like he had known that it was going to be something profound and that's why he picked it, but he was full of it. It was a God thing.

I couldn't stop reading. That was the question that I had been wondering for so long, even to the point that there would be times I would want to ask God something similar to this, and I so badly wanted an answer that I would actually pull up Google on my phone and hope that typing in my question would get me God's answer. But this answer was not going to be found in Google. Trust me, I tried.

I told my husband that I wanted to read more, so I backed up and started from chapter 1, verse 2. Here is what I read:

Habakkuk's Complaint:

How long, O Lord, must I call for help, but you do not listen? Or cry out to you, "Violence!" but you do not save? Why do you make me look at injustice? Why do you tolerate wrong? Destruction and violence are before me; there is strife, and conflict abounds. Therefore the law is paralyzed, and justice never prevails. The wicked hem in the righteous, so that justice is perverted.

The Lord's Answer:

Look at the nations and watch—and be utterly amazed. For I am going to do something in your days that you would not believe, even if you were told. I am raising up the Babylonians, the ruthless and impetuous people, who sweet across the whole earth to seize dwelling places not their own. They are a feared and dreaded people; they are a law to themselves and promote their own honor. Their horses are swifter than leopards, fiercer than wolves at dusk.

Their hordes advance like a desert wind and gather prisoners like sand. They deride kings and scoff at rulers. They laugh at all fortified cities; they build earthen ramps and capture them. Then they sweep past like the wind and go on—guilty men whose own strength is their god.

At this point, I paused, and my husband explained that basically God is validating Habakkuk's complaint and concern and that these people that are hurting Habakkuk and his people are as bad if not worse than what Habakkuk had said. God didn't respond with, "Buck up. It's not really that bad." Or He didn't say, "Quit complaining." He validated that yes, it is bad and yes, it is injustice, and it is wrong. I went on reading more out loud.

Habakkuk's Second Complaint

O Lord, are you not from everlasting? My God, my Holy One, we will not die. O Lord, you have appointed them to execute judgement; O Rock, you have ordained them to punish. Your eyes are too pure to look on evil; you cannot tolerate wrong. Why then do you tolerate the treacherous? Why are you silent while the wicked swallow up those more righteous than themselves? You have made men like fish in the sea, like sea creatures that have no ruler. The wicked foe pulls all of them up with hooks, he catches them in his net, he gathers them up in his dragnet; and so he rejoices and is glad. Therefore he sacrifices to his net and burns incense to his dragnet, for by his next he lives luxury and enjoys the choicest food. Is he to keep on emptying his next, destroying nations without mercy?

I paused in my reading again, and we talked about the boldness of Habakkuk. He was wise in starting out in the beginning, saying how great and holy God is, but then he goes on to say that they feel like they don't have anyone watching out for them and that these wicked men are virtually feasting on them. And it feels like God is doing nothing. We were amazed at Habakkuk being about to say such things to God. I have always been taught reverence for God and to fear God, so my prayers to Him have never been in anger mainly because I was scared to tick God off. I would say the right things in my prayers, ironically knowing that God still knew my heart. I continued reading.

The Lord's answer:

Then the Lord replied: "Write down the revelation and make it plain on tablets so that a herald may run with it. For the revelation awaits an appointed time; it speaks of the end and will not prove false. Though it linger, wait for it; it will certainly come and will not delay. See, he is puffed up; his desires are not upright – but the righteous will live by his faith – indeed, wine betrays him; he is arrogant and never at rest. Because he is as greedy as the grave and like death is never satisfied, he gathers to himself all the nations and takes captive all the peoples."

God then changes His focus and starts talking to the Babylonians who have been hurting the innocent:

"Woe to him who piles up stolen goods and makes himself wealthy by extortion! How long must this go on? Will not your debtors suddenly rise? Will they not wake up and make you tremble? Then you will become their victim. Because you have plundered many nations, the peoples who are left will plunder you. For you have shed man's blood; you have destroyed lands and cities and everyone in them.

"Woe to him who builds his realm by unjust gain to set his next on high, to escape the clutches of ruin! You have plotted the ruin of many peoples, shaming your own house and forfeiting your life. The stones of the wall will cry out, and the beams of the woodwork will echo it.

"Woe to him who builds a city with bloodshed and establishes a town by crime! Has not the Lord Almighty determined that the people's labor is only fuel for the fire, that the nations exhaust themselves for nothing? For the earth will be filled with the knowledge of the glory of the Lord, as the waters cover the sea.

"Woe to him who gives drink to his neighbors, pouring it from the wineskin till they are drunk, so that he can gaze on their naked bodies. You will be filled with shame instead of glory. Now it is your turn! Drink and be exposed! The cup from the Lord's right hand is coming around to you, and disgrace will cover your glory. The violence you have done to Lebanon will overwhelm you, and your destruction of animals will terrify you. For you have shed man's blood; you have destroyed lands and cities and everyone in them."

God basically explained to Habakkuk that the wicked will get theirs. It is most definitely coming, and it will not be pretty. The book of Habakkuk then finishes with a beautiful prayer from Habakkuk, and I won't share all of it with you, just the last four verses. You will see that Habakkuk had then put his trust in God, and even when things looked bleak and like there was no possible way for justice to come to the wicked, God will prevail and show His sovereignty and strength.

"I will patiently for the day of calamity to come on the nation invading us. Though the fig tree does not bud and there are no grapes on the vine, though the olive crop fails and the fields produce no food, though there are no sheep in the pen and no cattle in the stalls, yet I will rejoice in the Lord, I will be joyful in God my Savior. The Sovereign Lord is my strength; he makes me like the feet of a deer, he enables me to go on the heights."

My husband and I had a chance to talk more about our time of trials and that we must trust God and trust God's timing through this. That truth will prevail, that God's glory and goodness will be shown. We must trust and be patient just as Habakkuk was.

As we drove, I would start to feel my heart becoming overwhelmed again with fear or anxiety or sadness, and then I would pick up the Bible and read Habakkuk again out loud. I read it at least four times that trip. I needed that comfort and reminder in knowing that God's got this.

I will wait patiently for the day of calamity
to come on the nation invading us.
—Habakkuk 3:16b

The Lord God is my strength, my bravery. He will
walk me through places of trouble and suffering.
—Habakkuk 3:19

CHAPTER 21

My husband gives me the hardest time about the fact that I struggle throwing certain things away, things that have become unusable or no longer have a purpose. So many times in our marriage, he would just laugh at me as he opens up drawers and finds old debit cards that I can't part with, or he looks in my shower and finds multiple empty shampoo bottles that I hang on to just in case I could have a use for them later.

I'll never forget the time when we got my oldest son a large life-sized Mickey Mouse balloon for his second birthday. He absolutely loved that Mickey Mouse balloon that was twice the size of him. He played with it for at least a week, even when the balloon was slowly losing air. My husband was ready to trash the balloon, but I was emotionally sad about this loss. I struggled with putting him (the balloon) in the trash. My husband encouraged me that it was time to say goodbye to the Mickey Mouse balloon, so he went out to put it in our large trash can by the road. At least that was what I thought. What my husband actually did will forever be in my memory. He took off the weight that held Mickey Mouse down and had kept him from flying to the ceiling for the past week. My husband went out in our driveway and let Mickey go up into the sky.

I saw what he was about to do, and I yelled, "Nooooo!"

But it was too late, and I stood in the driveway with tears in my eyes as I watched Mickey float off into the distance. My heart was broken over a silly balloon.

Deep down in my gut, I think I struggle with throwing things away because I don't want to label something as trash. This had been something I remember doing all the way back to when I was a little girl, and it wasn't until my husband noticed it that I realized there was something odd about it. And yet understanding the mental abuse that went along with my trauma makes my feelings toward "trash" not as odd as you would think, especially when I myself was labeled as trash.

As the investigation was continuing, the visits from the men were still ongoing. But it was different. It was still threats and abuse, but it was mixed with constant mind games even more than before. They felt the need to remind me exactly what I am, trash and that I was worthless and deserved a life of being abused, that no one will ever believe me and no one will ever care.

The frustration was rising in me and also in the army that was standing around me. It was getting harder and harder to keep me protected. My mind was being triggered by these men, and even though I wouldn't go to the shed, men would show up unexpectedly at my house anyway. Sometimes I would later be able to recall some of what happened, but oftentimes, I couldn't. I would just have bruises or burns or other marks on me. My army was trying to get me to fight, to quit getting triggered, and to quit zoning out to where I couldn't remember what happened. They wanted me to fight. It was poured into me daily, the importance of fighting back and the truth about the fact that I am not trash and I am worth fighting for. They reminded me that people believe me and people care.

I was so thankful for their confidence in me and believing me and trying to empower me. But there was always a part of me that still questioned, "What about my parents?"

My parents have been my best friends for my entire life. They have been the people I have admired and looked up to the most. I had worked so hard my whole life trying to be the perfect daughter. I honestly made very few mistakes in my life growing up, and a big part of that was because I didn't want to hurt my parents. I knew my actions affected them as much as it did me.

So in this stage of life as an adult, I was still longing for their confidence and support. I felt like I still needed to protect them from the true hurt of everything I had gone through. But I do think I would've had more confidence to fight if I knew my parents were fighting with me. If my parents were a part of the army that was pushing me toward freedom and justice, I truly believe that my feeling of worth and my readiness to fight would've been much stronger. I believe it would've become a natural thing within me. I gained strength from those around me who were fighting and encouraging me, but there is something about having those who know you best believing in you and fighting for you. It somehow gives you that extra lift you need.

I'm not sure I can say that I gave my parents a fair shot at being there for me. I had several moments during my life where I would test the waters of opening up with them. I would mention little things. As a preacher's family, it was easy to feel like we weren't allowed to have any problems, that we should have it all figured out and never struggle. My parents described it as living in a glass house where everyone knows your business. So we became good at closing off the personal stuff in our life. As a result, it became hard to open up about something like this, something that I didn't know for sure if it was my fault or what would happen to my coach if I told them. I never sat down with them and poured out everything that I had been through. I had never shared with them all of my feelings of pain and shame and fear. I didn't know how to do that with them. And it's not because they were or are bad parents. But something in me felt the need to protect them instead of wanting them to protect me. Something kept me from wanting to ruin our good image of a "have it all together" family. Something kept me from wanting them to know the truth about what I had been through. So to say that they didn't support me or didn't fight with me is a bit unfair. Maybe had they known the whole story from the start to finish, they would've been more involved. Maybe given the chance, they would've been my biggest supporters and would've been the ones taking me to see the FBI and the state police and to the court house. Maybe they would've been there to hold me when I cried or encouraged me when I felt like staying in bed.

I think this is where our culture needs to pay attention. We have certain expectations of victims. They may not cry out for help in a way that makes sense to you. They may not be able to communicate about the abuse like you would expect. There is usually a lot of fear in a victim. You can't think to yourself that if it happened to you, you would've handled it in a different way. You're thinking from a non-traumatized brain, so your way of seeing things is different and not how your brain would function had you been through extreme mental, emotional, and physical abuse. You also can't think that if the victim would've explained things better, then you would've believed them.

Being a victim is not a choice. It is not a life that someone chooses. A victim is in a humbling position anyway and is dealing with flashbacks, underserved guilt, physical pain, emotional pain, and spiritual pain. They have doubts, and they have lots of fears. They can't remember certain things, and they start to feel crazy. They know it happened. They can see it. They can feel it happening to them again over and over. Anything at all that is said from a victim should be taken seriously. Judgment, disappointment, and doubts of your own need to be put aside. You have but a small window to help a victim feel worthy of being helped.

Don't take it personally if a victim feels like they can't talk to you about the trauma they have endured. You don't know what threats have been said to them and what type of people have hurt them. Don't get frustrated at a victim for reaching out to someone other than you. It's not a knock against you. The important thing is making sure that the victim is getting help, that the victim is gaining self-worth and getting back their fight.

If you find out that someone you love has been a victim, don't try to make sense of what they are saying because it may not make sense to you. Believe every word they say to you, and spend your time finding them help, not dissecting their words to what makes sense and what doesn't. They are already concerned that people won't believe them, so if you start telling them what is true or real and what couldn't possibly be real, then they will no longer feel comfortable sharing with you. There is not a victim out there who can recall all the trauma they experienced in a perfect *A*-to-*Z* way like you would be able to do about the day you took your family to the zoo. A traumatized event just doesn't work that way. And memories mesh, and certain things get blocked out. All of your senses don't always work, so they may not even be able to tell you what the temperature was that day. That doesn't mean it didn't happen. It just means their brains are processing as best they can, given what they've been through. If you question them, then they will begin to question their memories and will lose confidence in the healing process. They will also know that they have to be very careful with what they share with you because you will be trying to put their words together like a puzzle. What they will be expressing to you will not be something that fits together in a sensible way. Remember, evil is not sensible. Don't assume that if it doesn't make sense to you at first, it isn't true.

When someone comes forward with an accusation that they have been ritualistically abused, you won't find that their story makes sense. According to agents and officers that were working with me on my case, if the story is perfectly in order from *A* to *Z* with no confusion, it is less likely to be true than someone who struggles getting their story out, someone who can't put all the pieces together, someone who has memories that mesh together, and therefore, explaining them in detail becomes impossible. Trauma affects people in many different ways. Everyone remembers things differently. Remain encouraging and loving and showing them that they are worth fighting for.

There have been several people that have helped me, and none of them said the right thing every time. None of them knew how to handle it, but the ones that helped the most were the ones who never doubted my words, never questioned my memories or my thoughts, who wouldn't let me doubt myself or settle with being okay with what happened to me. Their supportive presence was used by God to help get me out of the pit I was in.

I believe that a great lesson can be learned in the book of Job in the Bible where you see how his friends handled the hardship that he was going through. The three friends did some things that are important for us to do when helping a friend a need. They went to Job when they heard of his suffering. They also empathized with him and mourned with him. It says in Job 2:12, "They began to weep aloud, and they tore their robes and sprinkled dust on their heads."

These friends also spent time with him. Job 2:12 says that they were with him for seven days before they offered their advice. They sympathized with their friend without passing judgment or trying to fix things. They simply sat with him and shared in the pain and suffering so that he wasn't alone. It wasn't until after those seven days when the friends started offering advice that they started to mess up. They started trying to fix things. Simply being a shoulder for your friend to cry on or the lap for them to lay their head can be the best thing you can do for someone who is going through a difficult time. So many times, I was too weak to do anything but lay my head in Granny's lap and just soak in her understanding, her sympathy, and her love.

Job's friends hurt with him and for him, but when they started sharing with him advice, then they strayed from God's Word and God's truths, and they left Job feeling worse.

Allow the person who is hurt time to actually hurt. It's part of the healing process. Allow them to feel that pain, but don't let them feel it alone. Be God's hands and feet to love on them during that time. I didn't allow my parents that opportunity because right away, I could see them questioning what happened to me. Whether it was from them feeling guilty for not seeing it or because they didn't want it to be true, I was still hurt by their questioning responses. Our communication skills were not very good when it came to talking about this as a child and as an adult. Even though they deserve answers, I also deserve that unconditional understanding, and that was what I most desperately needed from them.

Sadly, my parents continue to be on the outside of my fight. I continue to see them often, but I don't let my brokenness show. They knew at that time that the case was on going because of the huge raid that took place at my coach's house and his brother's house. But that's really all they knew. It was heartbreaking to me, but I couldn't deal with sorting through everything with them at that time and risking the feeling of not being believed. I needed to fight, and I had an army around me ready and willing to fight as well.

I praise God for my story in so many areas, but what happened next was just another moment when God showed me His goodness and mercy and strength. It is something that happened that I can't explain without fear that people will once again think I'm making up or crazy, but writing my story and leaving this part out would be wrong. So in light of knowing that I may come off as a bit nutty, I'm still going to share with you all that happened next and what miracles God performed in my life.

I was feeling the pull toward God more each day. I desired to be with God more and more, and I was going in my faith and in my pursuit of God, but I still had something inside of me that drew me back to the darkness, something that attacked my spirit way too often and would mess with my mind. I had believed that my issues with drifting back to the darkness were faults within myself, that I was simply a weak Christian. But memories were starting to submerge that gave me a better understanding of why my spirit felt like there was a dark hold on it.

I will not share the images of these memories that have come to the surface of my brain from when I was little mainly because it is simple that images and explaining in words is very difficult. But I became very concerned that the devil was in me. The thought began to overwhelm and scare me. Maybe this is why I struggled so much praying and why I could hardly open my Bible to read. It was a physical issue as much as spiritual. I wondered if this was why I couldn't get over the hump of letting go of the darkness and living fully in the light.

On a Friday, the four kids and I had gone out to Granny's to swim in her in-ground pool with several of her family and friends. I was able to get some time alone with Granny enough to express my concern to her. "The devil is in me."

She gave me a look like I had cracked a joke, "The devil is most definitely not in you."

"He is. I know he is. I can feel him. He's in me, and I want him out."

"Do you think I would let someone come into my house and sit on my couch that had the devil inside of them? No way. The devil is not in you."

I tried to take all that she said to heart and make it stick. I never in my life had believed in the idea of the devil being in someone in today's day and age, especially someone who also felt the Holy Spirit inside of her. This was not a normal thought for me and not something that I had heard much about, but I still was certain that the devil was in me.

Sitting on Granny's couch that day, I wanted to share with her all the reasons why I was concerned about the devil being in me, but in that moment, I just wanted to believe her words.

The next few days, I continued to try and remind myself that the devil was not in me, that I was a Christian and the devil could not be in the same place as the Holy Spirit. But in my heart, the fear was overwhelming and terrifying. I couldn't just accept Granny's word for it. I needed to explain to her exactly why I was feeling this way. And so through text, I started messaging her to explain one of my darkest memories that I had not yet shared with her from my childhood. It was the memory that left me feeling like there was something inside of me that was not of God. I explained the best I could to her in a way that probably made very little sense, but Granny listened and understood why I had the fear I did. Not only did she understand, but she also shared in the fear with me, and we were discussing what we needed to do to find peace about this situation. It was a foreign experience to both of us. New territory for sure. Granny prayed for guidance.

Sunday, I went to church, and I continued to struggle. I felt like I didn't fit in with the Christians around me, that it had to be obvious to them that something was wrong with me. I was ashamed and embarrassed and overwhelmed with fear and anxiety.

My youngest daughter was being antsy in church, so my husband ended up staying out in the lobby with her, and he listened to the sermon from there. I stayed in church amazed at what was being said. We had a guest speaker on this particular Sunday. This was a rare occasion at our church, but what made this guest speaker even more extraordinary was that he was there to speak on spiritual warfare.

I had never studied spiritual warfare. I didn't know a thing about it. I have heard stories but always doubted they were true. This speaker told story after story about experiences that he had been through where people were delivered from demons or from strongholds. Each story I slouched further and further down in my chair. I couldn't believe what I was hearing, and before long, I began to zone out, to shut off, and quiet his words.

I wasn't the only one amazed at God's timing with this guest speaker. When the service was over, I was slow to move from my seat. I eventually caught up with Granny, and she hugged me and asked what I thought of the sermon. I just looked at her with big eyes. We both felt that this sermon was spoken at this time and place for a specific reason, and we knew exactly what that reason was. We couldn't wait any longer to pray over me and make sure that I had nothing but God in me.

I met up with my husband in the lobby. He hugged me and asked how I was feeling, but I had no words. Nothing could describe the fear and yet hope that were swirling around inside of me. We decided to get some of the spiritual warfare stakes that the speaker had brought with him. They are stakes meant to place on the four corners of your property surrounding your house. These stakes have scripture on them that declares Jesus is Lord and proclaims that our property is no place for Satan to reside. The stakes and the scriptures on their own do nothing. There is no power in the stake, but there is power in God and in His written Word. It wasn't about believing in these stakes, but it was about believing in the scripture and shouting to Satan that he has no place in our home or on our property, that he is not welcome or wanted. And it's knowing and believing that God will protect us with a hedge of angels all around our home.

I could see the emotion in my husband's eyes. We were beginning to realize even more that our battle was not just with flesh and blood, that we had an even bigger battle raging around us, and seeing the tears welling in my husband's eyes, I could see the exhaustion of us trying too hard to fight this battle on our own. But I could also see a hope and a peace in my husband. He had an air about him that showed me that he finally felt that everything was truly going to be okay. Had God not placed this speaker at our church at this time, these revelations would not have happened.

I was pretty quiet the rest of that day. My husband was ready to post the stakes around our house and pray over our house and declare victory over Satan right then and there. But I couldn't. I was still wrestling with it a lot. I had shared with my husband about the feeling that something demonic was inside of me, and in a way, I shared with him my feelings and my memories as to why. But on this Sunday night, we agreed together that I needed to be prayed over. And so Granny set up a time at her house for me to be prayed over. The plan was to have several Christian women, Granny's husband, and one other man there to pray over me. This man had been my husband's boss a few years prior that I had explained had been a big part of my husband's spiritual growth. And he had encountered many miraculous things during mission trips that he had been on. This man had been praying for us as soon as he heard of our situation. He had been a shoulder for my husband and a support to our family. I trusted having him there, but I was still very nervous. He was going to be the one who led the praying over me because he had done this before. He was more familiar with spiritual warfare than the rest of us were.

My mentor and her husband were also very familiar with it, but they were gone on a work trip. I texted her often for encouragement, and she shared with me that she would be on her knees in prayer the entire time the others were praying over me.

I had asked Granny to ask the man one thing before I was prayed over, and that was if he was going to have to touch me. I still struggled with men touching me even if it was for a good reason like praying for me. It brought me a lot of anxiety and body memory of times in the past of being touched. So I was okay with him praying over me, but I didn't want him touching me. Granny sent me back a message that was reassuring, but looking back, I see how she was purposefully vague in her response to me because this man knew what was about to happen better. I didn't have a clue.

We decided that the next night, Monday night, would be when we would get together to pray. Monday morning rolled around, and I was really struggling. My heart would not stop racing, and the pain in my gut that was usually there was intensified times ten. I couldn't get any relief. I felt out of control, and I was scared. This wasn't necessarily uncommon for me. I dealt with this on almost a daily basis, but this was definitely the worst I had ever felt it. The thought didn't even cross my mind that Satan was attacking me. I just knew I needed relief, that I couldn't breathe, and I couldn't take the pain anymore.

I tried bingeing and purging. It didn't work. Within thirty minutes, I tried bingeing and purging three times, but it didn't even touch what I was feeling. I wanted to cry out to God, but the words couldn't even come out. I then felt a strong feeling inside of me that I needed to cut, that I needed to cut right then and fast. My kids were all around playing and watching TV, and they had no idea of the battle that was raging within their mom. I grabbed a knife and went straight back to my bedroom and locked the door. Then I went in my bathroom and shut that door too. Without hesitation, I pushed the knife to my skin and started cutting. I have no idea why I chose the spot that I did to cut except I was thinking it would be a spot I could easily hide from others. I chose a spot on my lower abdomen not too far from my hip bone. I was pushing down and cutting, and it didn't take long for me to realize it wasn't working. I pushed down harder and I expected pain, but I didn't feel any pain. I assumed it was because I was numb emotionally, but I pushed and cut and pushed down and cut more. Yet there was still no blood. This continued for probably ten minutes before I felt the need to text Granny.

"Are you praying right now?" was all I texted her. I picked up the knife again, still in shock of the fact that this knife was not going through my skin. With how hard I was jabbing the knife into my gut, it should've cut the skin easily and deep, but it didn't. I had tiny surface scratches on my skin that barely even had blood on them. I was about to try again with the knife when I heard a response from Granny.

"Yes, why? What's up?" she asked.

My thoughts instantly started spinning, and I put the knife down on my bathroom counter. "Were you praying for me?"

She responded quickly with an explanation about how she had been doing her Bible study that was on complaining, and she was filling in some questions that the workbook was asking her. It didn't matter what the question was. On each question, she kept feeling the need to write my name down even though my name wouldn't make sense for the answer. Finally, she took this as a cue from God that she needed to pray for me in that moment, and so she did.

I was speechless. She asked me again why I asked her this, and once I was finally able to wrap my head somewhat around what had just happened, I texted her back. "I've had a terrible, rough morning and couldn't find relief in anything. I felt a strong urge to cut, and I went in my bathroom, and for the next ten minutes I cut, but no matter how hard I tried or how hard I pushed, the knife would not go in my skin. It wouldn't even draw blood. I tried and tried, and the knife would not cut me. So then I thought maybe it was a God thing, and I decided to see if maybe you were praying for me at that time, and you were."

She was in tears and was praising God. I was wanting to praise God but was struggling with the truth of a miracle happening like that. What made it even crazier was the fact that I looked up online the spot where I was cutting, and it was right by a major artery. Had the knife gone through my skin, I very easily could have hit that artery and bled to death in my bathroom. I in no way wanted to die. I was just looking for relief from the pain, and even though I hadn't cut in a long time, I had remembered the relief it would give me in the past. It was a terrible decision, but it was a bad decision that God saved me from. He saved my life that morning, and He was about to save my life again that night, but in a totally different way. God was definitely working.

That evening rolled around, and my neighbor who was a good friend was going to come pick me up, and we were going to ride together to Granny's house where we were all going to meet for everyone to pray over me. In preparation, everyone had been praying leading up to the evening. Granny had also written scripture on pieces of paper and covered her house with it.

My friend pulled up to my house, and she came inside to get me. I was somewhat excited at this point. I was excited to see how things were going to work out. God had already performed a miracle that morning, and I was excited to see if more was going to happen, if I was going to be free of this pain and this anxiety and fear. I was hopeful that I would feel like a totally new person.

My husband hugged me and said that he would be praying the whole time. He stayed at the house and watched the kids, and I left with my friend.

The rest of my recollection from that night is from what I had heard from others who were there because my memory at this point goes blank.

As we walked out to get into my friend's large twelve-passenger van, my friend was talking to me about her day and just carrying on conversation. At some point while she was talking, I had stopped walking and froze. She didn't realize this until she was almost to the van and she saw that I wasn't standing by her. She looked back and saw me frozen. She instantly got scared. She had seen me try to run before when things got overwhelming. She had seen me refuse to go places that I needed to go to in order to get help. When I go to that spot in my head, it's very difficult to get me to function like I should. Questions were running through her head about how she was going to get me into her van. She smiled and tried to reassure me that we were just going to pray and that God was going to be with me the whole time.

I still didn't move. She tried to pull me, and I stood firm in that spot. Then she said some powerful statements to me that must have grabbed my attention enough to get me into the van. "Your kids deserve a mom who is free, completely free, free from slavery and from strongholds. And this prayer time is going to be about getting you back to being the mom they deserve."

I slowly walked to her van. She had a strong grip on my arm as we walked, and I would sometimes start to pull back, and she would reassure me and remind me that I was doing this for my kids.

We got in her van and I couldn't talk. She talked and prayed, but I was silent and had a look of horror on my face. We finally turned to drive down Granny's driveway. It was about dusk, and cars were all lined up and down her driveway. I instantly freaked and got up out of my seat in the front and quickly ran toward the back of her twelve-passenger van and squeezed myself into a small space. I'm not sure if I was scared or if I was hiding or if I didn't want to face what was going on inside of Granny's house.

Granny came out to get me, and she didn't see me in the front seat like she expected to. My friend explained that I had freaked out and that I was in the back on the floor hiding. Granny cracked some jokes about how big the van was and about how stuck I got myself in between the seats. She tried for a while to get me to listen to her and to move, but it didn't work. She realized that I wasn't going to budge. I wasn't leaving that van, and I wasn't going into that house. Something inside of me was screaming to run.

For the weapons of our warfare are not physical weapons
of flesh and blood, but they are mighty before God
for the overflow and destruction of strongholds . . .
and we lead every thought and purpose away captive
into the obedience of Christ, the Messiah.
—1 Corinthians 10:4–5

CHAPTER 22

I have no idea how they got me out of that van. I was sandwiched in between the smallest spot I could fit into. Granny and others came into the van to force me out. I'm not sure how long it took or how they did it, but they got me out of the van and began encouraging me and talking to me to get me to walk into the house. I continued to fight them. I pushed. I shoved. I did all I could to run. My head was on a swivel, looking all around me in fear. I did all I could not to go into that house.

Granny continued to encourage me and remind me to look around and see where I was. She knew that her house was my safe haven, but this evening was different. On this particular evening, I was unable to walk through her door. A crowd around me pulled me into the house and almost immediately, the man I spoke of earlier who had prayed for people like me started praying. He started rebuking anything that was not of God. He started reading scripture after scripture after scripture of how anything that was not of God was not welcome there.

I continued to fight. I ended up on the floor, trying to crawl away. I would sometimes stop fighting, but there was nothing in my eyes. Nothing at all. I would grab a hold of Granny and not want to let her go. And then certain scriptures were read, and my fight would come back. I would struggle again to get away. There were too many people there that I couldn't get them off of me, but the strength I was exhibiting was superhuman. This man wanted me to say Jesus's name. Over and over, he asked me to say the name of Jesus, and I couldn't do it.

The hardest part of the story for me was hearing that Granny was in tears begging me to act like the Rachel she had been helping for so many months. "Rachel, please. Please, Rachel, look at me. Look at where you are. You're safe. Please, Rachel, it's okay. You don't have to fight."

She so desperately wanted me to be free from the evil that was within me and the evil that had hurt me so badly for so many years. The man that was there had interrupted her and said, "This isn't Rachel."

Through her tears Granny responded, "I know. I just want her back so badly."

I know that these things I'm sharing with you is not something that Christians in the United States are used to hearing about. And honestly, I wouldn't believe it either had I not experienced it. The battle that night was scary. It was a group of God-fearing and God-loving Christians who were praying scripture over a young lady who had been traumatized so badly that Satan still had a hold of her. Most of the people there had never been a part of something like this. But they had faith. They saw a need, and they knew that the only way to fix it was to cry out to God, to fight the wrong with the right. And that's what they did. This was new territory for them, and yet the prayers and the scriptures were the common battle cries that they have used in many other situations in their life. God was there. And God was going to win.

Over and over, minute after minute, scripture and prayer, scripture and prayer, finally, after forty to forty-five minutes, this man grabbed a hold of my head. He held both sides of my head to where I couldn't move, and he got down in my face. This time when he prayed, it wasn't in English. He was speaking in tongues, a language that apparently the demon within me understood and responded to. My fight seemed to stop some, and this man continued praying in tongues. It went on for several minutes, and then slowly, I made eye contact with this man. He then asked me for the millionth time that night to say the name of Jesus. It was quiet in the house when I slowly moved my mouth and quietly said the name of Jesus.

Applause and tears filled the house. He continued to hold on to me. He started to tell me where I was and who was there. He told me that I was safe and that I was okay. He then asked me again to say "Jesus," and I did. He asked me to do it again and again, and I did. I lay there on my back, trying to gather myself and take in what was going on. I was eventually able to sit up. My hair was all over the place from rolling around on the floor trying to get away, and my clothes were soaked with sweat. I looked at this man, and he was sweating too.

I think everyone was anxious to see what was going to happen next. Everyone was very overwhelmed and taken aback by what they had just witnessed and been a part of. It seemed that all eyes were on me, and they asked me how I was feeling.

"Tired," I said quietly. But it was a different tired. It was no longer a zoned-out kind of tired. It wasn't this empty look of being worn out. I had a completely different look to my eyes and to my face. I was alive again. I had nothing but Jesus living within me. And there was an obvious difference right away to those who were there.

The man who led this then gathered us around, and he read more scripture to us. He read scripture to me about what just happened. He read scripture that focused on those around me to encourage them on how to be there for me as I walked forward from here.

At one point, one of the women there said something about me cutting earlier in the day. And I was confused. I had no idea what she was talking about. She stopped and just said, "Well, that obviously wasn't Rachel that did that then."

There was so much hope and so much relief in the room. We gathered around in the living room and started having a lighter conversation while that man went to my house to talk to my husband to explain all that had happened. I sat in Granny's living room somewhat quiet. I didn't quite understand what I was feeling. I felt lighter. I felt hopeful. I felt completely different. In my mind, I would keep saying "Jesus" over and over. I couldn't get enough of proclaiming His name. But while I was sitting there, I realized something. Yes, I felt new and restored, but something was missing. I couldn't remember things. I couldn't remember who I was, like, I knew my name and such. But so much I didn't know. My mind felt empty. And even though this was a very positive thing in some aspects, it was also very scary and overwhelming.

As the conversation started to die down, these women decided that they were going to take all the scripture that was around Granny's house and go and post it around my house and then pray over my house. I was so extremely grateful for these women. But part of me too was struggling to remember what my house even looked like in my head. People would keep asking me how I was doing, and I would say to them that I was good. And I really was good, but I was also very scared.

We loaded up, and Granny rode with me. I held on to her and I started to cry. She asked me what was wrong, and I said, "I can't remember anything. I don't know who I am."

"What do you mean?" she asked.

"I don't know who I am. What things do I like? What things do I do?"

She responded with lots of positive comments about how I get to decide all those things for myself, that I get to choose who I want to be and figure out what I like, that I could look at it as an adventure. And that did excite me some, but I was also overwhelmed. I didn't want to go home. I didn't want to see my husband. I was struggling remembering much about our relationship and where we stood on things. I just had so many blank spots in my head, and I was so confused.

Granny continued encouraging me and answering questions I had. I was so nervous when we pulled up to my house. I was glad that I recognized my house when I saw it and that things seemed to be making more sense as far as home was concerned, but I was still nervous about seeing my husband.

We walked up the back deck of the house, and he came out to meet me. It was a beautiful night. Stars were out, and the temperature was perfect, so we sat out on our patio furniture. He held me and he just cried. I felt at home with him, but I was also embarrassed. He assured me that everything was going to be okay and that he was proud of me. We both prayed together out on the back deck. We hadn't really had a heartfelt prayer like that together in a long time, and it filled me with even more power and strength and peace.

We went inside, and all the women had gone around and taped scriptures around the house. Every wall had at least three or four scriptures on it. Our bedroom was filled with them. We circled up and prayed together again, and then everyone said goodbye. My husband and I went on our couch, and he just held me. I tried my best to recall for him what had happened, but I couldn't. He then told me what the man had said. He told me about the superhuman strength I had and the fight I put up. I shared then with my husband that I was really struggling with remembering things and I didn't know what to do. He held me and said that it was God's way of protecting me again.

The next day, my husband and I went around our property and prayed at all four corners of the house as we hammered in each of those stakes.

We also prayed within our house. Satan was not welcome anywhere near our family. We were definite believers in the power of prayer and in the craftiness of Satan. We weren't going to go through that again.

I was still feeling the peacefulness of a full heart and an eeriness of an empty mind. I began to recall a lot of the basic stuff, but there was still so much missing. That same day, the guy who had prayed over me at Granny's house was still physically, emotionally, and spiritually exhausted from the battle the day before. Over the course of the next few days, his health started to go downhill. He was feeling really sick with a fever, fatigue, and pain. He decided to go to the doctor. When he got there, he told the doctor that he was pretty certain he knew what was wrong, but he needed the doctor to confirm it. The doctor ran tests, and everything came back good. He wasn't sick. This man told the doctor that was exactly what he needed confirmation on. This man knew that Satan was attacking him because of what had happened with me. This man went home, and he called one of his good friends from India who had been through a lot of these spiritual warfare battles too, and his friend explained that he was exhausted, that the battle took everything from him to pray over me to free me from that demon. His friend recommended that he get a lot of sleep to build back his strength. That is exactly what this man did. He slept and slept, and when he woke up, he felt completely better. Satan was still at work and was not going to give up easily. We knew that the battle was definitely not over.

Everyone around me could see a significant difference in my eyes. I was a different person. We were so excited about the future, and we were certain that things would finally be better. Over the next few weeks, my memories came back to me. I was able to discuss things easier with my counselor. I didn't struggle getting words out like I had before. He could tell a huge difference in me the very next visit that we had, and I was excited to share with him the good news. He started to tear up in excitement about it, and he shared with me that he hadn't been able to sleep since I started meeting with him. He was worried sick about me and would stay up all night praying. This counselor really truly cared about me and my safety and my recovery. I couldn't believe that he cared so much.

My small army was filled with the belief that I would not be hurt again. We prayed for a hedge of angels to guard me and my house and my family, and we believed fully that no more abuse would occur. It is hard to explain the hurt that followed when I was hurt again. And not just once. We felt defeated. We felt hopeless. Why wasn't God protecting me? We grew deeper in prayer and continued asking more and more questions. We were sharing everything we could with the police, but because I still would zone out and not remember much, I wasn't able to explain to the police what happened.

One time, I was able to keep from zoning out, and we declared it a victory. A man was in my yard approaching me, and I actually went after him and started punching him. After just a few punches, he was up and running. He didn't say a word to me. The more I thought about it, the more I realized that I didn't even know if this was a good guy or a bad guy. I didn't know if I just punched the lights out of a random guy who was passing through my yard.

From that fight, I ended up with a terribly busted-up hand. It was no doubt broken. It was deformed and swollen like you would not believe. I went to the doctor the next day, but because of all the swelling, they weren't able to get a good X-ray, so I was supposed to keep it in a brace and ice and then go back in a week.

During that week, the man who had originally prayed over me at Granny's house sent us a message and asked if he could come over one evening when the kids were already in bed. We agreed, and he came on over that night. You could see the nerves and excitement swirling around inside of him. He explained to us that God wanted to stretch his faith. He felt God calling him to do something outside of his comfort zone, something that he had never done before or even thought to do before.

He had been a part of many prayers that prayed against demons or strongholds, and he had become confident and comfortable in God working through him that way. But God put it on his heart to pray for healing over my hand. He felt God saying to him that Rachel needs to see the power of God. This man was very unsure of this and very nervous. He was obviously not comfortable at all with the thought of praying for healing. He had reached out to his mentors from all around the world and was able to get advice and guidance from them, and he then asked me if it was okay for him to pray over my hand until we saw healing.

In my mind, I had doubts. I kept thinking that this was something that they did in biblical times, not now. And I knew my faith wasn't strong enough to allow God to work. But I remembered what God had done for me at Granny's house, and I wanted to believe. I wanted to see God work, so in my mind, I started repeating to myself over and over again, *I believe. I believe.*

I felt like I was in the movie *Polar Express*, and I was the little boy shaking Santa's sleigh bell trying to hear the magic sound. I wanted to believe that God would heal me like this. This man held my hurt hand, and he began to lightly run his hand over mind while he prayed. My husband and I closed our eyes in prayer with him. And we all had belief that when we opened our eyes, we would see my hand healed.

This man prayed for probably fifteen minutes and when he said "amen," we opened our eyes and looked down at my hand, and we didn't see a difference at all. I tried to move my hand, and it hurt really bad still. The swelling was still huge, and I could hardly move it. This man reminded us that we must not quit, that God was working. We couldn't lose faith. He prayed some more and some more. My husband prayed some too.

And after an hour, we began to see the swelling going down immensely. You could start to see the knuckles on my hand whereas before you couldn't at all. And my range of motion was improving too. We went from prayer to praising God, and when we did, he then continued to pray for more healing. He prayed for every tendon that was torn, for every ligament that was torn, for every bone that was broken, and every nerve that was damaged to be healed. He prayed for each finger and each knuckle. And after another hour, my hand almost looked the same as my healthy hand. I had a tiny bit of swelling left and a little bit of pain but not bad.

While he was praying, I kept thinking that I needed to do something to fix my hand so that his prayers were answered. I was afraid that the lack of healing would be proof that I didn't have enough faith. But the fixing wasn't up to me. It had nothing to do with me. I couldn't fix my hand that day. And this man or my husband couldn't fix it either. Only God could, and I believed God was very pleased that we asked for his help. I have been a part of prayers where you pray for healing and then you go about your day or your week or your month, hoping that the prayer will be answered the way you want it to. This was new territory for me, and it was an incredible experience. I saw God's power work right before my eyes.

Later in the week, I returned to the doctor to do an X-ray. The doctors were shocked that my bones all looked great. Not a hairline fracture, nothing at all. They had several doctors look over the X-rays to make sure because they couldn't believe based on how my hand looked the week before that something wasn't broken or torn. It was an exciting feeling, a powerful feeling to know that it probably was broken but God healed it for me.

My hand seemed like an unimportant thing to pray about. There are so many terrible things going on in the world and so many illnesses and cancers and problems that praying for my hand seemed like nonsense to me, that having a broken hand isn't a big deal and I should just deal with it. But it didn't matter, the seriousness of the struggle, God healed me. And it gave me more faith and confidence, knowing that God loves me and is here for me in everything.

Over the next few months, I was triggered a couple of times. One of the times ended in me being hurt and unsure of what happened. Another time Granny was able to sense the change in me and was able to get me to work through the trigger and not run. We would feel like there was light at the end of the tunnel, and then in a moment, we would go back to feeling hopeless. We didn't know how to fight. The police were not helping us. I was still easily being triggered and would zone out. We felt lost.

One day, the Lord led me to start researching all I could about zoning out and triggers and why I didn't remember what would happen to me. I felt like the police thought I was crazy, and I was beginning to believe it too. I was beyond frustrated at myself. Nobody felt comfortable to leave me alone, and everyone was not only worried about me but also about my kids. My kids would beg to have their friends over for a playdate, but nobody felt comfortable leaving their kids here with me. So I began researching to see if I could find any answers. I typed all that I was experiencing with triggers and zoning out and ritualistic abuse in the past. I clicked Search, and immediately, I saw articles about something called monarch mind control. I clicked on the first link and began reading.

The description of someone who has endured monarch mind control was exactly what I was dealing with, to a *T*. I was completely blown away. There was a part of me that was very excited that I wasn't crazy, that this was real, and that I was not the only one. But when I read on, I realized that it wasn't an easy thing to fix. Monarch mind control is very deep in a person's brain, and it takes special training to deprogram someone's brain that has it. If it is dealt with in a wrong way, then the brain actually has been programmed to basically deactivate, and the person then will commit suicide. My stomach literally dropped when I read that. And I was scared. We were amazed at how identical my symptoms were to what the website was describing. We had no doubt that this is what was done to me most likely as a young child. It was infuriating to me to know that someone played with my mind so much. It brings tears to my eyes just thinking how much these people stole from me, even my brain. I wanted desperately to get it back. I didn't want anybody controlling my brain but me and God.

We read about triggers and how it is crucial to figure out what the triggers were that they used on me. Since I would zone out, I would never remember what was said or done. It could be a word or a phrase or a touch or just a sound. It could be anything.

We researched around to see if there were any counselors around here that had worked with people with monarch mind control. We couldn't find anybody nearby. I ordered a book online and was hopeful that with God and by studying, maybe I could figure it out on my own.

That next Sunday, my oldest son was sick, and I stayed home from church with him. According to my son, a mean old man came to the door and knocked, but Mom wouldn't let him in. My son doesn't say anything else about that day, but we later found several burns on my back. I had zoned out and had no recollection of what had happened. I wasn't even aware of the burns until the next day because I was emotionally numb from whatever happened and from zoning out.

I told Granny about the burns that next day, and it became more than obvious to her and everyone else helping me that I couldn't keep doing this. I needed to find help, and I needed to go away to get the help. My army had been doing everything they could to keep me safe, but because of the triggering and mind control, it was impossible to keep me safe and who knows what all my kids had seen through the years.

I didn't like this news. I begged them to please let me stay. I didn't have a way to explain that I would somehow do better because, honestly, I wasn't in control anyway during those times since I couldn't control zoning out. It was decided that my husband I would meet up at the man's house who had prayed over me. It was my mentor and her husband, this man and his wife, Granny and my husband all there trying to figure out what to do. Everyone was in agreement that I needed to go away to get help except me. If I was going to be forced to go away to get help, then I had to have my kids go with me. They were the main ones keeping me going. I couldn't stand to be away from them. But the possibility of finding a place to help that would allow my kids was very rare.

Sitting there hearing the conversation around me, I began to feel my world completely fall apart. I was about to literally lose everything. I was going to be sent away to get healing for something that I had no control over, and I would be away from my kids for who knows how long. At that point, my kids were six, four, two, and the youngest was ten months old. I couldn't bear the thought of leaving them. I had never been away from them. I had done everything I could think of to protect them. And now I was being told that it was best for them if I wasn't around because of the safety factor. I was literally losing everything.

In an attempt to catch my breath, I got up while they were all talking to step outside and to just cry. But because of my track record, my husband thought it was me running and quickly grabbed me from behind and picked me up in his arms to where my feet couldn't even touch the floor. I fought him and kicked and screamed and begged him to let me go. And he wouldn't. I explained that I just wanted to go outside to cry, and again he told me no. I begged him to let go of me, and again he said no.

Finally, I shouted out at him, "YOU ARE HOLDING ME THE SAME WAY THEY DO!"

And with that, he put me down. I crumbled into a ball by the front door of the house and cried. I was going to lose my babies. The women there came over and tried to reassure me, but they understood what I was feeling. They were moms. They couldn't imagine being told they couldn't see their kids. Most of the programs that they were talking about putting me in were two-year programs. There was no way I was going to be away from my kids for two years. I felt helpless. I felt angry.

There was discussion about what to do, and eventually they decided to call up one of my brothers who lives about seven hours away. We put him on speaker phone, and with everyone talking, they explained to him what has been happening to me the last few years. When he heard the news, we could hear nothing but sobs coming from his end of the phone. My heart broke for him. After much discussion, it was decided that my husband and kids and I would leave the next day in the middle of the night and go stay with my brother while we wait for a decision to be made for where I needed to go. I was happy about the thought of being with my brother and his family, and I was beyond excited that I was still going to have my kids with me. But beyond that, I was completely unsure of how God was going to lead us.

I will walk by faith even when I cannot see.
—2 Corinthians 5:7

Chapter 23

We had to be very careful while we packed. We didn't want it to be easily seen that we were packing. We had no idea what methods these men had used to keep track of me, but we weren't putting past them bugging the house in some way. Friends of ours packed up suitcases at their house with clothes that would fit my kids so I didn't have to worry about that. And so I just threw clothes for my husband and I in grocery bags to try and disguise what we were doing. It's hard to describe what I was feeling. It felt equivalent to planning my own funeral, like preparing for something that was going to rip me apart.

On that next day, I tried to keep my mind as busy as possible, but my heart was very heavy. I understood the concern for everyone helping me, and I understood that we had come to a point where this was the only way to go, but I still didn't like it. From everything that had happened to me, this was my worst nightmare, having to leave my family. And there was still so much up in the air that I didn't know what was going to happen.

I had friends stopping by throughout the day to say goodbye. Some of them stayed and hung out, and we decided to use that time to finish some of the decorating in my house. I had slowly been working on it, but there were some things I had ready but I just needed help hanging up, and so one friend came, and we tackled that project together. The air in the room was very heavy because none of us were wanting it to come to this.

Granny seemed extra busy as time got closer to me leaving. I wanted to soak up as much time with her as possible, but she was continually on the go. We ended up meeting her somewhere at our last stop before leaving town to get some suitcases from her and other things for our trip, and then it was time to say goodbye. I had no words and she didn't either. We had worked so hard for nine months to keep me safe, to find me freedom, to regain the life that I deserved. She did everything within her power to help me and my family. It felt like we had failed by having to send me away.

All we could muster up was a quick goodbye through tears, but maybe two hours into our trip, Granny called me. And crazy enough, she was calling to apologize. She felt like she had let me down, like she had failed me. Her tears somehow brought me strength. It reminded me how lucky I was to have her and my army. It reminded me that they all did everything they could. It reminded me that I was dearly loved and would always be loved unconditionally. And it reminded me that I needed to not only make this work for me and my family, but I needed to do this for everyone else who had tirelessly fought so long for me to stay. I did not want her feeling the blame or feeling like she failed me. She was the first person ever to fight for me, really fight for me. And I knew that if she hadn't stepped in when she did, I would not be alive.

On our drive to my brother's house, my husband stopped at Walmart and bought me a TracFone. I would have a new number, and it would be impossible for the men to know where I was. We weren't certain if they had bugged my other phone or not. We wanted to make sure that I would be safe wherever I was going.

We got to my brother's house around four in the morning, and since all the kids were asleep in the car, we decided that we would just sleep the rest of the morning in the car too. It was nice enough outside that we could turn off the car and just rest. My husband and I maybe got an hour or two of sleep before the kids started waking up. We then went inside.

It was difficult to face my brother. The shame that comes with being a victim, especially a victim of trafficking, is overwhelming. You know in your mind that it's hard for others to understand. You know in your mind that they are going to question things. I wasn't sure how he would handle seeing me. But we hugged, and we made things as comfortable and normal as possible for the kids. We had a nice breakfast and coffee waiting for us, and then we all sat down and started to talk. I was still hopeful that I would be able to convince my brother not to make me go somewhere for help. I was willing to stay near him and have my kids with me and seek help around his area.

The days passed, and I made phone calls to people my brother knew who had been survivors of trafficking or who had been connected to organizations involved in helping trafficked victims. At times, things were normal, and we were laughing and enjoying the kids, and other times, things were intense, and we would get into deep and hard conversations.

It was then decided that most likely the best place for me to go would be to a sex trafficking safe house that would provide everything I would need to get my life back. But what was devastating to me was that my kids couldn't be with me. It wasn't a two-year program like most places were, but it was a ten-month program. And the rules were that I couldn't even talk to my family. My kids wouldn't get to visit me, and I wouldn't get to talk to them on the phone. This was not at all what I wanted, and I begged my brother and husband and Granny on the phone not to make me go.

Picturing my life for the last six years, I spent every moment with my kids, every single moment. I loved them more than I could ever describe, and I knew that by going away for ten months, the separation for them was going to be just as hard as it would be for me. I would miss my husband greatly too, but my husband was old enough to understand that this wasn't a choice. My kids wouldn't understand.

I received a phone call from the organization that I was going to, and they went through an interviewing process to see if I was a good fit for their program. After hearing my story, they decided that it would be a good fit, and they were going to work on finding me a placement. They had several safe houses throughout the United States.

I begged again and again for everyone to not make me do this, but no one was budging. I went outside by myself and sat on the trampoline in the backyard of my brother's house. I sat there and I began to cry. This was the most intense, most gut-wrenching cry I have ever had. I cried as hard as I have ever cried, and finally, I was able to slow down and say out loud to God, "If this is what I need to do, if You are really calling me to lay everything and every person in my life down at Your feet, then I will do it. If it is best for my children to not have me around, then I will go. I give it all to You."

And immediately the sobs came back fiercely. I finally collected myself and walked back up to the house and told my brother and my husband that I agreed to go. And my brother's response was, "Good because you were going to go no matter what anyway."

The very next day, this organization called, and they had found me a placement that was going to be about five hours from my home. They said I could come as early as next week and that the last thing I needed to do was go over their rules and procedures and agree to those and then I would be set.

This man from the organization sent me an e-mail that had three pages worth of rules and procedures. I started reading over everything he had sent me. Tears began to well up in my eyes as I read things about what it was going to be like where I would be staying. They were talking about how during the first several months at their organization, they would be teaching me how to take care of myself physically and medically, how to function in the real world, how to overcome addictions like drugs and alcohol. They would be teaching me how to use food stamps and how to write resumes and go through an interviewing process for a job.

Granted these are all great things that I believe someone who has been living on the streets in that form of trafficking would benefit from. I, however, already knew these things. I had a home, four kids, and a husband. I cooked dinner. I went grocery shopping. I knew how to function in the world. I just didn't know how to keep myself from zoning out and being triggered.

At first, I just cried. I couldn't believe that not only would I be going to a place for ten months and not be able to see my family but I also felt like I would be wasting my time learning things I already knew. I was sad that I didn't have a choice in this. From my already swollen eyes, more tears began to fall. This was not at all the life I had envisioned for myself.

Something inside of me, I'm believing it was the Holy Spirit, stirred within me the strength to try and plead my case that this was not the place I should be going to. I first called Granny and I told her. She saw my point and said to go ask my brother. He was out on the lawn mower in his front yard, so I walked out toward him. He stopped the lawn mower, and I explained to him why I felt like this place was not a good fit for me, and he said, "Good because I was hoping that you wouldn't have to be away from your kids that long anyway."

He then suggested for me to do some research of my own to see if I could find a good fit for me. As I was walking back to his house, the thought popped in my head, the Holy Spirit again in my opinion, to try an eating disorder facility. I was still struggling with bulimia, and so it wouldn't be off the wall for me to go there. I would be safe, and I would be getting counseling. It seemed like a good idea to me.

I got back on the computer and typed in "Christian eating disorder facility." The first one that popped up I clicked, and immediately I had peace about it. It looked beautiful, lots of land. They had equine therapy, which is where you work with horses to help with trauma recovery. That sounded a whole lot better than the AA therapy I was going to be getting at the other place. I just had this overwhelming peace. Not to mention it was a minimum of six weeks, and my kids and husband could come and stay the weekends with me, and I could call them every night. That part made me very happy. It seemed doable.

But I thought about it, and this place was four hours away from home. I figured I probably needed a place closer. So I found one that was an hour away from home, and I decided to give them a call. Immediately, I could tell by the phone conversation that this was not the right place for me. I decided to go back to the first place and give them a call.

Right off the bat, I felt at ease with the woman I was talking to. She was easy to talk to, and I could tell that she really cared about me and my recovery and safety. I asked her if they would be able to help me. I gave her a brief snippet of my story, and she said that yes, they had dealt with several cases like mine. I was beyond thrilled to hear this.

After sharing the news with everyone, we prayed about it and the peace within me remained. I wasn't excited, but yet I kind of was. I was excited to learn how to fight, to learn how to keep from being triggered and zoning out. I was excited to find healing and to see God working in my life. The peace I was feeling had to be from God because even though there was some excitement in the knowledge that this would be good for me, it was also gut wrenching because of the thought of saying goodbye to my kids.

Over the course of the next week, I did an interview process with this eating disorder facility. They assured me again that they could help. We drove back toward home, but we stopped at my in-laws' house, and the kids and I stayed there while my husband continued to work. He had missed work too much as it was because of all we had been through, so he needed to be in the office, and I understood that. I made up a plan for the time that I would be gone to make sure that all four of my kids were taken care of during the day while my husband worked. I had a full schedule laid out. I would know who had them on Monday, who had them on Tuesday, and so forth. Hopefully it would make things easier on my husband and everyone else helping with the kids. It was going to take an army to get this accomplished. Good thing God gave me an army. I went shopping with my mother-in-law, and we got lots of things that I needed for my stay at the eating disorder facility. My parents were informed that I was going away, and even though at the time they had very little information, they were deep in prayer and had gotten me some things to take with me. I can't imagine the fear and anxiety they had, not knowing exactly what was going on, but for that times, I needed to wait for them to know. My brother had planned to drive to see my parents once I was in this eating disorder facility to explain what was going on.

The day before I was to report to what would be my new home for six weeks at the eating disorder facility, we loaded up and went back home for one night. We were careful to make sure no one saw us. I was terrified about the next day but still at peace with it. I held my kids extra-long that night. I nursed my baby girl, what I believed would be my last time. And I lay in my husband's arms as we fell asleep. This was my last night at home.

I got up and got ready early and was out the door at 4:00 a.m. I didn't wake the kids up, but I hugged my husband as long as I could, and then I walked out the door. I loaded up a large black suitcase and one backpack into the trunk of Granny's van, and we started on our way.

It was still very dark outside. She had her green tea and I had my coffee, but I couldn't drink it. I was nauseous and sad and scared. I had no idea what kind of world I was going to enter into. I didn't know what type of people I was going to meet. Everything happened so fast, but the peace never left me, and for that, I was so thankful. Yet no matter how much I knew that this was the right move, I still couldn't come to grips with actually going. I was certain that my ten-month old baby girl would forget that I was her mommy. I knew my six-year-old would wake up in the morning and be all out of sorts without his mom there. I was the one who would hold them when they hurt, and now I was the one causing them the most pain, and I couldn't be there to hold them through it.

The more we drove, the more I realized that thinking about how hard this was wouldn't make the situation any better. Granny would remind me the good things about going. She would give me pep talks like a coach. She didn't want me wasting any time there. She wanted me to soak up as much as I could from the experience, to start pouring out anything and everything to them. I would nod, but in my heart, I knew that would be really hard for me. It takes me awhile to trust people and feel like I can really open up to them. I could tell that Granny wasn't thrilled about me leaving, I think especially because she also knew how hard this was going to be on my kids. She wanted me to fly through the program and be home as quick as I could.

The drive seemed to fly by. We followed the GPS, and it told us to turn down this driveway amongst a lot of trees. We weren't certain if it was even a driveway or more like a path. But we took the turn, and then a covered bridge came into view that said the name of the eating disorder facility. It would've been beautiful had it not meant that we were actually there and it was time to say goodbye.

"Aw, that's really pretty," Granny stated about the covered bridge.

I just looked at her with eyes like, "Really?"

We continued down the driveway, and then a beautiful home came into view. We pulled in, and a lady right away came out to greet us. My heart was beating out of control. I turned to Granny and begged her to take me home. She said, "Come on. You can do this. It's a short time. It will go fast."

I continued to beg, but the lady was walking up to the car, so I stopped begging and we got out. When I got out, the lady who was greeting us was the same lady that I had talked to on the phone. She seemed nice, but she wasn't home. She asked if she could hug me, and I said sure. Granny told her that I was really nervous, and she understood. We grabbed my suitcase and backpack and followed her into the side building of the house. While we walked, I kept whispering to Granny to take me home. But we just kept walking.

As we got into the house, I saw that it was really nice and homey. This part of the facility was a modular that they had recently added to the big house where I would be staying. The lady who greeted us explained that this was where they did some group sessions and where some of the counselors had their offices. We all three sat down at the dining room table. I waited for them to sit, and I then proceeded to sit as far away from the other lady as I could. I just wasn't buying into this yet. I couldn't comprehend being left at this place. I needed to be with my kids. They were probably home and waking up and needing me. And I needed them. I was told to change seats to where I was sitting in between Granny and this other lady.

I'm not a person who is defiant by nature, but in that moment, I thought about simply not doing what they were asking just to prove a point. But that thought only lasted a second, and I got up and moved to the appropriate chair. This lady started going through rules and paperwork. I hardly listened at all and would simply sign where she told me to sign. I wouldn't make eye contact with her. Both these women were there to help me, but at the time, it felt like they were punishing me, that this place was my punishment for not being good enough.

I finished signing the papers, and she grabbed my bag to carry into the main house for me. She then said that it was time to say goodbye. I just sat there. I didn't want to get up because that would mean that the goodbye was really going to happen. But no matter how much I wanted to freeze time, I couldn't.

Granny and I got up and walked over to the door. And we hugged. And we cried. I continued to beg her to take me home. And she started begging me to be strong, that I need to be strong, that I needed to do this so I could get home and be healthy. It wasn't a long goodbye. She was quick to get out the door, I think because her tears were really starting to fall.

As she walked out the door, I watched her the entire way. She didn't even look back. She had her head down and was headed straight to her car. But just before she got to her car, she quickly did a 180 and came running back inside. My heart started racing that maybe she was going to take me home. She opened the door and she said, "I'm so sorry but I forgot something very important."

She grabbed me and held me even tighter, and she started to pray. I don't remember her prayer. I'm not sure I could even understand her prayer through her tears, but I believe those are the prayers that God hears the loudest. "Tears are prayers too. They travel to God when we can't speak" (Psalm 56:8).

As soon as she was done praying, she gave me a kiss on the cheek and told me she loved me, and she left, this time heading straight to the car and driving off.

I stood there and just watched. I didn't want to move. I'm not sure how long I stood there, but I was disappointed to then hear the lady say, "Are you ready?"

Do I say no because that's the truth> I wanted to run out the door and find Granny. But I swallowed the defeated feeling that this was really happening, and I nodded. I then followed this lady out the modular door, down a ramp, and into what looked like would've been a garage, but as we walked in the door, I saw that it was turned into an art studio. There was artwork hung all over the place. There were racks and bins full of supplies and big windows to let the light in. Had I not been in such a bad mood, I maybe would've thought it was neat.

It was explained to me that my first stop would be to see the nurse. As we walked through the art studio, we then turned down a long hallway, and the lady I was with knocked on the first door to the right. As she knocked, I started taking in all that was on the walls. Quote after quote was posted all over the walls. It wasn't in a tacky-looking way but actually really neat. And the quotes were positive and powerful. However, as I read them, I kept thinking that God was asking too much of me to be at this place, but then again, maybe this was all that I was worth to Him anyway.

A lady opened the door and introduced herself to me as the nurse. I went on in and sat in the medical chair. I was shaking terribly from fear and nerves. I wasn't certain yet what kind of place I was entering into. I could hear voices in the next room, and girls were boldly stating how much they hated their life and how much life must hate them, that they were ready to just be done. I could tell by their voices that these girls were not going to be people that I would easily connect with. I was already telling myself that I would be better off staying to myself.

The nurse began talking to me in a sweet grandmotherly sort of way. She started encouraging me and telling me that it was going to be okay. She explained more rules to me and had me go to the bathroom to change into a hospital gown. She explained that all the doors were locked, so the only way someone could come in the house was if a worker opened them. She also explained that the residents were not allowed to ever be in a room by themselves.

I went in to change, and she stood with the door cracked a few inches and waited right outside the door. I was already uncomfortable with this. As I changed, I realized they had more quotes all throughout the bathroom. They had the entire mirror filled with quotes to where you could only see your face. I asked the nurse if I could pee, and she gave me the green light, so I went ahead and flushed and washed my hands. As I walked out of the bathroom in my hospital gown, the nurse sweetly told me that I was not allowed to flush the toilet. My eyes got real big. I said, "What?"

"Yes, we have to have the door open, and we have to be the ones to flush the toilet for you. It's not a fun thing, but it keeps you from getting away with purging any of your meals. You also aren't allowed to go to the bathroom thirty minutes after snacks or an hour after meals. You will be allowed three caffeine beverages a day, but you will not be allowed to drink any more caffeine after 3:00 p.m."

I was pleased to hear that I would get coffee, but I felt like I was in a prison the more she talked.

"You will wear these three wristbands. One has your name and information on it. Another is red, which means you are not allowed to do any sort of physical activity. You won't be allowed to stand for very long. You can't walk out on the porch. You will also have to sit while you are in the shower. And then a white band, which means that you have to stay within arm's reach of a worker at all times."

This was getting better and better.

"You cannot be in a room without a working RC with you. An RC is a recovery care specialist. These ladies will take you to the bathroom, watch you shower, watch you get dressed, sit with you during your meals, and stay with you while you sleep."

Now I was really getting upset. I couldn't even shower without someone watching. Immediately, my mind went back to when I was a little girl, and I would get cleaned up by my coach's brother's wife in the shower after my coach had made love to me and made videos with me. My shaking had gotten worse at this point. Once the nurse got all of my vitals and my weight and bloodwork done, she then walked me down that long hallway into the main part of the house.

It was just as beautiful on the inside as it was on the outside. There was a large kitchen and an even larger living room. I wasn't able to get too much time to look around, but I noticed that the quotes continued throughout the whole house. I passed by a bathroom, and a lady was standing outside the door, and a girl walked out of the bathroom. I could tell she was a client. She smiled at me, and with her northern accent, she said, "Hi."

I told her hi back, but the wheels were turning in my mind about trying to guess what this girl's story was. I wondered if she was nice. I continued following the nurse, and we went into the living room, and she asked an RC that was sitting on the couch to go over the rules with me again.

The RC was really friendly and seemed very real. Before she went over the rules, she took time to ask me questions and see how I was doing, but I really didn't have much to say at this point. In my mind I was thinking, *I am one hour in and have a million more to go before I can go home.*

I told the RC I was fine, and she went on explaining the rules. While she was talking, some of the clients walked in. There were only three from what I could see, and they quietly said hi to me. It felt like high school all over again. I was trying to figure them out, and they were trying to figure me out. I just couldn't imagine what this was going to be like. I was given the tour of the house after the rules, and I was taken to a large room that had four beds in it, three up against one wall and one against the other. Two beds were taken, and I was given the choice of which bed I wanted. I chose the single bed on the opposite side of the room.

It was a weird feeling to see that my things had all been unpacked and put away. I had a section of the closet that was mine with shirts and pants hung up and shoes down below. They put my toiletries in a drawer in the bathroom and my books and binders in a drawer by my bed. I also realized that there were some things that I had brought that they wouldn't let me have, like my spiral notebook. Everyone there had eating disorders but several also struggled with cutting, so nothing sharp was allowed. You weren't even allowed to staple your papers. They also confiscated some of the pants that I brought with me because they looked too athletic, and wearing them could trigger someone to want to exercise. And since over-exercising is a common behavior for people with eating disorders, they had to take those away from me too.

We had a small break before our first snack, so we got to go out on the back deck. I stood and stared out at the tiny pond not far from the house. I hadn't been standing long before an RC reminded me that I needed to find a seat. They were very nice about it, but I was still perturbed at all these rules.

One of the main rules about this place was confidentiality. We were, and still are, not allowed to talk about each other. It would violate HIPAA. So as I write about my stay at this eating disorder facility, I have to be very careful what I say about other clients even if I am keeping their names out of it.

The next thing on the schedule was a 10:00 a.m. snack. I wasn't forced to have a snack, so I didn't. The RCs were pretty aware that most likely I wasn't used to keeping very much food in my stomach, so we were going to start off slow. Instead of doing snack with the girls, I was called in for a meeting with different members of my recovery team. I had a psychiatrist, a therapist, a family therapist, and a nutritionist. I was given an overwhelming amount of information, and my mind was still only on one thing—the shower.

I couldn't handle showering at this place with someone watching me. It felt too similar to past experiences, and I couldn't do it. I ended up getting myself all worked up, and I found the person that I had connected with the most up until this point, the nurse. She also seemed the easiest person to let me do what I want, and what I wanted was to call Granny.

I explained that I needed to go home and I couldn't do this. I begged to call Granny, and the nurse went in and got her phone and asked me her number. I told her, and she dialed it up for me. I was beyond grateful. The only person who would understand how I was feeling was Granny because she knew everything I had been through. She would help me. I knew she would.

I knew that Granny was playing in her weekly golf league at this time, so I was really hopeful that she would answer her phone. I was relieved to hear the nurse start talking and explaining who she was and that I was there and that I needed to talk to her. The nurse then handed me the phone.

"I need you to come get me. I can't do this," I cried out as broken and shattered as you could ever imagine. "Please, please come get me and take me home."

"Rachel, stop it," Granny said in a comforting but stern way.

"No, I can't do this. This isn't right. Please trust me. This isn't right, and I need to come home." I wasn't able to explain about the shower. I struggled with words and sharing hard things, and sharing about the shower at that moment was too hard. I really just needed Granny to understand and come back and get me. But she wouldn't even consider it.

We went back and forth for a while, and I kept trying to hint that something was wrong, but since I couldn't explain what was wrong, she couldn't help. The nurse was sitting right next to me, so that made it even harder to talk. Finally, I said to Granny, "They watch us shower."

"So?" Granny said.

"I can't do that, and you know why I can't do that."

"Okay, that makes sense, but you can't let that keep you from getting the help you need for your family. They will work with you. I have a huge amount of peace about you being there, and yes, that will be a hurdle for you, but you can do it. Talk to them. Explain to them what you're feeling and why. They aren't there to hurt you. They are there to help you. But they can't help you if you don't communicate with them."

I was upset and just handed the phone back over to the nurse. I couldn't believe that she was still going to have me stay at this place. When the nurse hung up the phone with Granny, she told me that she would talk to my therapist and they would work something out to where I was comfortable showering. This helped. But I still wasn't thrilled.

I was on high alert the whole day and was trying to keep up with the schedule. The first group session I went to was chapel, and the chaplain was an older woman who had been through a lot—you could tell just by looking at her. You could also tell by talking to her. She cussed like a sailor and had one of those real and bold type of relationships with God. She asked all of us to start the group by answering the question, "What is the hardest thing about being here?"

She went around the room and asked the other three girls. Then she turned to me and said, "Rachel, what is the hardest thing about being here for you?"

And instantly, four of the sweetest faces popped into my head, the faces of my four precious babies, and I couldn't even get out the words as the tears started falling.

What we suffer now is nothing compared
to the glory He will reveal to us later.
—Romans 8:18

CHAPTER 24

The first week at the eating disorder facility is hard to remember. I must've been exhausted from living in survival mode for so long. At home, I was getting just a couple hours of sleep a night and was always feeling unsafe. But the first week at the eating disorder facility, I couldn't stay awake. My body just crashed, and any time I sat down, I was out like a light. It must've been a pretty common thing for new clients to need to catch up on sleep when they get there. They didn't harp on you for sleeping, knowing that most of us finally felt safe and our body needed the sleep in order to be able to get anything out of counseling and the classes. Another typical symptom of an eating disorder is always being cold, so the house had big soft blankets in almost every corner so that we could wrap them around us to keep us warm.

I got used to meal time. The staff would portion the meals for us and then serve us. We were not allowed to leave the table until everyone finished their plate. When we left the table, all of our pockets and sleeves had to be checked to make sure we didn't hide any food.

I was still pretty quiet in groups and at meals. The girls would often play different games at the table to keep their mind off of the fact that they had to finish their plate. I didn't participate much. My mind was on other things.

You maybe remember my excitement when I heard that this eating disorder facility would have equine therapy. It was originally pictured in my head that we would be around horses a lot, that we would get to love on them, and just like how they say that a dog is good medicine, I was guessing that simply being around a horse would be good medicine. That was not what equine therapy was like at all.

My first time going to equine therapy, I got to meet two equine therapists. We had the whole group of girls there, and I was still at the point where I wasn't talking much during sessions. Equine therapy was no different. One of the equine therapists seemed to be someone I thought I could connect with, but at the time, I wasn't willing to get close to anybody except maybe the girls.

It was explained to us that equine therapy will be a chance for us to learn to take control of a situation. We would be going into an arena where we would have to use our voice or our actions to get the horse to do whatever the equine therapists told us to do. Sounds easy enough except these horses didn't necessarily know any certain commands. And the tasks they were having us do seemed almost impossible. As I stepped out in the arena for the first time, I tried my best to blend in with the crowd. As a group, we were given a task, and we were unable to complete the task, but in the process of trying to get the horse to do what we asked, I said the words, "Please, please, please, please go over there."

The two equine therapists stopped us, and the lady equine therapist asked me about my comment that I had just made to the horse. I shrugged my shoulders. I really didn't know, but I also didn't want to dig down deep and figure out why. This sweet but feisty lady kept pushing me. She asked if in my life I find myself begging for things a lot. And I instantly thought back at all the times I've begged people not to hurt me or I begged people not to send me away or I begged God to help me. So I nodded yes to her question, but I was really hoping she would move on to someone else. My arms were crossed, and my head was down.

"Why do you think you feel like you need to beg people to listen to you?" she then asked me.

I shrugged my shoulders and said, "I don't know."

She quickly snapped back, "Bulls#%^!"

I was a little bit ticked off at this point and wanted her to leave me alone and move on to somebody else, but she didn't. After going back and forth for a bit of me saying, "I don't know" and her saying "bulls#%^," I finally blurted out, "Because my voice doesn't matter!"

Then she gave me a sad look and nodded her head. She then asked, "Why do you think your voice doesn't matter?"

I thought about saying, "I don't know," but that didn't work for me the first time, so I said, "Because when I do try to use my voice, nobody listens to me."

She nodded a sad nod again and then moved on to the next person.

My eyes were a little bit misty at having to say those words out loud. When the session was over and we walked out of the arena, I noticed a strange feeling come over me. It was confidence. And then it hit me that when I was in the arena with an overpowering horse, I instantly turned into that nine-year-old girl. But as soon as I stepped out of the arena, I felt thirty-one again and had more confidence. I became aware that I tend to turn into a young child when I am put into overpowering situations.

I ended up having a love-hate relationship with equine therapy. I would gain a lot from it, and I enjoyed my time with the equine therapists, but it was usually a deep and hard session.

The very first weekend, my husband and kids came to visit me. It was so nice to see my babies. I just wanted to hold them and not let them go. It was a very bittersweet feeling because when our visit was done and they had to leave, the kids didn't want to go. They wanted to stay with me, and they weren't going without me. My husband had to rip my oldest out of my arms and force him into his seat in the van. All the way home, my oldest was angry and yelled at his dad that he hated him. From that moment on, we saw a big change in our oldest, and it absolutely killed me. I wanted to fix it for him.

As they pulled away, I was broken apart all over again. I needed to go home with them. I could not understand God's plan in all this. I no longer felt the peace. Something that hurt children like this could not be in God's will. I needed to be home with my kids.

The RC and the nurse working at that time gathered around me and allowed me to cry as my family drove away. They didn't have to say anything. They knew I was hurting, and there wasn't anything they could do to take that pain away. After several tears, they reminded me that I need to get better so I can get home to my babies and never have to leave them again. I knew they were right. So I decided to try.

That next week, I didn't sleep as much. I was more motivated to get better. I wanted my treatment plan to not involve anything from my past but instead be solely focused on the future. I started talking in groups and talking at meals. About a week into my stay there, another client came. She seemed to be close to my age and was actually a preacher's kid too. Oddly enough, three out of five of the clients there were preachers' kids. The new client was shaking like a leaf when she joined us in our first group session. I just wanted to hug her, to tell her that it was going to be okay. My heart broke for her.

In that session, I spoke up more than before, and around that time, I started finding myself thumbing through my Bible almost constantly soaking up all of God's Word. This new girl and I were connecting more than the others because of our faith, but the other three girls were starting to open up more too. And before I knew it, we all were laughing and joking and having a good time throughout the day. When sessions were hard and someone would cry, we would surround them and be there for them. We began encouraging each other and pushing each other. It took just a week and, it felt like these girls were my family.

Over time, more girls continued to show up, and instead of wondering about their story or trying to figure them out just by looking at them, I actually would be ready to love on them and be there for them. Knowing their story or what they were like didn't matter to me anymore. God had completely changed my view on people.

One time, I was sitting out on the front porch because I had graduated to a yellow band instead of red, which meant I could stand longer and walk out to the porch. I was sitting there talking to the client near my age who had become a dear friend. We knew that we were expecting another new client that morning and that this new client was already in the modular doing the check-in paperwork. I then saw a woman who was probably in her fifties quickly walk out of the modular toward her car. Even from where I was, I could see the tears streaming down her face. My mind immediately flashed back to Granny walking away from the modular the same way just a few weeks prior. Without thinking twice, I hopped out of my seat and walked toward the driveway to meet this woman. God was really opening my eyes to the hurt in others, and I was thankful for that.

"Excuse me, miss." She looked up and saw me. "Hi, I'm Rachel. I've been here a couple of weeks, and I just wanted to tell you that your daughter is in good hands. And we are going to love on your daughter every day."

This lady looked at me and burst into tears and grabbed hold of me in a tight mama-bear hug.

"Thank you. You have no idea how much peace that brings me to hear that."

About that time, a few other girls started coming up to her too and hugging her and encouraging her. She asked our names, and we told her and we told her that would be praying for her. The front door to the house opened up, and out popped two RCs swiftly walking out to us.

"Girls, you aren't allowed to walk off the porch," one RC said to us.

Even though I broke a rule, I felt blessed to get a change to encourage this mom who was broken for her daughter.

I still missed my family terribly, but time was ticking along, and I was starting to feel like my purpose was showing more and more each day. More girls came and added to our group. One girl felt the need to come up and tell me that she was an atheist. I simply said okay, and we went on with our conversation. Nothing else was said about it. But all of us girls continued to get closer and closer. None of us wanted to be there. We all had a life outside of this eating disorder facility that we hated to leave. So I would try every day to have a smile on my face, and I would usually try to crack jokes, hoping to make the girls laugh and more at ease. The house was less gloomy and more bright. God was definitely working.

I have always loved quotes, and I learned that all the quotes on the walls were called affirmations. I started to make and write my own affirmations, for myself and for my friends. I began using many affirmations and scriptures that I had highlighted in my Bible. I have never been more in my Bible than I was at that time. I just couldn't get enough of the good news in it. Certain affirmations or scriptures would touch my soul in a way that I needed right in that moment. I knew that was God's handiwork.

I remember the day I found a neat passage in 1 Kings 19 where Elijah said, "Lord, I want to die," and instead of answering his prayer, God gave him strength to live instead. I had to stop and share this with others especially since the way God gave him strength to live was to send an angel who told him to "arise and eat." And God had waiting for him a heavenly baked cake sitting on a hot stone and a jar of water. Not once but twice God commanded him to "arise and eat." It was fun to share that with the girls since eating was such a difficult thing for all of us to do. And dying seemed like the thing each of them had hoped for often.

I could feel myself improving a lot, but in the back of my mind, I also knew I wasn't digging down to the root of my problems. I hadn't talked about my problems. I wouldn't talk about my struggles or my past in any of the group sessions. I would offer advice, and I would love to hear others speak and see them have a breakthrough moment, but I wouldn't open up about myself mainly because I didn't want to burden them with all I had going on. But as time went on, I realized that I wasn't fooling anybody there. They could see right past my humor and even past my love for others. I still wasn't doing the work to take care of myself. And that's when I realized I needed to start sharing more. I started off small, and as time went on, I began to open up more and more.

The girls weren't scared of my story. They weren't doubtful of my story. Not one of them acted like this couldn't be true, which is much different than the people I had encountered most of the time back home. These girls believed every word, and they were mad about my story and mad that I had been through so much. It didn't change how they looked at me, but I do believe it brought us closer.

One girl had mentioned to me that she had been wondering what my story was for weeks, but she didn't want to just come out and ask me. I felt bad for being closed off to them for so long when they had been willing to open up to me. It was easy to talk to them because in many ways, they understood and had been through similar things and also because they had been through trauma so they knew how to treat someone struggling with trauma.

Not long after opening up and sharing my story, I had girls starting to ask questions about God and Jesus. Even the girl who proclaimed to me that she was an atheist was asking a lot of questions. Granny even ended up getting her a Bible and bringing it to her. It didn't make sense to these girls that I could smile and be okay after all that I went through, and I think they knew that God was the one behind it all. Not to mention all of the staff was constantly praying for us and loving on us. This was the first time these girls had a Christian man or woman love on them. They only knew Christians as people that judged them, who wanted to correct them and tell them that they were wrong for how they felt or what they believed. They never saw the love of Christ in the Christians they met until now. And the transformation in these girls was like nothing I had ever seen. I literally saw dark eyes turn light and sad faces turn to joyful ones. They were new people simply because the love of Jesus was being shared with them. They began thinking about their future and really wanted to live.

Due to finally letting go and trusting and opening up, I was able to truly start healing. And somewhere in that process, I also found a new understanding of God. Once again, God was working. The eating disorder facility had a small library of books in the house. I had been moved to an upstairs room, and it was up there that they had this little library, so one day, I started looking through the books. I wasn't really wanting to read a book, but the nudge inside of me to look through the books was strong.

There was one book that really stood out to me. There was nothing special about the cover, and I didn't recognize the name of the author, but the pages were worn down, and there were probably a dozen or more sticky notes stuck within the pages. After thumbing through it, I decided I would try reading it. I have started many books in the process of wanting and seeking healing, but none of them would have the advice that made sense for where I was in my relationship with God. I was tired of reading the cookie-cutter Christian answers.

The book I started reading was by Christa Black Gifford, and it was entitled *Heart Made Whole*. It is about turning your unhealed pain into your greatest strength. In this book, Christa explains her trauma and hurts. It was one of those moments where I finally seemed to find someone who could relate and understand. And then she shared her testimony of how she overcame her doubts about God. Everything she wrote about I could relate to, and I was able to personally see God transform my thinking to better understand Him.

When the serpent slithered into the Garden of Eden, whispering poisonous lies into the ears, minds, and hearts of sinless Adam and Eve, Satan had one primary goal in mind: to make sure that God's children began to question the goodness of their perfect Father. I can only imagine him hissing deception into their pure innocence.

"Are you sure you can trust God? See, He doesn't want you to eat the fruit because you will be like Him. This world He's set up for you and the parameters He gave you, they're not in your best interest. You need to take matters into your own hands to protect yourself. Eat of the fruit and you will be like Him – knowing good from evil. Believe me, guys, He cannot be trusted. God is not a good father!"

As Adam and Even let into their minds the possibility that God didn't love them completely, that He was withholding His best, that His intentions weren't good, and that His Word couldn't be trusted, their hearts opened to deadly deception. As a result, they made a decision to eat the fruit, releasing sin and death upon the world—the same fallen world that continues to smash our hearts with pain today.

The deceiver knows that if he can get you to question God as a good Father—believing that He doesn't love you fiercely, that He doesn't fight to protect you, that He didn't send His only Son to restore you to His embrace—then you will begin to withhold pieces of your heart from Him, just as I did.

Our scheming enemy also knows that as long as parts of your heart aren't on friendly terms with God, even though you might be born again, those places will remain barren, tormented, fragmented, and broken—the way mine was for decades, even as a dedicated follower of Jesus. I had been like Adam and Eve in the garden, letting the serpent hiss into my ear and convince the broken parts of my heart that God wasn't good. I built a secret case against Him over years of pain, and as the case file grew bigger, filled with truthful facts of personal trauma and tragedy in a fallen world, my heart divided into the healed parts that truly loved Him and the wounded parts that were more than skeptical.

I realized that at its core, the offended, broken pieces of my heart didn't believe that God was good. How could He be, when so many bad things continued to happen, causing so much pain? My wounded heart had built a solid case against the goodness of God through a lifetime of bad experiences, and it wasn't going to be convinced otherwise by listening to another sermon telling me facts about God's faithfulness." (Christa Black Gifford, in *Heart Made Whole*)

I had no idea just how confused I was about God. I would often say that there wasn't anything wrong with God—there was something wrong with me, that I am in a lower class than everybody else. Those thoughts came from the brainwashing that was done to me as a child, but even still believing that is saying God isn't good enough to love me, to protect me. And that's simply not true.

After reading *Heart Made Whole*, I had an amazing eye-opening moment of realization. And it has forever changed my outlook on God. Earlier in my book, I talked about a time when I was still in grade school and I was taken to the white country house. But on this particular occasion, I wasn't escorted right away. In fact, I lay there on the floorboard of that car, and I began to pray that God would rescue me, that the next person who opened the door to the car would be an angel, somebody to take me home. I prayed and prayed and truly believed with all my heart that God was going to protect me that night.

Instead, the door opened, and the brother grabbed me and pulled me out and led me into the shed where I experienced one of the worst nights of my life. For so long, I struggled with what the point of praying was. Why pray? Why pray with a childlike faith for God to protect you if God is going to do whatever He wants anyway? I had recently began to understand that if given the chance, God could turn those bad experiences into something positive, but it still didn't change the fact that going to God in prayer didn't seem like a logical thing to do anymore.

However, God opened my eyes to see that on that night, lying on the floorboard of the car, praying that God would send someone to protect me, someone to take me home, He actually did answer my prayer. God was there with me that night. I know He was. I felt Him. And He never left me. God lived inside of me, in my heart, so whatever I experienced He also experienced with me. Physically, I maybe still went through the trauma of that night, but I see now that God did in fact protect me. He protected my heart. He kept my heart from being hardened by these events. He kept my heart from being so broken that I could never love again. The proof that He protected my heart is in the fact that I am married with four kids. With what I went through, if God had not protected me, emotionally I could not have trusted a man enough to marry him and have children with him.

God also protected my mind. As I learned more from my counselor at home and at the eating disorder facility, I began to see that my dissociation was a good thing. It was a God thing. It was how God kept my mind safe during unsafe moments. And God waited till I was ready to handle the events that happened before He placed them back in my memory. And there are still memories that He has not revealed to me, and I am definitely okay with that.

So on that time when I prayed for protection, God most definitely protected my heart and my mind from all that took place. Physically I was hurt, but my heart was not touched. And now I know that anything could happen to me physically, but no matter what, my heart is safe with God.

But that wasn't the only thing I prayed for that night. I also prayed for someone to come and take me home. When that door opened and it was the brother, I was devastated. It was heart wrenching and was one of the hardest things for me to get over. But I now know that God did in fact answer that prayer too. Let me explain.

When I was at the eating disorder facility, we would sometimes do what's called inner-child work. Basically this is when we connect with the inner child within us and give our inner child whatever it was that she needed years ago. On one particular afternoon, a client was actually leading a group and she had us do some inner-child work. We found a comfortable spot in the room and closed our eyes. We had almost an hour to simply drift back in our mind to that little girl. I allowed my mind to choose what age I wanted to go back to, and instantly, the night in the car where my prayer was seemingly unanswered was what I thought of.

I let my mind drift back. Tears again started to fill my eyes as I remembered the fear followed by the peace, followed once again by fear. Going back to this moment was difficult, and I was proud of myself for going to such a hard place in my mind. I was pretty sure that some of my friends were simply using this time to sleep, but I could feel God leading me to something. It was in that moment when I went back to my child self that I was able to be there to hold her, to comfort her, to tell her that everything is going to be okay. I could explain to her that she is not alone, that God is in her heart, and because of that, she is going to be okay.

And because this was all within my control of going back to my inner child, I was able then to pick my inner child up from that car and carry her all the way home. And I laid her in her bed and tucked her in. It may sound like a stretch to you, but it was very healing to go back and rescue my inner child from that traumatic moment. It gave the control back to me, and it completed the prayer I had prayed. As a little girl, I had prayed for an angel to come and take me home. I had no idea that the angel would actually be me.

"I don't have the answer to why some prayer requests materialize on this earth and some don't. I don't understand why some people are healed miraculously and some aren't. What I do know is that there is a tumbling ball of pain, sin, death, disease, and destruction that will continue to have power in this fallen world, because that is where we live. But even though my physical body bleeds in its mortality my spirit is alive with Christ as a citizen of heaven" (Christa Black Gifford, in *Heart Made Whole*)

As I continued to improve and stretch myself, I was transferred over to what was called the PHP house, which stood for partial hospitalization. It was right next to the horses and was an even more beautiful and amazing home. At this house, we all shared one large bedroom that had eight beds in it. And we shared one large bathroom. At this house, we were allowed to flush our own toilets, to go into rooms without having an RC with us, and we were allowed to have our phones. I could call and talk to my husband and kids a lot more often. And I could receive pictures from them. I was getting closer and closer to being ready to go.

I felt like I was really making strides, but there came a moment when something was brought up in a random conversation in the kitchen, and it triggered me. In that moment, I bolted from the kitchen, but nobody noticed except the equine therapist who happened to be near the kitchen. Apparently, I headed off to a corner in the art room and sat down. It took quite a while for someone to find me and for them to get me snapped out of the zone. My therapist was called, and she came in and helped get me out of my zone.

Once I was no longer zoned out, I just cried. I can't describe how scary it is to zone out and go back in your mind to the place where you were hurt. You can see it, smell it, taste it, and feel it all over again. It's as if you're facing past circumstances again.

That setback caused my treatment team to discuss extending my stay. As it was, my six weeks was over in just seven days. I was going to be getting home just one day before my youngest daughter's first birthday. It seemed perfect, but my treatment team talked about it and decided to extend me another two weeks. This was also bad because my oldest son had a countdown going for when his mom would come home, and it went from seven days to twenty-one days, which is a big deal in a six-year-old's mind. And it was a big deal in my mind. My heart was broken. But I also knew that I couldn't go home still zoning out. It wouldn't be good for anyone, especially my kids. In the long run, I would be giving my children the best present ever by finding healing and restoration, and that was what I had to keep my focus on.

I can do all things through Christ who strengthens me.
—Philippians 4:13

CHAPTER 25

One of the positive things about the PHP house was that we got to do individual equine therapy sessions. I was beginning to make a connection with one horse in particular named Star. They had probably nine different horses in the stable at the PHP house, but they always chose Star as the horse for me to work with. She was a large thoroughbred with a stubbornness to her. But she was very sweet and kind. She just seemed to have a mind of her own and wasn't interested at all in what you were asking her to do.

I had no idea how intuitive horses were. I absolutely love telling these stories about my time with Star because it goes to show that God will use anything to get our attention.

On one particular day, I had individual equine therapy with Star, and after completing the task that the equine therapist asked me to do, I was then standing by the fence talking to both equine therapists. I had a way of making things harder on my therapists by either answering questions with a question or by answering with the generic obvious answer. Luckily, these therapists were patient with me and would continue to push. It wasn't that I didn't want the help because truly in my mind, I would be thinking that I was wasting this precious time, but I didn't want that. But I think deep down, I was scared to allow the therapist to see the broken pieces inside of me because I wasn't sure if I would be able to get the pieces back together again.

As I was talking to my therapists, they asked me a tough question, and as usual, I responded with an answer that was generic and vague. I kept my answers surface level without even trying to dig deeper to see the meaning behind the pain that stirred within me when they asked the question. I kept the smile on my face and continued to be ornery with each of my responses. But the next thing I knew, Star walked right in front of me and stopped to where she was in between me and the therapists. I couldn't even see the therapists anymore because of where Star was standing, which made me comfortable because then I could take a second to gather myself.

The therapist asked me if I knew what Star was doing. I said that she was standing in front of me. They rolled their eyes at my response once again because of my obvious answer. "Yes, she is standing in front of you, but do you know why?"

I stood there and pondered for an answer in my mind. Finally I said, "Because she wants to be near you, guys."

"She could be near us by standing in several different places, but she chose to stand between you and me to where we can't see you. Why do you think that is?"

I was really beginning to think this therapist was pushing it with this horse thing. I really didn't think the horse had any particular reason to be standing where she was. I finally said that I didn't know.

"Horses are very good at being able to read how people are feeling. And it really bothers horses when you don't act the way you are feeling. Star is standing between us because she can sense that you are feeling something different than what you are trying to tell us and she feels like that is a danger, and so she is trying to protect you from us."

I'm glad the therapist couldn't see my face because I'm pretty sure my facial expression showed something like "yeah, right."

"Really?" I said. "Is that true, Star?" And I looked over at Star in an ornery way, and right away, Star started nodding her head up and down. I was a little taken aback by this and tried not to read too much into the coincidence of her nod.

The therapists continued to dig deeper with their questions, and before long, I was allowing them in to see some of the broken pieces in my heart, and with that came some tears. They would ask me a question, and if I would take too long to answer, then Star would turn her head toward me as if to encourage me to speak. As the tears were falling, I looked over at Star, and I saw a teardrop fall from her eyes.

"Is Star crying?" I quickly asked in amazement.

"I don't know. Is she?" the therapist responded.

"Water just fell from her eye."

"Then I guess she is crying. She knows you are hurting, and she hurts for you."

"No way," I said. "That can't be true." And I turned toward Star and jokingly said, "Is that true, Star?"

And right away she nodded. I was beginning to become a believer at this point. Or else there was a lot of coincidences. I mean I know that God used a speaking donkey in the Bible. I suppose He could use a horse in my story. But there was still a lot of skepticism in my mind. The therapists climbed up the fence a ways so they could see over Star to see my face, and as they did, Star raised herself up higher to where again they couldn't see me. I tried to walk around her, and she would move with me to stay in between me and the therapists. It became comical, and once I was true to my feelings and was able to express how I was really feeling, then Star went ahead and walked off.

We talked in group about how our society doesn't want you to be real and show what you are feeling, that it is looked down upon for you to feel and act sad. Even if you hurt, it's important in our society to pretend you aren't hurting. I'm sure there are times when it's not appropriate to show exactly what you are feeling, but it's sad to me how fake our society has become, how ashamed people are to share their pain with others. Star definitely called me out on being fake.

I was gaining strength like a snowball rolling downhill. I was gaining confidence and believing in myself. I began to work on my final project as my last day at the eating disorder facility was approaching. I had only zoned out one other time, and that was when I got word from the state police that all charges were being dropped against my coach. It didn't make sense to me. They had told me a long time ago that they had found evidence of everything I had told them, that they found child porn in his house. I had three or four different officers tell me that. I didn't understand how it could all be dropped. And I was instantly scared to go home.

It was a hard day, and it took me a few hours, but I was able to remember that God is in control and His timing is perfect. I can't hold this weight. I had tried everything I knew on how to expose the truth. I had so many feelings and thoughts swirling around in my head. Most of them were truths from God that I had been filling my head with. But one was a feeling of embarrassment. What if this meant that everyone wouldn't believe me anymore?

I had a chat with one of the main group therapists at the PHP house, and my primary therapist and I were reminded that it doesn't matter what other people think of me. I have to follow God

We later had a group session where we were asked to take some time and write some positive things to ourselves to encourage us. Here is what I put down on my paper:

> I am strong.
> Stronger than
> I was ever allowed to be.
> I have a life to live,
> Not rules to follow.
> Not a line to walk.
> No one else to please.
> Just being who God made me to be.
> I am strong.
> I have a future.
> I am not a slave.
> Or a prisoner.
> My kids deserve a healthy,
> strong, determined
> mommy
> with a purpose.
> I am strong.
> I am worth
> the fight
> I am about to face.

As the days drew closer to my last day, I was beginning to get antsy. I was excited to be going home, but I also wasn't certain if I was completely better from zoning out. I knew I would be going back to my counselor and working with him. I joked around with the therapists that I really didn't have an eating disorder, but they would just laugh. My eating disorder had served a purpose to get me through moments when I couldn't breathe. But now I have tools in my toolbox that would help me through those tough times. And my biggest tool was the Lord. Knowing He always had my heart, I could face anything and be okay. I started to realize that God didn't call me to this earth to be comfortable but to push myself constantly to do more and be more for Him. My goal in this life is not happiness. My goal in this life is not accomplishing my dreams. My goal is to go where God leads, to give Him my whole life.

That morning a few months earlier, out on the trampoline at my brother's house where I literally gave everything to God, that was one of the biggest moments in my life and one of the hardest. But never again do I want to have control of my life. Never again do I want to deal with the burdens of this world. I give my life to God every single day, knowing that my life in His hands is a life I want to live.

It was finally the day that I would get to go home. It was a surreal moment, but as I packed my things, I began to feel the questions enter my mind on whether or not I was ready. I knew that I had tackled everything I needed to and that it was time to go back home stronger and empowered to take control of the life God has given me. Nerves were really high. I had a feeling that I was going to be faced with a trafficker at some point when I got home and I needed to have the strength to not let his trigger affect me, and I wouldn't know for sure if I would be able to do it until I was faced with it. I was trying really hard to focus on the strides I had made and the excitement that by that night I would be back in my home, holding my babies and laughing with my hubby. I couldn't wait. I was so unbelievably proud of myself for making it through. I thought back many times to the first week when it seemed impossible to stay. I cleared every hurdle that was placed before me. I had the chance to see that I was stronger than I thought. I found God again and was able to understand where He was through all of my pain. And I was able to find out what it's like to love someone that you barely know and through loving them you can begin to see a light turn on in their eyes simply because you are showing them the love of Jesus.

At the PHP house, I had several occasions where girls would huddle around what everyone called Rachel's corner. These girls would mosey their way over, and in a shy, quiet voice, they would say, "I want to know more about Jesus."

I felt so unworthy to answer the question, and yet a fire from within my soul could not wait to share about Jesus. I couldn't wait to explain what God was doing in my life and what He wants to do in their lives. I would have to take deep breaths to slow my heart down and say a prayer for God to lead me. Otherwise, my excitement would make me have no rhyme or reason to my words.

These girls would then come up and join me in my corner, and we would open my Bible up and start from there. They would ask questions, real sincere questions. They would share where they were at with God, and I would share some of my testimony with them. God would remind me of certain scriptures and thoughts to share with them, and hours later, we would finish up. It was going to be really hard to leave these girls. I loved them dearly and loved watching them bloom into women who wanted to not only live but they also wanted to live a purpose. They were excited about their future. These were my sisters for eight weeks and would continue to be for the remainder of my life.

Three of these sisters were able to come to my house for thanksgiving not long after we all had returned home from the eating disorder facility. And two of them decided to get baptized during their trip. One of those girls happened to be the girl that early on made it known to me that she was an atheist. Another cool thing is that I got to be the one to baptize them. It was an incredible moment where only God could receive the glory for what was taking place. It was a miracle.

Back to the last day at the eating disorder facility, the commencement ceremony for my graduation from the program was planned for three o'clock in the afternoon. My husband wasn't able to take off work and the kids had school, so we decided to see if Granny, my mentor, and some other friends and support ladies would like to come. And four of those ladies were able to make it, and so they were going to come and be there for the commencement and then take me home. I would then surprise the kids that night when I got home. I was a ball of nerves but also very excited. I had figured that it would be a fairly easy last day at the house, but around one o'clock, I got a surprise visit from my favorite equine therapist. She ended up being a rock for me at the eating disorder facility, and she had planned just one more equine therapy session.

I told her okay but to take it easy on me, that I was already very nervous and anxious about leaving. She said okay. So we walked down to the stables. When we walked in, inside of the arena were two horses. One was Star, and the other was a horse I had never met before named Spirit. When I walked in, both horses were standing right next to each other at the front of the arena as if to say they were ready to work. I changed into boots and went on into the arena expecting a fun light session.

As I opened the gate and went into the arena with the two horses, the equine therapists introduced me to Spirit and then gave me my instructions.

There were cones set up in the arena similar to how we would set up cones on the basketball court for dribbling drills. My job was to weave both horses through the cones without a lead. I immediately said okay and started walking out to the horses, but as I did, Spirit took off galloping straight toward Star. Within the next minute, Spirit kept going after Star, and it seemed like she was even nipping at her. Star kept letting out this cry. I quickly moved out of the arena and closed the gate. I was spooked myself, but I was also really mad. Spirit kept going at Star, and I turned to the equine therapists and told them to do something. They needed to do something to stop Spirit from hurting Star.

They looked at me with big eyes and said, "What should we do?"

I was shocked at their response. I said, "I don't know. You're the equine therapists. Just do something."

They looked at me again and said, "This arena represents your world. You have to tell us what to do."

"I don't know what to do. This isn't a game. Just help her."

Again they responded with asking me what I wanted them to do. At this point, I had my arms crossed, cheeks covered in tears, and my body was shaking in fear and anger.

"Please just help Star. Spirit is hurting her. Make it stop." I wanted to run. But I couldn't turn my back on Star. I couldn't bear seeing her hurt by Spirit, but I didn't know what to do about it. I was furious at the equine therapists for acting like this was just part of the session. I was not at all okay with this. "Please do something," I begged again.

They responded with, "You tell us what we should do, and we will do it."

"Get Spirit out of here!" I yelled out.

"Okay," one of them responded, and then she grabbed the lead that was on the fence. She went out into the arena and hooked it up to Spirit and led her out into the pasture. As soon as she led Spirit out, then Star started to let out a terrible cry and whine. I immediately knew what was wrong with Star, and I figured the equine therapists would be quick to ask me the question I was expecting. And I was right.

"What is Star doing?" the other equine therapist asked.

"She's crying," I said.

"Why do you think she is crying?"

"Because she misses Spirit."

"But Spirit was hurting Star, so why would Star be sad that Spirit is gone?"

The tears continued to fall silently as I responded, "Because now she is alone."

Star's cries continued until the equine therapists came back in from leading Spirit out to the pasture. Once the therapist walked back into the arena, Star ran up to her and nuzzled against her. Her crying was done. She was okay. And she was safe.

The therapists let me gather myself together. Here I was hoping for an easy last equine therapy session, and I was standing there feeling like I had been through war.

"What do you think Star was trying to teach you through this?" one of the equine therapists asked me.

"You think she did this on purpose?"

"What do you think?" they responded. I was not a fan of those questions.

"I first walked in, they were both standing next to each other and were fine. Why did they start fighting?"

"I'm not sure what happened," they said. "What did this represent in your life?"

I kind of rolled my eyes, knowing the answer was obvious. That was usually when I would respond with an "I don't know," but I knew that wasn't going to fly for my final session with them. "It represents someone hurting me and me not knowing what to do. It represents me crying out for help and nobody doing anything."

"But you used your voice, right?"

"Yes."

"And what happened next?"

"I told you to get Spirit out, and you did," I explained.

"Exactly. You told us what needed to be done. You knew what needed done. You didn't have to ask. You didn't have to say please twenty times. Your voice mattered."

My head was swirling. I had so many emotions flowing through me.

"Who does Spirit represent in your life?" they asked me.

I let out a huge sigh. "Spirit represents the men coming after me trying to hurt me."

"And what can you do now when they approach you?"

"I can demand them to leave."

We stood there a while, Quiet. Finally, one of the equine therapists asked if I was okay.

Sarcastically I responded with, "That was one heck of an easy last session."

I don't know what caused the chaos in the arena that day. I don't know if Star was actually wanting to teach me something or if God was working through her to show me that I have strength to never let anyone hurt me again. My guess is the latter. I walked up to Star and spent some time with her. It was hard to leave her, knowing I would never see her again. But it was amazing to me how much she helped me, how God could even use a horse to open my eyes.

I made the walk up the hill back up to the house. Before long, Granny and the other women would be there, and it would be time for the commencement ceremony. I was still trying to put myself together again from the equine session. I had so much nervous energy. I went into a small room where my nutritionist was working and sat down. She asked if I needed to talk. I explained to her what had just happened in equine therapy. I was still physically shaking, and now I was going to have to present at my commencement. I needed something to help calm me down. One of the tools that I had learned to use was self-talk and speaking truth to myself. So that's what I did.

Rachel, don't do this. You've been waiting for this day for so long. You've done the work. You are stronger than this. God is ready to use you and your story, and it starts now. You got this.

I had to continue the self-talk all the way up until Granny and the other ladies arrived. I couldn't believe it was finally time. My bags were packed and my papers were signed. The last thing left to do was to commence, and then I would be on my way, on my way home, on my way toward allowing God to use me however He sees fit.

After your season of suffering, God in all of His grace
will restore, confirm, strengthen, and establish you.
—1 Peter 5:10

CHAPTER 26

My commencement ceremony was very personal and extremely touching. There were lots of tears and lots of laughs. It started with the presentation of my final project, which happened to be a video that I put together that explained the reality of sex trafficking in the rural towns and in our backyards. After the video, there were lots of comments about how important it was to get the word out and how God was going to use this video and my story in miraculous ways. The second portion of my final project included some thoughts I had written down about my journey.

My Journey

Barbara De Angelis was quoted saying, "Between who you once were and who you are becoming is where the dance of life really takes place." To imagine my journey as a dance seems inappropriate, but even though the journey has some dark moments, it is still my journey, my dance, a journey that I wanted to erase but now I fully own. My past no longer owns me. My story, my life, is mine to own, mine to live, and mine to love.

For so long, I lived in two separate worlds, both real, both a part of my journey, but both oblivious to the other. One world held me captive to the pain and hurt that was forced on me for years, memories that I worked hard to shield from the other world, one that left me with shame and guilt and nothing to hope for.

The other world felt like an oasis, my vacation home away from the pain. God was in the lead of this world. I followed close behind Him and clung tight to His people. In that world, I had so much joy and purpose in my life. My way of survival became simply dissociating from the two worlds that lived within me and around me, dreaming of the day when I would have complete freedom from the world of pain and shame. My understanding of healing meant freedom from all that has hurt me in the past, that to be healed is to be cut off forever from that which hurt me. I am learning now that this is incorrect. Losing that which hurt me is amputation, a severing of an experience, a dissociation. Healing, instead, is a process that works from the inside out, reordering our experiences, placing them in a greater framework, adding depth to the story of my life in a way that simply forgetting could never do. I cannot change the past. But I can weave it into my story, creating a tapestry for others to better understand the world around them.

My journey has given me so much. I am now a storyteller. I have the power to create understanding through pain. So much of me wants to hate my story, my journey, but I would lose so much of who I am if I subtract all the dark moments in my life. This doesn't mean that every experience makes sense to me. Sometimes there is no way to fight your way through it with logic. Evil is evil, plain and simple, but God can use anything or anyone, even me.

Pain is part of our experience as humans, and so is happiness. I understand that some days will be seemingly insurmountable while others will glitter with joy beyond words or expression. Because I haven't reached my final destination, I am still on my journey, my dance. What I have experienced may go beyond the realm of my understanding, but it cannot diminish my ability to find the calm, the peace, and love in every passing moment. So I choose to love myself. My little imperfections, my quirks, my accomplishments, and achievements, all that I am proud of. And not least of all, I choose to love myself for the small everyday moments of overcoming pain, understanding that I am healing from within with each passing breath.

I am strong. I am a survivor. I have gotten back up more times than I have fallen down. One of the most powerful words that has entered my journey is *forgiveness*. Forgiveness, especially in the face of immense pain or trauma, can seem beyond our reach. My biggest challenge along my journey has been forgiving myself.

Human beings are hard-wired for survival. We do what is necessary to keep ourselves alive, to protect our loved ones, to continue on our journey through life. I am a survivor. I am strong. I am important. Yet through my journey, I have made mistakes that leave me with regrets, with guilt, with shame. However, I am learning that human instincts, the drive to help us survive, sometimes continues to rule our lives even when we are safe. The fear or compliant behavior or the dissociation that helped me get through what I experienced is no longer serving me. The forgiveness and love can still be mine. So I begin to let loose of all that I hold against myself.

For the shame and pain that have followed me, I forgive myself.

For the things that happened that I could not have changed, I forgive myself.

For the choices I made that helped me survive but hurt someone else, I forgive myself.

For the guilt I carry deep within me, I forgive myself.

For the nightmares, the doubts, the self-loathing, and the fears, I forgive myself.

For all the coping behaviors that have damaged my relationship with myself and others, I forgive myself.

For the times I have spent sobbing, raging, or completely stone still, I forgive myself.

For living in fear, I forgive myself.

For functioning in robot mode in the amazing world that God has blessed me with, I forgive myself.

For ignoring my intuition or loved ones advice, I forgive myself.

For all the costs physically, mentally, spiritually, emotionally, I forgive myself.

For not knowing what I didn't know until I lived through it, I forgive myself.

I am a survivor. I am not alone as my journey continues. When doubts start to fill my mind, I will look back on my journey, my dance, and I will be reminded of just how far I've come. I will remember everything I have faced, all the battles I have won, and all the fears I have overcome, for the devil intended to harm me. He intended my journey to defeat me. But he must not know *my God*, for even though the devil's intentions were for evil, God's intentions were for good. God's plan has been all long for my journey to not end in defeat but triumph in victory, for the accidental stumbles in my dance to only add to the beauty of my story, for this is my journey, my dance, that I take ownership of and choose to live my life as God intended it, strong and courageous, full of joy, mounted up with wings like eagles, clothes in the full armor of God, with hope of a future, serving an almighty God.

As I sit here now, I have been home from the eating disorder facility for almost three months. I was faced with a trigger, just as I had expected, and it did cause me to zone out. However, I did not follow the trigger. I did not run. I was able to gain control, and I explained to my loved ones what had happened and that I simply needed to sleep it off. And that's what I did. I slept for a chunk of the day and woke up feeling stronger. It wasn't the perfect outcome. I had hoped that I wouldn't zone out, but I was definitely stronger in my recovery from the trigger.

Over the course of the last six months, I had a lump in my left thigh. I had concerns about it and had my husband feel it, and he said that sometimes he gets lumps like that too and that it would go away. Mine didn't go away, and as time went on, it began to feel more like there was something actually in there working its way out. And I was right. In my leg was a small metal piece that was about the size of a grain of rice, maybe a little bigger. It had numbers on it, and everyone became concerned that it was a tracking device or a chip of some sort that someone had placed in me in the past.

We contacted the authorities, and they said to get medical documentation. So I had someone watch my kids, and a friend and I headed up to an urgent care in town. We were looking for them to write down what they saw and take a picture of it and put the documentation on file. That was it. We figured we would be in and out.

Mind you, this was a difficult process for me because I was going to have to communicate with the doctor about what has happened and be honest that I was a victim of sex trafficking. I had never done that before. I was embarrassed. For the correct medical documentation to take place, I was going to have to tell them.

The first nurse that did my vitals came in and asked what we were in for. I responded with telling her that I was a victim of sex trafficking. Her eyes were like saucers at this point. I went on to say that I found a metal piece in my leg, and we aren't sure what it is. Our fear is that it could be a tracking device or some kind. I was definitely not expecting the response she gave me.

"All right! This is way better than the flu." She was so excited, too excited.

When she left, then the nurse practitioner came in and again asked us what we were in for. Again I explained about the trafficking and tracking device. Her eyes got big too, but it was for a different reason. She was scared. She immediately started explaining all the reasons why she couldn't help me and that I was going to have to go somewhere else. Some of her excuses were that she didn't know how to document this, that she was going to be moving soon, and that she didn't have a good camera to take pictures. It was obvious that she wasn't going to help us, so we asked to see the other nurse practitioner that was working there. The lady responded quickly, saying that the other nurse practitioner heard it was sex trafficking related and wouldn't even step foot in my room. It felt like I had leprosy, like I was being reminded again that I am trash. My friend who was with me at urgent care was adamant that we were then going to the hospital to get the documentation that we needed. We couldn't believe the way we were treated.

The ER nurse was very kind and understanding and treated me like a normal human being. Then the doctor came in and asked what was going on. My friend explained that I was a victim of sex trafficking and that I had found a possible tracking device in my leg. The doctor then turned to me and stared at me for a second before asking if I was in sex trafficking for the drugs.

The conversation got worse from there, and I eventually completely shut down. He was pushing and prodding, and it felt like I was a circus animal and he was just interested in the lowdown. He kept trying to explain that his questions were just for doctor purposes, but I knew better. He just wanted to know for his own mind. He then got offended when I acted frustrated at his questions and comments. I could see his eyes roll at the fact that I had shut down and wouldn't talk to him anymore.

Before we left, my friend walked out of the room to go to the bathroom, and the doctor stopped her. He began asking questions that gave the impression that he was concerned for his own safety if he were to document what he saw. I left the hospital feeling no more like a person than I did when I was being sold at a brothel. I knew that it would be hard for people to comprehend, but the fact that these professionals had absolutely no idea what they were doing made things ten times harder than what they should've been. I felt like the trash I was always told I was. I realized there is a lot that our society needs to open their eyes to. They need to be educated so they can provide the help and love that these victims deserve.

I am more determined than ever to not only seek justice, rescue girls, and help them recover but also I am feeling led to educate others on trafficking, on seeing the signs and knowing how to handle a situations involving a victim. Helping victims is a very selfless act because you are putting your life on the line for someone else. You can't expect immediate results and outcomes. It's a roller-coaster ride, but it's these roller-coaster rides that God has called us to go on. These girls are worth the fight. They are worth the trouble and the tears. They are worth sleepless nights full of prayers. They are worth disrupting the fake persona that our country displays that says we are the land of the free. They are worth taking a stand for.

Choosing to stay silent speaks volumes to the women feeling hopeless in the slave trade. I know what it is like to feel like no one cares or nobody will love me if they know the truth. Let's expose the evil and the lies that were purposefully placed inside these victim's minds.

There have been many times where we have felt like our case would finally break open only to be disappointed that the evidence disappeared or the police would choose to not follow our lead. But we've continued to fight.

My time at the eating disorder facility gave me a chance to find myself. It gave me a chance to truly find where God fits in all of this, and it opened my eyes to what God is wanting me to see. I am hanging on to hope. I always have. But before, the sliver of hope I had was in finding comfort and freedom. And now my hope looks more like opening a safe house, writing a book, making a documentary, sharing my story, speaking out against trafficking. I am no longer in search of comfort. Nothing great ever happened in comfort. I am not in search of freedom either, for I am not a slave. No one owns me. They never have. I am a servant to the One True King. I am not looking to freely do as I please but to follow His plans for my life.

Now that my story is coming out. I have had many people surround me and show their support. People often ask how I am doing, which is a complicated question to answer because in so many ways, things are good. I can see God working miracles, but it doesn't necessarily keep it from being hard. It just makes it worth it.

It is hard for others to comprehend the magnitude of the trauma I have endured. And it is even more difficult for them to understand the effects it has had on me. I appear completely healed and normal in so many facets of my life, but nothing about my mind, heart, and soul is healed or normal. It can't be. Not for what I've experienced and seen. However, I'm learning how to let God guide me to where my broken and abnormal spirit can be something He uses for His glory.

I see the frustration in my army as I continue on a roller-coaster ride. I want so desperately to see life the way others do, but I just don't. I don't feel life the way others do. I don't know how to express my feelings the way others do. It's complicated and discouraging for those who desire for me to see life as they do. Not long ago, I had a day where I was struggling the whole day through. A day or two later, I was able to sit down with some of my army and share with them how my mind actually worked during that day when I was struggling. And I was also able to hear how their minds worked. It was a good learning experience for all of us. This is how I explained it to them.

Tornado

Another tornado strikes.
Another trial.
Another pain.
The tornado destroyed bits and pieces of me again.
I am still alive. But I am broken.
This pain is too common to my every day.
"Breathe, Rachel, breathe."
I need someone to help me.
I feel like I can't breathe.
I don't know what to do.
Panic starts to set in.
Maybe this is the end.
But I keep my face stoic.
"Breathe," I remind myself again.
A million thoughts run across my mind.
The same thoughts run across my mind again, the same thoughts that always scream loudly at me after I've been hurt.
I'm worthless. I'm dumb. I'm trash. I'm crazy.

What if these thoughts are true?

What if everyone is thinking the same things about me?

I begin to feel like I'm falling.

I hold my breath and shut my eyes, faster and faster down a dark pit.

Does anybody care that I can't breathe, that I'm falling?

I start to scream out for help, but I stop myself.

Last time I cried out for help, I hurt people.

I can't cry out for help.

"Be strong, Rachel. Think."

I cycle the same thoughts through my mind again.

I'm worthless. I'm dumb. I'm trash. I'm crazy.

I harden my heart to the words.

I literally feel the tingling in my chest as my heart hardens to the feelings behind these words.

Who cares if I am these things?

Who cares if this is what others see in me?

I don't need these people anyway.

I know the truth.

I know I am not these things even if others disagree with me.

The thoughts start to cycle through again.

This time I have the strength to stop them.

I realize this time they are lies.

I realize that others really don't believe these things.

I realize I am not falling.

My heart rate slows down.

I can breathe again.

I made it through.

I look at the clock and see this time it lasted only a couple of hours where before it would've lasted the whole day.

I look at my phone.

My heart sinks as I realize that I hadn't stayed silent after all, that I wasn't hiding my feelings like I had thought.

I realize that all my thoughts during the last two hours I shared with my friends.

I realize I had cried out for help, that I had shown my pain, my fears.

Frustration and regret follow.

I hurt people again.

I shared too much again.

I see how I must look to others and I cry.
Just ten minutes before, I felt on the brink of death, unable to breathe.
And now I am back to the reality, and I see the destruction that I caused from my tornado of emotions.
I am the tornado.

I was told that it was helpful for some of my army to read so they could get an idea of how my mind works in those moments. We discussed having patience with each other, but I know that this is new territory for them. I know it's difficult for them. I'm just so thankful they are willing to try and to not give up.

I know of at least two people who would never give up on me. One is God, and the other is Satan. No matter what, they both will never give up on chasing after my soul. And the one I give the power to, the one I allow to reign in my life, will be the one who wins me for eternity. So often I wish that Satan would just give up on me, that he would realize that I am going to be on God's team no matter what he throws at me. Nonetheless, Satan continues to throw me struggles, and obstacles.

When I got home from the eating disorder facility, I was set up to right away meet with my counselor, and I did. He was in tears with seeing the obvious change in me, the confidence I exhibited, the light that shone in my eyes, and the purpose I was living with. Each week I would see him, and I would always leave challenged and a bit more put back together.

Just a month from being home, I got a phone call from my counselor's office saying that he needed to cancel my appointment that week because he was sick. They went ahead and set me up an appointment for the following week. However, that next week, I received a letter in the mail stating that my counselor was diagnosed with acute leukemia and would no longer be able to see patients. My heart dropped to the floor. This man couldn't be sick. He was the one who sat across from me one a week for ten months. He had cried with me. He had been all in when it came to my fight against trafficking. He never questioned me and always showed that he cared. I didn't want to go see a different counselor. I wanted him.

In my mind, I decided that I would wait until he got better, and then I would start seeing him again. Counseling was in his blood. I knew once he was better that he would be back at counseling again. I didn't want to have to start over with a completely new counselor only to switch back to him.

A week and a half later, I received a text from a friend of mine who had just found out about my counselor.

"I just heard the news. I'm so sorry about your counselor. He was such a good man," she said to me. I was surprised by her wording with saying he *was* good man.

"I know it. It breaks my heart," I responded. "I'm praying that he is healed completely and can get back to counseling." I waited. In my gut, I began to dread her text back to me. I was hoping that the *was* she put in her text was just a typo.

"Oh, Rachel. I'm so sorry. I was just told that he passed away yesterday."

This was easy for me to separate from immediately. I tried convincing myself that I would be okay with my counselor. I tried to shove the pain down. For about a week, I was able to do that. The family of my counselor decided to have a gathering time to honor him and to allow his clients and friends who weren't able to make the funeral to be there to pay their respects. A friend and I went together. She had been seeing my counselor for three years.

As I sat in this ceremony and listened to all that was said about my counselor, God opened my eyes even more to not just live a life of comfort but a life of purpose as well. This man had impacted thousands of people. He had stayed up several nights praying for me. He had lived this chaos with me. It wasn't easy for him, but he did it. And because of him doing that, I was able to find healing quicker and feel like I mattered.

I still will catch myself and think in my head that when I see my counselor next, I will have to tell him about this or ask him about that. Then I remember that he's gone. It really felt unfair. I needed all hands on deck as I continued to recover and stay safe. I especially needed a counselor.

This was not the only obstacle that was placed before me by Satan. Just three months from being home, there was a break-in at our house. I was home with three of my four kids, and I had been cleaning up the basement. Toys were everywhere as usual, so I began to organize and pick up. There were even bicycles and riding toys from the garage piled up in the playroom, so I started grabbing those big items and began carrying them out into the garage. The garage door was shut, so I wasn't even the slightest scared. About the third trip of walking in the garage to put away toys, I saw a man start walking toward me.

I had no time to think, and instantly I charged back at this man. Just inside the house was my three kids, and I was going to fight with everything I had to keep that man from going in there. I punched him and scratched him. I pushed him away from me the best I could. He threw me to the ground. He was able to physically hurt me, but not easily. Looking back at this even now, I'm afraid that for a bit, I did zone out, which gave him more time to hurt me, but when I wasn't zoned out, I was fighting. He wasn't in there long. Maybe four minutes tops and then I watched him crawl out of the window in our garage. I didn't know we had an open window in our garage, but somehow he went through it and was gone.

I was hurt, and I knew that I needed to call for help. I went back inside the house, trying to play off the fact that my stomach was bleeding through my shirt. *My* kids were all unaware of what just happened, and I wanted to keep it that way. I kept trying to take a deep breath, and I couldn't.

I found my phone and saw where Granny had texted me, "Are you still feeling strong?"

Her timing was remarkable, a God thing. I texted her back that I needed her, and I needed her now. She asked what happened, but before I could text her back, she called me. I guess I wasn't speaking very clearly to Granny, but I begged her to come. Within five minutes, she was there.

I was awkwardly trying to talk to her when she came in. She had already called the police, and she began trying to reassure me that everything was going to be okay. I kept commenting on how I fought back. I noticed that Granny kept looking at me with concern in her eyes.

"Why are you talking like that?" she asked. "Did this man hurt your mouth?"

I had no idea what she was talking about. I was just so proud of myself for finally doing everything the way I was supposed to. I knew the police were coming, and this time, they would be able to catch the man who broke in.

"Seriously, Rachel, why are you talking like that?" she asked again.

"I don't know. What am I talking like?"

Granny decided to drop it, but later, she explained to me that I sounded like a small child who had just won a ballgame. I had gone back mentally to that little girl. I assume the reason was because I was faced with similar situations when I was a kid, an overpowering situation.

Not long after Granny got to my house, the policeman showed up. Granny started to give him a quick synopsis of what I explained to her happened. The man then came up to me and asked me what happened. I told him that a man broke into my garage, that I fought him and he ended up leaving through the window just after a few minutes.

"So this happened in the driveway?" the police officer asked me.

"No, it happened in the garage," I politely but agitatedly responded. I was pretty certain I had just said *garage*.

"Are you hurt?"

I lifted up my shirt to see where I was bleeding. When I did, I could see exactly what the man had cut into my stomach. It was in large letters the word TRASH. Granny told me to show the policeman, and so I lifted my shirt enough for him to see the words. His eyes became like saucers.

"Who did that?" he asked. This seemed like a really dumb and obvious question.

"Uhh, this man did it, that broke in."

"When did this happen?"

"Just now."

"Okay, so this happened in the driveway?" he asked again.

"Nooo, it happened in the garage."

I could tell that this police officer didn't believe me. It was shown in everything he did and said. He insisted I take an ambulance to the hospital mainly to preserve any evidence that was on my body and clothes. I did not want to go in an ambulance. I did not want to go to the hospital. But this police officer made me so that I was going to be able to document what happened to me.

As soon as I was in the ambulance, the police officer was already gone. He had not done anything to find evidence from my house. In fact, when he asked me again if it was in the driveway, Granny offered to him to go see the garage. So he did. Right away, the police officer stated that there was no way the man went through the window.

The police officer left around the same time I left in an ambulance. Granny stayed back at the house, trying to get someone from the police station to come back and do a correct report. My husband came home, and friends came over. Some of our friends went in and out of the window in the garage easily, the same window that the police officer stated there was no way the man went through that window. They also found blood splatters on the garage floor. None of which was seen or documented by the police officer.

I had always been told to scratch when I'm being hurt so that I can collect DNA under my fingernails so the police can catch who the person is. I was proud of myself for doing that this time, but the police officer told me that since I didn't know who the man was that supposedly hurt me, they couldn't run a DNA test. It didn't surprise me when I heard nothing back from the police officer except to see what my kids' birthdays were.

And then two days after the assault, an employee of children services came to our door. The woman asked me if I knew why children services was called in.

"Yes, because a man broke into my garage a couple of days ago," I replied to her.

"No," she quickly stated back. "The police report indicates that you are the one who hurt yourself, and the police are concerned about your mental health and being around your kids."

I wanted to throw up or punch something. This is exactly what I was told would happen from the men who were telling me to keep quiet. I answered all of the woman's questions, but nonetheless, I was mad. She was simply doing her job. It was the police who continued to frustrate me. It was the police who weren't believing me, and now they were even calling me crazy.

In my mind, I knew that I would never again call the police. I couldn't, not if the only way they would respond is by calling me crazy and taking my kids. I felt like I had no safety. I had no one I could trust in the system who would take me seriously and keep me safe.

Something along this journey that God has continued to teach me is that I must put my faith and trust in Him, not people. That people will let me down, but God's ways are perfect. I'm so thankful to be where I am at in this fight, knowing that I have God going before me, that He has already won this battle. He has the victory. So many times along the way, just when it would look like we were at a dead end, when there appeared to be no answers after we would rack our brains trying to find a solution to a problem, God would step in. He would provide not only an answer, but He would also already be going before us, lighting the way.

In those moments, I am reminded of how important it is to wait patiently on the Lord, to allow Him to work miracles before you jump in trying to fix things yourself. Prayer is key followed by patience and obedience.

I am currently sitting in my living room while some men from my church work around my house, putting up cameras and a new security system. I have a new guard dog lying at my feet. We've hired a nanny to be here with me during the day when my husband is at work. I am finished up my book and in the beginning stages of preparing a documentary, plus raising money toward opening a safe house in our area.

We were devastated when we heard that my coach was being able to go back to teaching because the investigation on him was closed. It was hard to not feel like everything we did was all for nothing. And yet by being obedient and following God's plan, now there are more girls coming forward, girls who had been hurt by my coach. Parents and teachers have started standing up against the school for allowing my coach to be around kids. And the school has hired an attorney to collect all of these personal stories of what he had done to so many. After the interviews are done, then the attorney will present the information to the state board of education, and they will decide if my coach should be allowed in the school.

Blind eyes are starting to be opened. Slowly, but they are definitely being opened. Legally, we will wait to see where God leads. We will be in prayer with how we should go about that in the near future. We plan to meet with the chief of police and the city manager soon in attempt to educate them on trafficking in our area. The first step will be simply getting them to believe that what I am saying is true. The last conversation that we had with the city manager he promised to keep an open mind to this "bizarre" story. That has exactly been my prayer—that blind eyes will be opened.

For four years now, I have been in this fight. During those years, I would long to go back to before I had the realization about my coach, to before I felt the need to fight this battle, back to when I was living comfortably. But that is not my feeling anymore. That last four years have been treacherous, an absolute nightmare. None of it I would like to relive. However, I am thankful for the ministry God has been able to use from it. I'm thankful for the ability to reach out to girls in similar situations and love on them. I'm thankful for finding my purpose in my life. I'm even thankful that I no longer live comfortably. I am constantly pulled outside my comfort zone. I'm constantly challenged to dig deeper in my faith and to reach out to more people. I am thankful for it all. This is where God needs me, and this is where I want to serve. Doing things my own way may feel comfortable for a time, but it won't last. Following God may be difficult and challenging, but it will be proven completely worth it in the end. God's ways are always better even if we don't understand it at the time.

Our battle continues as we work to keep safe and away from these men and in finding a way to expose this evilness. When I began writing my story, I had hoped that the last chapter would be filled with victory and triumph, but instead, I write about the battle we are still fighting. My coach is still a free man and is still in the school system. My family is still not safe. However, God is working, and I end this book in excitement for how God plans to work it all out. I also end this book in prayer for all I hope to see come to pass.

Dear Heavenly Father,

I praise Your name, Lord, and thank you for Your goodness. I am thankful for the path You have led me and the story You gave me. I am thankful that today I am stronger in my faith than I have ever been. I pray, Lord, for blind eyes to be opened, for parents to understand signs of grooming, for schools to make sure that children have a safe person that they can talk to if something in their life is making them uncomfortable or if someone is hurting them, for the justice system and the authorities to be educated on how to talk to victims and to understand someone who has been through trauma, for Christians to stop judging and start loving, for the church family to be the people we share our lives with and our burdens with and our joys, both inside the church building and out, for God's army to stop fighting so hard to achieve the American dream and instead fight the battle God has equipped them for—to save lives—for the good people in the world to start using their voice to call out the bad. It's better for our country to know the truth instead of hiding under the false belief that sex trafficking doesn't exist in America.

Thank you for this assignment that You have given me, and I pray that I am obedient in all that You need me to do. I am thankful for the fight You put inside of me, the fight not just me but also for Kaitlyn, for the girls in the camper, and in the shed, for my four babies, for the little girls in my life that I would die to protect. I am also going to fight and pray for the men who have allowed Satan to use them for evil and that they will find You, Lord, and change their ways.

In Jesus's name, I pray. Amen.

God is asking us to be the hands and feet of Christ and to open blind eyes.

EPILOGUE

It has been close to three years since the last chapter was written of this book, and I was told by several people that an epilogue was definitely needed. I had originally written down my story in book form for my own healing but also to have a way to explain to people how trafficking can go unnoticed and undetected in normal society. I also hoped my story could be a voice for others who are in similar situations and can't explain in words what is happening to them, or who have people around them who don't understand the effects of trauma, or worse yet, don't believe them. As far as what happened with this book after I wrote it, I was leaving it completely in God's hands.

I didn't know the first thing about publishing a book or even if that was what God wanted. So I prayed and let it go. Fast-forward three years, and I have been presented with an incredible publishing opportunity that blew me away, and even more mind-boggling to me was how much my book had circulated already without even being published. That can only be explained by the work of God. He started opening eyes, and people were reading my story and believing, and then they were passing the book on to others.

It was a scary feeling at first, knowing so many were reading my raw thoughts and memories that I had put down on paper, but I had to remind myself that I had put it completely in God's hands. This must be what God had wanted. I had only shared my story with people close to me, so the fact it got out and spread like wildfire must've meant God was truly using it to open blind eyes.

Unfortunately, over the course of the last three years, my story has continued in its typical roller-coaster form. I have continued to heal, and with that, I've remembered many more memories from the several years of abuse both as a child and an adult. Those memories have come back in the form of awful flashbacks that often take days to recover from. Dealing with the traumatic effects of my past is hard and challenging. So much of me wants to live every moment in the present, but too often, my healing mind has other plans. And it brings back to the forefront of my mind events that took place long ago as if they were happening in this very moment. The healing process is definitely a life long journey.

On top of dealing with flashbacks that feel like they are happening in the here and now, I also have had to deal with the evilness of this ring of men that are still causing problems in my life to this day. It's been extremely difficult trying to function in a normal way and going through the healing process while these men continue to make their presence known almost on a daily basis.

There hasn't been much normal in my life as a result. From awful evil and disgusting text messages being sent to me and my support system to being followed, watched, and harassed, these men have continued to bring a never-ending sense of fear and unsafety to me and my family. We've taken all sorts of steps to try and stop the tactics of these men. I no longer have a phone, and I stay home most days, never leaving anywhere alone, leading to a life of isolation. My support system works hard to stay connected to me, but these men have made it extremely difficult. I know it is all a part of their plan. The mental distress from the everyday harassment has been challenging, and it doesn't seem to show signs of stopping any time soon.

We have had to consult many professionals for help in deciding where to go from here, especially since even in the last four months, the harassment has amped up to more physical harm being done again and there is no law enforcement who believe. We have come to the conclusion that so much of what has been happening since I left the world of trafficking is not about getting me back, but about getting me to keep my mouth shut. The more I remember, the more people I remember being involved, the more I want to scream from the mountaintops what is going on. But this ring of evil men knows that the knowledge and memories I have could put a lot of people in jail if the right person finally hears my case and pursues it. And they can't let that happen. We have figured out, based on their threats and attacks the last four months, that they either want me crazy or dead.

So how do we function and live with that knowledge and understanding? How do we raise our four kids, financially support our family, and live a life of safety? After talking to professionals who deal with trafficking and the injustice with it, we have found that our case is not uncommon. Our country has many people living like me because of this heinous crime and the injustice that follows. So not only do trafficked victims suffer immensely, but so do trafficked survivors as well. Even the survivors go almost as unnoticed as the victims still in the life. And their lives continue to be controlled by the evil men who work so hard to keep them quiet or seemingly crazy.

I am thankful that eyes are starting to be opened to the reality that trafficking exists in one of its evilest forms in America, but we can't stop there. Action must follow. Changes must be made. And it won't be easy because many higher-ups are involved in trafficking throughout our country, from celebrities to the wealthy and the political influencers. It's not just the gangs that stay hidden in the dark selling people. It's also the influential people in our society. It's those who have a say in our judicial system. It's those who have the means and the power to cover up their crimes.

The action that is required to stop trafficking in our country is massive, but the consequences that will come if we don't take action is insurmountable. If we don't take action now, we will be so overtaken with slavery that our country will never recover. We honestly aren't far from it now. But I can't help but believe that this is why God is bringing trafficking to the forefront of the news and social media now, that it's why he is opening eyes to the truth. He has been trying to open eyes in more subtle ways for years, but our society didn't see it, or they chose not to see it. They would simply brush the signs that God was giving them under the rug. But now it's gotten to the point where the enslaved are our neighbors, members of our church, or in our child's circle of friends. It might not be your son or daughter yet. But we need a country who chooses to fight before it gets to the point that it is directly impacting every family in America because that is honestly the direction we are heading.

As I write this epilogue, I am sitting outside of my house in a lawn chair. I have no phone, and I haven't left to go anywhere by myself in I don't know how long. I am virtually a prisoner to my own home, trying to function normally in a very toxic and unhealthy situation. My lack of a life is still being controlled by the ring of men that have hurt me and used me for so long. My voice is still not being heard, justice is not coming, and my family suffers as a result. And as I watch car after car drive by in front of my house, I can't help but think of how little they know. I am sure when they see me sitting here, they don't see a slave. They don't see a prisoner to their home. They drive by clueless of how big of a problem our country is dealing with and how close it really is.

My dream for the future is still freedom, but if I'm being honest, I can no longer picture what that looks like for me. I can't imagine a life that is free from all this. But I will continue to pray for it and fight for it. I will use my voice to share the truth, whether people choose to listen or not. And what I hope is that God will bless me with another opportunity to write another book, hopefully a book that is written on the other side of slavery and not still in it, that He will give me the chance to share more of what He has taught me and shown me through this journey, and that there will be a large number of people eager to learn more so that more action can be taken so that the numbers of those enslaved will go down and the numbers of survivors receiving justice and true freedom will go up. That's my hope, my prayer, and my dream.

My hopes for you are that this book changed your thinking on trafficking, that your eyes are now open to the reality of this dark world, and that your heart and soul are moved to do something about it, that you choose to be one of the people who take action, who use their voice to speak truth, who rise up and say enough is enough, who join the fight. Not everyone can be involved on a daily basis to stop trafficking, but everyone can do something. Right now, you are being given the choice of fighting against trafficking. Don't wait until you are directly impacted by trafficking, and then you're fighting because it's a life-or-death situation for someone you love. Start now. That's my hope, my prayer, and my dream for you.

May God bless you!